THE SUBURBAN MYTH

THE SUBURBAN MYTH

by Scott Donaldson

COLUMBIA UNIVERSITY PRESS · NEW YORK

Permissions have been granted to quote the following:

"Housewife," pp. 200–01 of this text, from *Poems 1930–1960* by Josephine Miles. Reprinted by permission of Indiana University Press.

"To An American Poet Just Dead," pp. 201–02 of this text, from *Ceremony and Other Poems,* copyright, 1948, 1949, 1950 by Richard Wilbur. Reprinted by permission of Harcourt, Brace & World, Inc.

"June in the Suburbs," p. 203 of this text, from *Times Three,* copyright 1953 by Phyllis McGinley. Reprinted by permission of The Viking Press, Inc. and Martin Secker & Warburg, Ltd.

❧ To Janet

PREFACE

THE IMPRESSION that the American suburb has been grossly and unfairly maligned first developed when I was covering a suburban "beat" for a metropolitan daily newspaper in the mid-1950s. After I became editor of a suburban weekly newspaper and our family moved to the suburb of Bloomington, Minnesota, in 1959, the impression solidified to conviction. Bloomington turned out to be a far better place to live than we could remotely have suspected had we listened to the tirade of critical abuse printed in such best-selling books as *The Organization Man* (1956), *The Crack in the Picture Window* (1956), *The Split-Level Trap* (later, in 1961), and in countless magazine articles. The first thing I wanted to say, then, was that suburbs have been unjustly, and irrationally, accused of all sorts of vices which they neither produce nor harbor.

The often emotional attack on suburbia reached its virulent peak during the Eisenhower years of the middle and late 1950s, and it has persisted to this day despite the publication of recent, reasonable studies by such scholars as Bennett Berger, William M. Dobriner, Herbert J. Gans, and Robert C. Wood. In this book the attack is examined, point by point. Playing the role of advocate, I have tried to dismiss those charges that are unsupported by the evidence and to admit guilt in those cases where no other plea is possible. *The Suburban Myth,* in other words, consists largely of a critical review of the literature on suburbia appearing in the years since World War II. Where it has seemed applicable I have referred to the experience of Bloomington or of other Twin Cities suburbs I came to know during seven years as a reporter, editor, and publisher, first with the Minneapolis *Star* and later with Twin City Suburban Newspapers, Inc., a corporation publishing more than twenty suburban weekly papers. The book is *not* another case study of a single suburban community. Instead, it is the attempt of a generalist to look at the suburbs whole—to assess the mountain of material composed by sociologists, architectural critics, planners, political scientists, ministers, psychologists, educators, popular social commentators, novelists, poets, and film-makers. Obviously, I do not have competence in all these fields, and my argument has often been based more on common sense than on disciplinary expertise.

After establishing that the suburbs have been much maligned, the book attempts to perform a still more important and difficult function: to understand *why*. Why did the liberal-intellectual establishment of the 1950s take such delight in sticking pins in the suburban doll? There are several reasons. First of all, the *post hoc* fallacy accounts for much of the attack. Critics in the 1950s watched conformity spreading across the land, for example, and attributed its spread to the concurrent phenomenon of suburbanization. People moved to the suburbs, such arguments ran, and the suburbs made the people conformist. The location was blamed for a universal malady. Another source for the attack was provided by the many writers who tended to generalize about all suburbs from the example of a single one. This practice frequently resulted in unjustified conclusions, and explains why some critics found too much neighboring in the suburbs, while others found too much loneliness. But neither the *post hoc* fallacy nor the generalizing tendency provide an explanation for the viciousness of the attack. The onslaught against the suburbs has been so violent as to make it clear that another, less rationally explainable motive is at work.

This motive, which is, I believe, the dominant one supporting the attack, can be traced to man's myth-making imagination in general and specifically to the champion American myth of all time—the myth of the virtuous and healthy yeoman farmer, at

once individualistic and altruistic, simultaneously at one with nature and with his fellow man. It is the persistence of this myth,
most persuasively expressed by Thomas Jefferson, that has caused
most of the disillusionment about the suburbs. The depth of the
disillusionment, reflected in the bitterness of the attack, testifies
to the staying power of this myth and its ability to create un-
justifiable expectations.

The word *myth* is not defined here simply as a widely believed
cultural lie. It refers to such a lie that has outlived its time, but
which continues to shape the minds and actions of a people. The
myth *of* suburbia, in other words, refers to the Jeffersonian ideal,
an ideal which persists among almost all Americans but which
has had especially disillusioning effects *on* the American suburb.
The persistence of this myth accounts for many of the misconceptions *about* suburbia, misconceptions which sometimes, but not
in this book, go by the name of "myth."

A *suburb* is defined simply as a community lying within commuting distance of a central city. Usually, but not always, suburbs
are dependent on central cities economically and culturally; usually, but not always, they are independent of those cities politically.
The persistence of the Jeffersonian myth has had, and continues to
have, deleterious effects not only on suburbia but on the nation
generally. There are welcome signs that the myth is gradually losing its stranglehold on the American imagination; hopefully, this
book will help to loosen its grip still more.

If I have been successful in achieving this, much of the credit
must go to some good teachers, not all of them professionally en-
gaged in teaching. I am thinking of John Tilton and Don Heinzman, Bernard Casserly and Paul Swensson, all newspapermen, and
of Mary Turpie and Bernard Bowron, Mulford Sibley and Charles
H. Foster, Gregory P. Stone and Donald Torbert, all professors at
the University of Minnesota during 1963–1965. A still greater debt
is owed to Professors J. C. Levenson and David W. Noble. Professor Levenson contributed his keen stylistic advice, proposed
valuable bibliography, and is jointly responsible with Professor

Noble for whatever historical-mindedness I may have achieved on so "modern" a topic as suburbia. Professor Noble not only provided encouragement when it was most needed, but suggested lines of strategy and key readings which, hopefully, have resulted in a coherent argument. None of the above, of course, can be asked to bear accountability for my shortcomings.

SCOTT DONALDSON

October 1968

CONTENTS

THE SUBURBAN MYTH

I. ONSLAUGHT AGAINST
THE SUBURBS

People need to believe in the value of the communities in which they live,
the goals that they seek, and the satisfactions they receive.
—*Maurice Stein, 1964*

In the last two decades, the American suburb has been the victim
of a critical onslaught of monumental, and largely nonsensical, pro-
portions. Time and again, journalists and social commentators have
typed out staccato blasts at the relatively inert target of suburbia.
So far the suburbs have survived the onslaught, but they may suc-
cumb in the end. People need to believe in the place in which they
live, and it is becoming increasingly hard to believe in a suburbia
that is a battleground under continual bombardment. Such concentrated pressures lead to demoralization and despair.[1]

The critical attack which peaked in the mid-1950s contains little
that is intelligent or constructive; for the most part, it is composed
of whopping irrelevancies, galloping over-statements, and poorly
concealed animosities. A great deal of intellectual and emotional
energy has been expended in the onslaught, energy which might
well have been invested more profitably.

What accounts for this venomous attack on a place in which
seventy million Americans now live?

Part of the explanation comes from the bandwagon effect: once
it has become profitable to criticize any particular facet of Amer-

ican life, it is likely to become fashionable as well. A recent rash of books on invasion of privacy bore witness to this phenomenon, as did the production of diatribes directed at advertising. This bandwagon effect is aggravated by the human susceptibility to stereotype. As Louis Gottschalk remarks, ". . . those who know Germans to be ruthless and Englishmen to lack humor generally find . . . ruthless Germans and humorless Englishmen" in their study of history.[2] When we are led to expect a vast wasteland of conformity in suburbia, we have seriously hampered our chances of finding anything but a vast wasteland of conformity. Important though this dual tendency may be, however, in determining the *direction* of the suburban onslaught, it hardly accounts for its violence. Other, deeper motivations are at work.

When mentally competent men commit obvious errors of logic, it is surely a sign that irrational elements are busy in their thoughts. And the attack on the suburbs abounds in fallacious thinking, in unresolvable inconsistencies and contradictions, in the illogical *post hoc* conclusion that all our ills can be traced to a particular location. *Most critics of suburbia write out of a set of convictions which have been basic in American thought, and which have persisted past the point of usefulness or validity.* They are infected by myth. This is true to a degree of social commentators who have launched their weapons from the pages of the nation's magazines. It is even more true of such scientifically sophisticated critics as William H. Whyte, Jr., whose section on "The New Suburbia" in *The Organization Man* remains the single most influential statement in the attack on the American suburb.[3] Whyte, like his few predecessors and many followers, accuses the suburbs of nothing less than failing to live up to the American dream, a dream he defines as the world of the individualistic, self-sufficient yeoman. It is no wonder then that the suburbs remain passive, refusing to enter a plea when faced with this accusation; they are obviously guilty as charged. So, however, is everywhere else, though the city and small town do not face the accusation. The wonder is that anyone should have expected to find the independent yeoman living in the suburbs, in twentieth century America.

Magazine articles on suburbia (the very word, "suburbia," carries unpleasant overtones, suggesting nothing so much as some kind of scruffy disease) since World War II reveal a near unanimity of opinion. The consensus is simply that the American suburb is no place to live. In elaborating this basic conclusion, the critical commentators frequently trip over each other's arguments. Sometimes, they accuse the suburbs of directly contradictory vices. It becomes clear that there is no escape for the critics' chosen target: the suburbs are damned when they do, and damned again when they don't.

But what does it matter? Why bother with those people out in the suburbs? Understanding is its own reward, of course; but it does matter, and it is necessary to bother with those people out in the suburbs because those people are you, or me, or the next fellow. Everyone knows that the farm population has been rapidly declining throughout this century, as has that of the small rural towns which serve as market centers for farming areas. Everyone knows also that the population of this country, as of others, is growing at rates capable of producing new Malthusian prophecies of doom. Fewer, however, realize that most of America's cities have reached or passed their population peaks, and are now only holding their own, or actually declining in total population. It is obvious that the nation's people are moving to the suburbs, and the figures bear out the logic.

As recently as 1934, in his article on "Suburbs" in the *Encyclopedia of the Social Sciences,* Harlan Paul Douglass proclaimed that the possibility of suburban life was "virtually limited to the most highly paid types of labor and to the upper middle classes." At the same time, though, he noted that suburbs were growing faster than cities. In the decade from 1920 to 1930, Douglass wrote, suburban population grew by 39.2 per cent, "more than twice that of both non-suburban cities and central cities of similar size." [4] During the depression thirties, rates of home building and home ownership remained relatively stable. But a combination of influences—practically universal car ownership, the expanding highway system, the baby boom of the forties, and most important of all, the availability of cheap land, cheap homes, and cheap financing after World War

II—extended the possibility of living in the suburbs to more Americans than Douglass would have thought possible.

In two decades, between 1934 and 1954, the suburbs grew by 75 per cent while the total population grew by 25 per cent. Between 1950 and 1954 people living in 168 'standard metropolitan' central cities increased by 14 per cent, those in the suburban rings around the cities increased by 35 per cent, and those living in the semi-suburban rural rings around the suburbs increased by 41 per cent.[5]

Specific examples of growth make such overall figures look conservative by comparison. San Fernando Valley outside Los Angeles, a garden of fruit trees before World War II, now houses a million people. The Levittowns on Long Island and in Bucks County, Pennsylvania placed 17,000 homes apiece on land formerly used for truck farming.[6] Suburbs are becoming cities in their own right, even spawning other suburbs.

In 1955, the Bureau of the Census, always conservative between decennial headcounts, estimated "that the suburbs [harbored] 30,-000,000 persons." [7] But by 1957, *Newsweek* estimated that suburbs had grown six times faster than cities during the preceding six years,[8] and according to the 1960 census, "about 84 per cent of the 28 million population increase during the decade 1950–1960 occurred in the nation's metropolitan areas," with the suburbs alone accounting for 18 million.[9] The total number of suburbanites in 1960, then, was approximately 50 million; by 1965, it was more than 60 million and still rising. By the 1980s, the population experts predict, *one hundred million Americans will live in the suburbs.*[10] Critics carp at such figures, maintaining that they perceive a trend back from the suburb to the city, but neither the census figures nor common sense support such a view. The long-term outlook, statistician A. W. Zelomek writes,

is for continued growth in population. The large crop of babies born in the "baby boom" of the 1940s is just about reaching maturity, and the rate of family formations should spurt in the 1960s. There will be no satisfactory housing for these new families except by additional building in the suburbs, and this is where they are expected to go. The central cities are built up, and their population should remain relatively stable in numbers.[11]

One-third of a nation now lives in the suburbs; some day, perhaps, half of all Americans will reside there. The type of life they will be able to lead in the suburbs is obviously a matter of considerable importance. The chances of living a good life, the critics assure suburbanites, are not good. If they can convince enough people, the critics may turn out to be right.

The process of conviction has advanced so far already that the image of the suburbs has become stereotyped. At the mention of "suburbs" or "suburbia" two reactions are permitted. You may comment indignantly (preferred) or giggle nervously (permitted to those who happen to live in the suburbs but are right-thinkers). As Bennett Berger writes, the very "ubiquity of the term suburbia in current popular literature suggests that its meaning is well on its way to standardization—that what it is supposed to connote is widely enough accepted to permit free use of the term with a reasonable amount of certainty that it will convey the images it intends." [12] William M. Dobriner, like Berger a social scientist who takes his subject dispassionately and seriously, has listed the intended images in this way: suburbs are pictured in the popular mind as "warrens of young executives on the way up; uniformly middle class; 'homogeneous'; hotbeds of participation; child centered and female dominated; transient; wellsprings of outgoing life; arenas of adjustment; Beulah Lands of return to religion; political Jordans from which Democrats emerge Republicans." [13]

Dobriner's catalogue pretty well sums up the stereotype, but in its objectivity lacks the bite and the color of the popular indictment. As Phyllis McGinley observed in 1952, "Spruce Manor [the fictitious name she applies to her Connecticut suburb] has become a sort of symbol to writers, a symbol of all that is middle class in the worst sense, of smug and prosperous mediocrity. I have yet to read a book," she adds, "in which the suburban life was pictured as the good life or the commuter as a sympathetic figure." [14] Few such books exist, even today. Almost all of us have seen magazine articles like that of Stanley Rowland, Jr., entitled "Suburbia Buys Religion," in which it is proclaimed that suburbs "have few of the opportunities for individuality found in the big city. One moves there, buys the right car, keeps his lawn like his neighbor's, eats crunchy breakfast cereal and votes Republican." [15]

The image has met some resistance, usually expressed by people who (unlike most of the critics) actually live in the suburbs. Such level-headed sociologists as Herbert J. Gans and William M. Dobriner have tried to correct the balance. For example, Zelomek comments, it may come as a surprise to suburbanites that:

> they and their communities are the source and center of all kinds of evils, that they are homogenized, excessively conformist, live in potential slums, see, hear, and know nothing beyond their picture windows, belong to too many organizations, are dominated by the children who practically never see their fathers. . . . If the suburbanite sees life through a picture window, many of his appraisers see life in the suburbs through the keyhole; the view may be sensational but it's always very narrow. The failures and ironies of suburban living are all too obvious and easily exaggerated into "good copy." [16]

And McGinley challenges the cliches, observing that "for the best 11 years of my life I have lived in suburbia and I like it." [17] But such counter-criticism has not significantly brightened the tarnished image of suburbia, and makes little headway toward understanding the root causes of the onslaught. For some reason, Spruce Manor has become a stereotyped symbol of most of what is wrong with our society. To get at the reason or reasons, it is necessary to particularize the attack and search for those indications of illogicality that reveal the deeper, more irrational, and emotional beliefs that have given shape to the stereotype.

Since the criticism of suburbia assumes that location forms the basis for social ills, it is fitting to follow the example of anthropology and begin this book's review of the criticism with a discussion of the use of space, a discussion of suburban architecture. There follows a brief summary of the attack as it relates to life style, to politics, and to certain institutions—the school, the church, and the psychiatric couch. In each instance, the sources of the criticism will be, principally, articles in popular periodicals.

No one loves the suburbs less than John Keats, whose indictment of the suburban home is contained in the best-selling *The Crack in the Picture Window.*[18] Keats concentrates his fire on the postwar housing development, where he finds ticky tacky homes and a landscape laid waste. The dwellings are shoddily built, and it is the fault of get-rich-quick developers. In vitriolic style, Keats disposes of the builders: "The plain fact was, the chisel was the tool most often used to construct the postwar development house, and the chisel's popularity with builders has not decreased with the passing years. It is one of the touching love affairs of all time." [19] To illustrate the effect of these jerry-built development houses on the people who live in them, he invents an imaginary couple who move first to Rolling Knolls, then to Merryland Dell. The couple's names are John and Mary Drone (the author cannot be accused of subtlety). Just about everything that *could* go wrong with any home goes wrong with the Drones' first suburban home in Rolling Knolls. "Their street is not paved, their plaster is cracked, and their floors are warped; their neighbors are repulsive; for lack of a basement they have to hang the wash on rainy days in the living room, and for lack of space on the same rainy days the children have no place to play except under the indoor clothesline." [20]

Such shoddy building will eventually result in suburban slums, the critics feel sure. What is needed is more planning, obviously. Thus magazine writer Hal Burton praises the virtues of the Country Club district of Kansas City, a planned community, while deploring the practices of "the fast-buck developer [who] is far more prevalent around the country building houses in a hurry and moving on without bothering to consider the problems he has left behind." [21]

Such criticism fails to take into account the very real service rendered by builders to a nation desperate for quick housing after World War II. But, more important, the notion of thorough planning as a solution to suburbia's ills runs into an obvious inconsistency: it is just those new, carefully planned communities, such as Park Forest near Chicago and Long Island's Levittown, which have been the most often studied and most roundly criticized. What the critics seem to want is not planning for the future, but planning which will result in restoration of the past. Burton's approval of the

Country Club district supports this view; this "in-town suburb" (it lies entirely within the political boundaries of Kansas City, Missouri) "started under a sound architectural code back in 1907," long before the suburban migration became numerically significant. And in his description of Country Club, the community sounds very much like a restoration of small-town America. Keats is even more explicit, contrasting the unlovely housing development with the good old days on Elm Street. Anyone who recalls the small town America of Sinclair Lewis or Sherwood Anderson can only echo the exasperation of the reviewer who asked:

Does he really believe that, prior to World War II, everyone lived in a comfortable old two- and three-story house on Elm Street? [Didn't *anyone* live over those drab small town storefronts Edward Hopper painted in "Sunday Morning"?] Does he really believe that our vast amorphous developments sprang from nothing more than the cupidity of real-estate con men? [22]

The answer, incredibly enough, is yes. It is as if Keats were wearing a set of clip-on, flip-up sunglasses. When he looks backward in time, the tinted glasses are flipped down on top of his spectacles, and he pictures a world of individualism and self-fulfillment in a lovely old home. When he focuses on modern suburbia, the sunglasses are flipped up, and in the clear light of day he finds "idiots" subsisting in cramped, stifling boxes. This practice of judging the modern suburb by the impossibly high standards of a nonexistent utopian past is not at all unusual. Keats is at once more explicit and less thoughtful than some other critics of suburbia in acknowledging the standard of comparison; the flip-up sunglasses are standard equipment for them as well.

But it is not really the shoddiness of housing development dwellings that rouses Keats's wrath. It is their intolerable standardization, row on row of "identical boxes spreading like gangrene" throughout the country.[23] There can be no question, of course, that the charge of standardization (like that of shoddiness) has its basis in the facts. If you have driven through the streets of most American suburbs, you have seen the row houses of equivalent design, decoration, and setback. Such standardization seems depressing to you, but the important thing is that it seems even more depressing to the suburbanite. As a consequence, an enormous amount of effort has been spent by suburbanites to make their houses somehow different from those on either side and across the street. The more identical things are, the more he seeks some distinctive touch to symbolize and validate any particular tract house as *his* house.

Harold Wattel has traced this process in Levittown, where individuality has been expressed on the small, originally identical homes in a variety of ways. Levittown residents have repainted the outside of their homes, shifting colors; they have rearranged the grounds and planted shrubbery; they have altered the original design of the house by additions; and, most of all, they have differentiated the interiors of their homes. Wattel found homes furnished in "contemporary, Chinese modern, early American Colonial, overstuffed borax, and individual make-shift. . . . The Park Avenue interior decorator might well turn up his nose at the poor taste with which some of the decorating has been handled. The point of the matter is, however, that it was individual taste that carried the day." [24] That is the point of the matter for Wattel, a practicing sociologist who apparently carries no excess baggage from the past. It is not the point at all for those social commentators who continue to bombard the suburbs with criticism. For them, the point is that all these alterations and redecorations are not efforts to express individuality at all, but merely attempts to keep up with the Joneses. The suburbanite, clearly, can't win. If he leaves his home as he found it, he is accused of standardization and conformity; if he attempts to alter his home, he is accused of a shallow competition for status.

The most severe charge of the critic of suburban architecture is that standardized dwellings produce standardized people. "Whoso would be a man," Ralph Waldo Emerson wrote, "must be a nonconformist." But this great individualist was wise enough to allow men to conform in minor matters, among which he would certainly have included similar house facades and uniform situation of plumbing facilities. The important thing for Emerson was self-expression, self-development. Beyond that, he advised men to accept "the place the divine providence has found for you, the society of your contemporaries, the connection of events. Great men have always done so, and confided themselves childlike to the genius of their age, betraying their perception that the absolutely trustworthy was seated at their heart, working through their hands, predominating in all their being." [25] The modern critic of conformity is stricter; he finds it lurking behind the picture window, and blames it *on* the picture window. Keats, for example, states that Mary Drone lived in a "vast, communistic, female barracks," which was "much closer in every way to 1984 than to 1934" (There was a golden year!) and that this "communism, like any other, was made possible by destruction of the individual." [26] It is the house, he maintains, that has turned Mary into an impossible nag of a wife, and John into a weak, weary imitation of a husband and father.

Life in the suburbs has dire effects both on the individual and on the family, according to the critical attack. Working against the individual is a social climate composed of conformity and continual neighboring, with a consequent loss of privacy. The family contracts money ills, weakens because of Dad's long commuting hours away from home, and collapses into a permissive child centered matriarchy.

That, in a short paragraph, is the sociological complaint against suburban life style. The single worst element in the charge, of course, is that of conformity. As Daniel Bell has pointed out, Americans have rarely been able to stand the idea of conformity, and it is just as easy to score a hit with the accusation today as it was thirty years ago.[27] Then, you had only to call a man a "Babbitt" to produce acute discomfiture; now the term "suburbanite" has been virtually equated with a shallow conformity.

Appearances seem to justify the equation of suburbia with conformity. Many (probably most) suburbanites live in row houses which vary widely in quality but narrowly in home design: they live in little boxes. The standardization is made even bleaker, Max Lerner writes, by "the uniformity of age, income, and class outlook," [28] by homogeneity, in other words. A good case can be made that the suburbs (or at least the new, postwar suburbs) *were* inhabited principally by families of approximately the same age, social class, and level of advancement. A generation of mostly middle class veterans occupied the houses as quickly as they were built, aided by a combination of necessity and liberal GI loan policies. But what was true in 1948 is much less true today, as William Dobriner has shown in his book, *Class in Suburbia*. Long Island's Levittown may have begun as a "monotonously middle class" bedroom community, but times have changed, and so has the population, with many upper lower class and lower middle class families now intermingling with the middle class residents.[29] Such half-way measures do not satisfy Lerner, for ". . . in time the suburban dwellers and planners were to learn that a community must embody a balance between industry and residence, as it must also have variety and surprise in its outward aspect, and a balance of age and class groups, of ethnic groups, of innovation and tradition." [30]

This idealized community sounds very much like a loose collection of diverse individuals. The "balance" of social and individual is jiggered in favor of the individual. Suburban conformity will destroy the individual, Keats tells his readers, and the more moderate Max Lerner would probably agree. Surely the attack on conformity is motivated largely by a powerful individualism. A suburban minister, for example, complains that "a lot of people don't have convictions of their own. They're living by standards set up by friends and relatives." [31] Does he believe that each person should live by his own code of ethics? If so, he holds as idealistic a view of the nature of man as does Lerner of the nature of the community. He does not regard social restraints—"standards set up by friends and relatives" —as useful or worthwhile. Institutions are not to be trusted; if each man does away with them and thinks and lives for himself, the result will be a state of happy Veblenian savagery, in a community of isolated individuals.[32]

This mindless, herdlike conformity, born of homogeneous people living in standardized dwellings, breeds what suburbia's attackers regard as the silly, stifling habit of neighboring. The women Kaffee-klatsch all day and then with their husbands play bridge in the evening, interrupting the bidding with discussions of childbirth or child rearing. These friendships are the product of proximity and nothing more; they have little meaning, and can easily be exchanged for similarly dull, strictly temporary relationships in the next suburb. Such neighboring is but a substitute for individual thought and action. Commingled with the group, man gives up his right, even his duty, to be himself. The groups themselves are formed for callous instrumental reasons; the women socialize because they can't escape one another, the men regard their neighbors with all the warmth required to borrow a lawn mower. People in the suburbs, it is charged, regard each other as tools, or commodities, to be "used" as needed to fill idle time or increase one's comfort.

But it is at least possible to credit the notion that suburbanites make real friends with each other, partly because suburbs "assemble people of similar ages and interests." There *does* seem to be more social life than among comparable groups in, say, a city apartment building. "The people involved in this socializing . . . don't think it's so reprehensible. Many people, in fact, move to the suburbs hoping to make new friends. And critics are in the position of condemning the suburbs for making friendship easier." [33] The position seems particularly untenable, since some of the critics are the same ones who condemn cities for making friendship difficult. Again, there is no escape from the barrage: live in the city and you're indicted for alienation, live in the suburbs and you're charged with a meaningless togetherness.

The critics of the suburbs condemn the practice of neighboring because, they say, it becomes compulsory. Visiting is so ritualized that any attempt to break away from a pattern of continuous contact is regarded as evidence of being "stuck-up." In short, one gives up all claims to privacy in the suburban group, or risks total ostracism. The argument is illuminated in J. D. J. Sadler's satire on the suburban life of Byron and Wendy Quilp. The fictional Quilps live in "an abandoned onion barn" up in Connecticut and have acquired title to land "which extends away from their house for more than 20 feet in every direction." A tract development soon surrounds their reconverted onion barn, but "skillful planning has insured the young family's privacy." They have planted trees for the purpose, and it "is ridiculous," according to Byron, "to suppose that *sequoia gigantea* will not flourish in this climate." [34] This rather broad satirical touch assumes that the readers of *House and Garden* will have a picture in their minds of the suburbs, and that this picture will include the difficulty of achieving privacy. But it is a real question whether this picture is representational or whether it reflects the impressionistic palette of super-critical commentators. At least two sociologists, in recent studies, have produced findings which contradict the charge of lack of privacy.[35]

Suburban life is not only supposed to destroy the individual; it is also supposed to disintegrate the family. People are constantly in debt; with credit stretched past the breaking point, the family comes apart at the seams. In a nation of consumers, suburbanites are the prototypical consumers; "they're buying everything at one time and some make payments running higher than their incomes." [36] The Quilps, for example, watched helplessly while their monthly budget ran up to $1,500, for which only $4 per month was set aside for entertainment. More than half the budget went to heat, maintain, and pay off the three mortgages on their house. Sometimes it seems to Wendy Quilp like a case of "so few never having owed so much to so many, at the same time, that is." [37] Constant debt leads to worry, worry leads to irritation, irritation leads to family fights, and family fights lead to the divorce court. Such is the presumed result of suburban consumption patterns.

In lamenting the tendency to buy now and pay later, the critics have of course isolated nothing that is peculiar to the suburbs. Western civilization generally, and the United States particularly, now operate on a credit basis. There may be *more* use of credit by suburbanites, for a good reason: these are, by and large, young and growing families, with needs for appliances and furniture that older, more established families have long since satisfied. What probably really distresses the attacking forces is the shift from a production to a consumption economy. They would return to that hazy past when indistinct men were dimly seen producers. With Veblen, they deplore an age when people consume not merely to satisfy their needs, but to differentiate themselves from others. Again, the critics have aimed their ammunition at too narrow a target. It is not only in the suburbs that people consume conspicuously, although there may be more consumption, both conspicuous and functional, in suburbia than elsewhere. "It is . . . noticeable that the serviceability of consumption as a means of repute, as well as the insistence on it as an element of decency," Veblen wrote, "is at its best in those portions of the community where the human contact of the individual is widest and the mobility of the population is greatest." So it is that conspicuous consumption claims more of the urban income than the rural income, Veblen added, and so it is that the urbanites "habitually live hand-to-mouth." [38] The substitution of suburbanite for urbanite makes sense, considering the apparent friendliness (wide human contact) and the high turnover rates (mobility) of most suburbs. But there can be nothing *exclusively* suburban about a phenomenon the philosophical economist noted at the turn of the century as existing everywhere, though most notably in the cities of the day.

However that may be, the critics insist, an economic environment which keeps Dad away from the youngsters during their entire waking hours is not a healthy one for the family. Holding down several jobs, forced to spend a good part of his day commuting, the father is too occupied with his task as breadwinner to play his proper familial roles. The result is "a matriarchal society, with children who know men only as nighttime residents and weekend guests." [39] Mom, by default, assumes the customary male roles: she disciplines and plays with the young as well as feeding and comforting them. In this indictment also, suburbia appears to be a scapegoat for a tendency in modern life which can hardly be limited by location of residence. Women do have more say in the suburbs, but they have more say everywhere else, too: "this is a universal trend, not a suburban one," as Gans reports.[40]

Mom gains none of the normal privileges accruing to the family boss. She is at the mercy of her children, and her life is "merely motherhood on wheels," an endless round of delivering children, "obstetrically once and by car forever after." [41] This version of the indictment contradicts the one just expressed. Suburbia's social organization is not only not that of traditional patriarchy; it is not that of matriarchy either. The system is one of filiarchy; the children are in control. Youngsters in the suburbs are hopelessly pampered and coddled and coaxed along. They are overprotected, and learn nothing of the trials and difficulties of life from their permissive parents. "Suburban parents and teachers are prone to do *for* youth rather than to spur youth to do for itself. . . . Too zealously we shield our children from a knowledge of the realities of life. . . ." [42]

Even granting that this charge may be true, can it be reasonably argued that it is true only of the suburbs? Helen Puner, after assessing the "many, mean and sometimes contradictory" pronouncements about suburban life styles, ends with a restatement of this question:

Life in the suburbs is too over-organized. It's too homogeneous. It's too competitive—for parents and children alike. There's too much pressure to conform. Families are too child-centered. On the other hand, they're not child-centered enough, for the suburbs are 'rootless' and rootlessness robs children of stability. . . .

Question: whichever of these observations—or accusations—are true, and to whichever degree is it just Suburbia? Or have we found ourselves a new kind of scapegoat for follies not really limited to people who happen to live on the outskirts?

Do these pressures on the individual and the family come from within or from without, from the individual in contact with his culture generally, or from the suburb itself? "Isn't it always people, in the end," she concludes, "who form the character of the place they live in?" [43] And not the other way around?

At the end of a harsh article about suburbia's growing problems, the magazine *America* comments editorially: "Perhaps the moral to be drawn from this rather gloomy catalogue is that no community can long remain an island in modern America. Forces that work for good and for evil have a way of intruding on the most secluded spots. For the suburbanite the lesson is plain: a mere change of address is no longer enough to free him from obligations that rest on all of us." [44] The statement assumes that suburbia was once a place where man could escape his obligations, but that this is "no longer" true; and it assumes that modern man is still motivated by hope of such an escape. The flight to the suburbs is nowhere more bitterly condemned than by those who see in it an escape from political responsibility, an escape achieved by electing not to participate, by refusing to plan for the future, by clinging to outmoded forms of government at the expense of the whole metropolitan area, and by casting only conservative ballots.

Some critics thus depict the suburbanite as an apolitical animal, apathetic, unintelligent, nonparticipating. Others paint him as *too* dedicated. C. W. Griffin, Jr., in a review of Peter Blake's *God's Own Junkyard*, agrees with Blake that the sprawling suburbs are "eating up open space, fouling up transportation, raising costs of utilities and services, and creating a stultifying homogeneity." But Blake, when he writes of "some suburban ignoramuses [who] don't even know what community they belong to, and . . . are unconcerned with local government," has missed the point, according to the reviewer. Suburbanites, he argues, are far more political than their city cousins, but their political interests derive from the "wrong" motivations. "Actually, to the suburbanite local government is a shield protecting him from the outside world, a Declaration of Independence from the big cities." [45]

This declaration is not, however, to be confused with an earlier, more justifiable one. For in retreating from the problems of the city and the entire metropolitan area to concentrate on his own local problems, the suburban resident has retreated into an inefficient, wasteful, out-of-date community while trailing the really important problems behind him. The worst sin of all is the insistence on local control, an insistence derived from an old American idea about self-government at a level where the individual can be seen and heard. The unwillingness to give up this "outmoded" idea has led to scatteration and inefficiency. The proliferation of small government units means that each unit is too small even to deal with its own problems, according to the attack. As the suburbs grow, so do their headaches. Streets and highways are inadequate to handle the unanticipated crush; water and sewer systems are inadequate to serve mushrooming communities; schools are built too small and too late. The basic difficulty is that "we are still attempting to meet the crushing problems of suburban chaos with a horse-and-buggy system of government that belongs in the last century." [46] And the chaos forgotten in the city is even worse than that in the suburbs.

What is needed, the critics proclaim, is more planning. More planning and more metropolitan government. In the suburbs, people lose track of such acute societal ills as wholesale poverty. The suburbs, Michael Harrington writes, have built a wall around the city's slums, and do not care to look over the top at the world of the other Americans. "Living out in the suburbs, it is easy to assume that ours is, indeed, an affluent society." [47] The solution to such blindness is to consolidate; when central city and suburbs work together under one governmental bureaucracy, instead of at cross purposes under many, the problems can be cleared up.

This argument is the most persuasive of all those advanced by the critics, and for a curious reason. Suburbanites commonly resist metropolitan government in the name of the Jeffersonian ideal of the small community, made up of individualistic, selfsufficient yeomen who meet occasionally to solve their mutual problems. By this ideal do suburban residents justify their blindness to problems affecting the larger community, and feel virtuous about it. The curious thing is that much of the criticism leveled against these suburbanites has been written by commentators whose thinking is far more powerfully influenced by this same myth than is that of the normally non-ideologically oriented suburban homeowner.

The critic of the suburbs is nearly always liberal, liberal enough to be idealistic about the Jeffersonian yeoman and liberal enough to be disillusioned by the large majorities of Dwight D. Eisenhower in 1952 and 1956. Almost to a man, the liberals blamed Eisenhower's success on the Republican suburbs, although such an easy explanation does not bear the light of close inspection. It was during the height of President Eisenhower's popularity that the indictment of life in the suburbs reached its peak. During that period the American public—and for the liberals, the American public of the time were suburban Yahoos—was choosing Eisenhower for a second term, the months between March 1955 and February 1957. Whyte wrote and published his attack on the organization man and the new suburbia during this time, and Keats brought out his vitriolic book. *The Reader's Guide to Periodical Literature* lists 60 titles for suburban life or suburbia during these 24 months, as opposed to 15 for the March 1953–February 1955 period and 29 for the two years from March 1957 to February 1959. Since that time, magazine writing on the suburbs has fallen off steadily.

The attack on government was paralleled by forays against other suburban institutions (the church and the school) and complemented by a barrage against suburbia's supposedly inherent psychic disorders. That there has been a revival of religion in the suburbs is an established fact; more than three dozen churches were formed in fifteen years to serve the burgeoning population of Bloomington, Minnesota, for example. But this development has been greeted with grave misgivings by the critics. There may be some suburbanites who are "searching for meaning in life where the better barbecue pits have already been built," they admit, but the "main mood of many a suburban church on Sundays is that of a fashionable shopping center. . . . On weekdays one shops for food, on Saturdays one shops for recreation and on Sundays one shops for the Holy Ghost." Once more, the suburbs are identified as the home of the consuming life. This tendency of the churchgoer to purchase a certain status and respectability on Sundays is unfortunately fostered by some ministers themselves, who go out of their way (as in offering drive-in services) to make worship "more convenient and comfortable," as does the merchandiser of more concrete products. "The house of the Lord," the critic bitterly concludes, "is being reduced to a comfort station." [48]

This attitude does not seem particularly Christian, or at least it implies a view of Christianity which is no longer held by most people. The viewpoint is Calvinistic, and is reminiscent of the American Puritans, in two ways. In the first place, the writer apparently has little confidence in the nature of man; even on entering the doors of his church, the suburbanite is judged guilty of base motivations. The churchgoer, or at least the suburban churchgoer (are people *better* in the cities, or small towns?) is innately evil, and acquires no title to virtue by following the commandment to worship on the Sabbath. In the second place, the condemnation assumes that religion is not real unless it is uncomfortable. For his ideal church, the critic faces squarely into the past.

In assessing the suburban school, the critical attack runs afoul of another contradiction. One-half of the attack is based on the inadequacy of schools. Thus one writer remarks that adequate school facilities "just don't exist in or near thousands of new communities" and another observes that parents "are becoming reconciled to having their children go through school on a half-session basis more or less indefinitely.[49] The other half of the attack maintains that schools in the suburbs are good only for the bright students, that their concentration on a tough college preparatory curriculum fails to take account of that percentage of their students who are not fitted for college either by ability or desire. This is the point James Bryant Conant emphasizes in *Slums and Suburbs*.[50]

Actually, there is some truth in both charges. Many new, rapidly growing suburbs have great difficulty in financing and building enough classrooms to accommodate their huge populations of school-age children. The suburb of Bloomington, to take an example, constituted the youngest city in the United States, with a median age of less than twenty years, according to the 1960 census. Many other suburbs were not much "older." Where nearly half the population is in school or on its way to school, the costs of education can be astronomical, and the chances of keeping ahead of the demand remote. On the other hand, in more traditional, long-established suburbs like Newton, Massachusetts, or Evanston, Illinois, the excellence of the school system may indeed take too little account of the student who is poorly equipped for college preparatory training. The apparent contradiction results, obviously, from a reluctance to distinguish one kind of suburb from another, a reluctance which characterizes and confuses much of the social commentary about suburbia.

Another contradiction, however, is less easy to explain by the process of differentiating between types of suburbs. This paradox starts with the idea that suburban teenagers are under almost intolerable competitive pressures to perform in their school work, as opposed to the notion that school-age youngsters are coddled and secured against any pressure at all. Students work and worry their fool heads off, one camp maintains. They take it easy and spend their time being popular, the other responds.

Whatever his school orientation, the youngster in suburbia is often portrayed as a delinquent. Sensational incidents lend credibility to this notion: vandalism at a coming-out party; drinking followed by automobile death after a graduation party. Such events, it should be remembered, tend to make news largely by virtue of the prominence of the families—or of the suburbs—involved, and are not to be regarded as more typical of the suburb than of the city or small town. Certainly, they do not justify the statement of Kenneth Rexroth that the "most serious delinquency problems in the San Francisco area, where I live, are not in the slums but in the garden suburbs . . . the habitat of drag racers, switchblade artists, motorcycle girls and infant hopheads." [51]

Moving away from the children, the popular version of suburbia's psychic troubles says Mom is very lonely. Just *how* she can be lonely in an environment where there is no privacy or escape from neighborliness is not clear, but lonely she is supposed to be. Such loneliness turns out on inspection to be nothing more sinister than the customary difficulty faced by people in adjusting to any new community. The difference is that in the suburbs, where there is more open friendliness, it is easier to make this adjustment. While mother is supposedly frittering away her day in lonely isolation, father finds that the suburb may look idyllic but that actually "it's an ulcer factory." Among the sources of his ulcer-producing strain, according to *Newsweek,* are high taxes, a fear of failure, and "crab grass on close cropped suburban lawns." [52] Crab grass warrants some round, resonant cursing, but such an outlet is supposed to be psychologically healthy. It is not likely to bring on an ulcer: "There is no reason to believe that the move from the city to the suburb, or suburban life itself, has any effect on mental health, other than a positive one. Most interview respondents report improvement in health and disposition." [53] Life in the suburbs, in short, is not nearly so unpleasant as the critics maintain; in fact a great many people like it so much that for them suburbia is a fulfillment of the American dream. The attackers object that such a fulfillment is only possible if the dream is an unworthy one, but in so objecting they take a position of omniscience. Not only do they tell the suburbanite what is wrong with his way of life; they presume to teach him a new set of goals and aspirations.

The social commentators who find suburbia so dreadful are disillusioned men. Disillusionment, of course, presupposes the existence of illusions, and the depth of the disenchantment is usually proportionate to the height of the expectations. By and large, the attackers have approached the subject of suburbia with great expectations— too great, in fact, to be possible of realization. The verbiage of magazine articles is remarkably consistent in illustrating this point; time and again, such phrases as "American dream" and "utopia" and "paradise" are used to depict what is expected of suburbia.

This rhetoric is then employed in reverse to portray the various serpents which have invaded paradise. The critics warn that young dreamers face rough sledding. They caution that drastic measures are needed to make suburbs "Paradise Won instead of Paradise Lost." [54] They write articles entitled "Suburbia: Lost Paradise?" and "Utopia Reconsidered." As their disillusionment becomes more bitter, so do the titles of their journalistic critiques. The question mark drops out of "Suburbia: Lost Paradise?" in such forthrightly hostile headings as "Life and Love in the Split-Level Slums," "Trouble in the Suburbs," "The Ugly America," "The Crab-Grass Roots of Suburbia," and so on.

When the people occupying these chaotic, ulcer-ridden, fouled-up suburban slurburbs or slums are given names, they too reflect the bitterly disillusioned attitude. John Keats, for example, calls his leading characters John and Mary Drone; among their neighbors are the Faints, the Amiables, the Wilds, and Mrs. H. Ardis Voter. And the "amount of either charity of intelligence meted out to the lot of them by the author could be put in a jigger with plenty of room left for a stiff drink." [55]

The critics have apparently fallen victim to what has been called the IFD disease, "the triple-threat . . . disorder of Idealization (the making of impossible and ideal demands upon life) which leads to Frustration (as the result of the demands not being met) which in turn leads to Demoralization (or Disorganization, or Despair)." S. I. Hayakawa traces the downward progress of this disease through an examination of the love lyrics of popular songs, which he regards as liable to lead to human demoralization, disorganization, despair, and disillusionment.[56] A set of too high expectations, whether about the love object or the place of residence, will result almost inevitably in a state of disillusionment. What is disturbing in the critical onslaught against suburbia is that it asks its harangued-at audience to share the disillusionment, even though it may not share all of the underlying expectations.

What is it, exactly, that the critics expected to discover, and found lacking, in the American suburb? Their expectations can be summed up as nothing less than the realization of the American ideal—a return to nature, a return to the small village, a return to selfreliant individualism. The American suburb, many social commentators came to believe, was the twentieth century place in which this eighteenth century ideal could and should come true. Reality stands little chance against such illusions.

II. CITY AND COUNTRY: MARRIAGE PROPOSALS

Town and country *must be married*, and out of this joyous union will spring a new hope, a new life, a new civilization.

—*Ebenezer Howard*, 1898

David Riesman, in his essay "The Suburban Sadness," acknowledges that he writes as "one who loves city and country, but not the suburbs." [1] Riesman's position is not at all unusual. Most social commentators regard today's suburbs more with loathing than with love, finding them homogeneous, conformist, adjustment-oriented, conservative, dull, child centered, female dominated, anti-individualist, —in a word, impossible—places to live. It was not always thus, with intellectuals.

For one thing, the American intellectual has not, until recently (until, in fact, the suburb came along as a scapegoat to replace the city) been willing to confess any affection for the city. For another, as the epigraph from Howard suggests, there was a time when the suburb was thought of as the hope of civilization, as the happy, healthy offspring of the marriage of town and country. [2] Howard's Garden Cities represented the apotheosis of the suburban dream, places which were at once *real* communities, collections of people who would work and live together in civic and social harmony, and at the same time totally self-sufficient units, made up of discrete individuals able and willing to pursue their own private goals. Indeed, if hopes had not once been so high for suburbia, it surely would not have fallen so low in critical estimation at the midpoint of the twentieth century. For Howard was by no means the only theorist to envision the suburb as the product of a happy marriage between town and country, a union to resolve one of the most troublesome paradoxes of American civilization.

The paradox is, of course, the continuing worship of rural, countrified life in a nation where the pull of progress has created an unmistakably urban civilization. The roots of the agrarian myth stretch back to the beginnings of Western culture and the paradisiacal garden. But the most powerful expressions of the myth came with the new nation and the Enlightenment, in the voices of such men as Hector St. John de Crevecoeur and Thomas Jefferson. Jefferson's fondness for the farm and dislike of the city are legendary, and Crevecoeur located his ideal Americans on the farms of the "middle settlements," midway between sea and wilderness, where the simple cultivation of the earth would purify them. These men expressed beliefs which have demonstrated amazing staying power. Their persistence can hardly be denied in a land where the Supreme Court must step in to assure city and suburb dwellers of fair legislative representation, where farmers are subsidized not to grow crops, where it is still expedient for a politician to claim a rural heritage. And the beliefs persist despite their obvious lack of relevance to reality. Men mouth agrarian sentiments, but go to the cities, where the money is to be made. The American thinker, almost since the first days of the Republic, has been confronted with this paradox, and as time proceeded American thought arrived at a potential solution. It would be the suburb which would represent the best of both worlds, which would preserve rural values in an urbanizing world, which would enable the individual to pursue wealth while retaining the amenities of country life.

After the Civil War and owing to the development of the railroads, the first American suburbs were developed around New York, Boston, and Philadelphia. From the beginning, these suburbs were regarded as ideal places to live, representing a rather wealthy middle landscape between crowded, unhealthy city life and the coarse and brutal frontier.[3] "So long as men are forced to dwell in log huts and follow the hunter's life," Alexander Jackson Downing wrote, "we must not be surprised at lynch law and the use of the bowie knife. But, when smiling lawns and tasteful cottages begin to embellish a country, we know that order and culture are established."[4] Downing had in mind rural villages full of tasteful "cottages" of real elegance, like those going up at Newport, Rhode Island.

Efforts soon began to scale down the lavish Newport cottage to the pocketbooks of the middle classes. Suburban homes and lots served as promotional bait in a 1876 *Harper's Weekly* advertisement aimed at attracting readers to "the Fourth of July Centennial Demonstration at the Third Avenue Theater." Two two-story cottages and ten $100 lots in Garden City Park, on Long Island, would be raffled off at the demonstration, the advertisement announced, as well as 100 silver watches and 388 one-dollar greenbacks.[5] Later in the same year, this magazine celebrated the joys of suburban life with a cover picture and article on "Summer in the Country." The picture, which shows a young boy and girl "walking side by side in the sweet summer fields," was designed to remind readers, "by contrast, of the sad lot of poor city children, who rarely have the opportunity to breathe the pure air of the country, and refresh their eyes with the sight of flowers and grass."[6] The "flowers and grass" make it clear that the "country" *Harper's Weekly* finds so desirable is somewhat nearer at hand than the Iowa corn fields. If such country was inaccessible to most readers of the magazine, as it probably was in 1876, it still represented a popular goal. Then as now, the place to bring up children was out in the open air, far from noise and smoke.

Three years later, in 1879, the radical Henry George proposed in *Progress and Poverty* that his single tax on land would have the effect of creating a sort of ideal middle landscape. Such a single tax, George maintained, would do away with wholesale speculation in real estate, and:

The destruction of speculative land values would tend to diffuse population where it is too dense and to concentrate it where it is too sparse; to substitute for the tenement house, homes surrounded by gardens, and to fully settle agricultural districts before people were driven far from neighbors to look for land. The people of the cities would thus get more of the pure air and sunshine of the country, the people of the country more of the economics and social life of the city. . . .[7]

Certainly most Americans agreed with this urban politician in an emotional preference for country over city; certainly most desired above all that union of country and city, sunshine and social life, he envisioned as a consequence of the single tax.

It remained for Ebenezer Howard, the London court reporter, to propose specific arrangements for this marriage of city and country in his influential 1898 book, *Garden Cities of Tomorrow*. Howard's proposals were welcomed on both sides of the Atlantic, and they remain today the guiding principles of so important an American critic and theorist as Lewis Mumford. Clearly, the proposals are motivated by agrarian sentiments: "It is well-nigh universally agreed by men of all parties, not only in England, but all over Europe and America and our colonies, that it is deeply to be deplored that the people should continue to stream into the already overcrowded cities, and should thus further deplete the country districts. . . ." How should we go about restoring people to the garden, "that beautiful land of ours, with its canopy of sky, the air that blows upon it, the sun that warms it, and rain and dew that moisten it—the very embodiment of Divine love for man?" The restoration can be accomplished, Howard wrote, only if we reject two-valued, black and white thinking, and consider instead a third alternative.

"There are in reality not only . . . two alternatives—town life and country life—but a third alternative, in which all the advantages of the most energetic and active town life, with all the beauty and delight of the country, may be secured in perfect combination. . . ." To illustrate the point, Howard constructed the metaphor of the magnets. Each person may be regarded as a needle, attracted by magnets. Until now, he wrote, the town has had the most powerful magnet, and so it has pulled citizen-needles from the no longer all-powerful magnetic "bosom of our kindly mother earth." To remedy the situation, "nothing short of the discovery of a method of constructing magnets of yet greater power than our cities possess can be effective for redistributing the population in a spontaneous and healthy manner. . . ." Howard set about to construct this more powerful magnet, which would combine the best of both town and country. There was social opportunity in town, but it was balanced by a "closing out of nature"; there was beauty of nature in the country, but it was measured against "lack of society." The town-country magnet would merge the country's beauty of nature with the town's social opportunity. In economic terms, the town's magnetism resulted at least partly from the high wages paid, but rents were high in town as well. In the country, rents were low, but so were wages. In the new town-country land, however, the citizen would make high wages and pay low rents—he would have his cake and eat it, too.

The town-country magnet became, in Howard's theory, the Garden City, which was to be economically self-sufficient while still at peace with nature. Population would be restricted to a workable size in the Garden City, and jobs, including industrial jobs, provided for all inhabitants. Homes would be surrounded with greenery; the presence of nature was never to be lost sight of in a pell-mell drive for the dollar. In his conception of the Garden City, Howard constructed a new version of the middle landscape, closer to town than Crevecoeur's. In Crevecoeur's version, the middle settlements were located halfway between the city seaports and the wild woods; Howard had moved his middle landscape so that it was now placed between the city and those rural settlements which had served as Crevecoeur's ideal. The ideal middle landscape, in short, was coming closer and closer to suburbia. It would be more explicitly located by intellectuals in the early decades of the twentieth century.

This movement of the middle landscape closer to the city reflected a growing awareness, already obvious in the negative features of Howard's country magnet, that rural life left something to be desired. The farm could never be subject to the vilification the muckrakers brought to bear on the American city, but the agrarian life was not all milk and honey, either. The Country Life Commission appointed by President Theodore Roosevelt in 1908 reported that drudgery, barrenness, and heavy drinking characterized rural regions.[8] The town boy did not have to visit Paris to pack up and leave; the question was rather, "How you gonna keep 'em down on the farm," after they've seen the farm? Young people continued to desert farming for the city, but the standard rhetoric of all Americans, whether they were urban or rural by birth, continued to praise and celebrate the virtues of life on the land. In their hearts, Americans knew that the good life was agrarian; but they listened to their heads, which told them to seek their future in the city.

Somewhat in the manner of Al Smith, who believed that the ills of democracy could be cured by more democracy, Teddy Roosevelt's Country Life Commission recommended a revival of rural civilization as a solution to its apparent degeneration. This revived rural life was to be different, however. In the words of the Commission chairman, Dean Liberty Hyde Bailey of the Cornell Agricultural School, it would be a "working out of the desire to make rural civilization . . . a world-motive to even up society as between country and city." [9] The scales were over-balanced in favor of the city. Something was needed to give more weight to the country's side of the contest. That something, several turn-of-the-century observers were convinced, was represented by the suburb.

Adna Weber, writing in 1900, surveyed suburban growth, then scarcely beginning, and pronounced it the happiest of social movements:

The 'rise of the suburbs' it is, which furnishes the solid basis of a hope that the evils of city life, so far as they result from overcrowding, may be in large part removed. . . . It will realize the wish and prediction of Kingsley, 'a complete interpenetration of city and country, a complete fusion of their different modes of life and a combination of the advantages of both, such as no country in the world has ever seen.' [10]

Court reporter Howard had located his town-country magnet in carefully planned Garden Cities of the future. Weber was more optimistic: mere dispersal of population to the suburbs, a trend already going its merry, unplanned way, would accomplish the modern utopia.

Frederic C. Howe, in his 1905 book, *The City: The Hope of Democracy*, qualified the title's message by suggesting that suburbanization, not urbanization, represented the democratic hope of the future:

The open fields about the city are inviting occupancy, and there the homes of the future will surely be. The city proper will not remain the permanent home of the people. Population must be dispersed. The great cities of Australia are spread out into the suburbs in a splendid way. For miles about are broad roads, with small houses, gardens, and an opportunity for touch with the freer, sweeter life which the country offers.[11]

Avowedly pro-urbanite, Howe could not resist, at least rhetorically, the charms of the countryside. These, he thought, could be made available to every man in the suburbs of the future.

Two eminent Harvard philosophers took much the same view as Weber and Howe, though they did not advocate suburbanization by name. Josiah Royce, who deplored the excessive mobility, the homogenizing tendencies, and the "mob spirit" of city life, maintained that the individual was swallowed up by the city, and could avoid this fate only by fleeing to the provinces. In the "provinces" (what he seems to have meant by this term might be designated "rural villages") were located the small social groups in which freedom was to be found. The individual could best exercise his individualism in a socio-economic-political community of limited size: the message, basically, of Thomas Jefferson, restated in twentieth century terms by the leading idealist of the age. George Santayana blended a strong strain of the bucolic with his urbane philosophy. Describing his boyhood town of Avila, Spain, he "expressed his admiration of situations that he described by the phrases *rus in urbs, oppidum in agris,* or *urbs ruri,* some combination of city and country." [12]

The search for the ideal middle landscape persisted along with the belief that city life was stifling to the soul. Louis Sullivan, in his *Autobiography of an Idea,* tells of the sinister effects of being taken to Boston as a young lad. "As one might move a flourishing plant from the open to a dark cellar, and imprison it there, so the miasma of the big city poisoned a small boy acutely sensitive to his surroundings. He mildewed; and the leaves and buds of ambition fell from him." He would surely have run away, the architect recollects without tranquillity, had it not been for his father's wise excursions with him to the suburbs, "on long walks to Roxbury, to Dorchester, even to Brookline, where the boy might see a bit of green and an opening-up of things. . . ."[13]

Perhaps the worst thing about the twentieth century city, as such observers as Robert Park and John Dewey examined it, was its very bigness. In the urban maelstrom, the individual lost the identity that had· been so assuredly his on the farm, in the village. The primary group tended to dissolve in the city, Park wrote in 1916, and people lost sight of the values of the local community in a search for excitement. "Cities," he wrote, "have been proverbially and very properly described as 'wicked.'" It is both ironic and appropriate that Park, the nation's first great urban sociologist, should have revealed a nostalgic preference for the secure values of an agrarian civilization, of the family on the farm.[14] Dewey, like Park, noted the frenetic quest for excitement in cities and suggested that it might be simply "the expression of [a] frantic search for something to fill the void caused by the loosening of the bonds which hold persons together in [an] immediate community of experience." As Morton and Lucia White point out in their valuable survey, *The Intellectual versus the City*, Dewey and Park were both playing modern variants on an old theme of Jefferson's, "divide the counties into wards." Like Jefferson, these public philosophers of the twentieth century regarded the small local community as the fit habitation of democratic men.[15]

In 1917, John R. McMahon published a remarkable book entitled *Success in the Suburbs*. He agreed with Park and Dewey that the city failed to provide man with a healthy environment. By some mystical process, nature refused to function inside the city limits, as O. S. Morgan of Columbia University's Department of Agriculture wrote in the foreword: "Soil somehow has ceased here to function normally on root systems, has become dirt and dust. Tonic sunshine has ceased to function in chlorophyll bodies in the leaf, has become an unrevered model after which to pattern an enervating midnight glare." The elect of the city, if they followed the good advice of author McMahon, would throw off this city spell. The advice was simplicity personified. Take yourself to the suburbs, he told his readers, where you can find true success. What was meant by success? Simply "an independent home establishment in a fairly countrified suburb; a household that is self-supporting as to fruits, vegetables, eggs, broilers, and such-like, produced for home use and chiefly by the efforts of the family itself. . . ." Such a successful life means not only health and happiness; it also means financial independence. There will be no *cash* dividends, but in terms of food produced and economies effected above the cost of living in the city, suburban life "returns an annual profit on the investment of something like twenty-five percent." In the suburbs, then, a man and his family can enjoy the moral and physical benefits of contact with the soil, and they can make a pretty penny as well.[16]

McMahon's was a "how to" book, as the subtitle makes clear. To achieve *Success in the Suburbs,* one must know "How to Locate, Buy, and Build; Garden and Grow Fruit; Keep Fowls and Animals." McMahon provides the answers. For him, clearly, "suburbs" seem to connote little value until they are transformed into farms. But as the future site of a nation of subsistence farmers, providing economic as well as spiritual gain, the suburbs would represent the Jeffersonian paradise regained. This paradise is within your grasp, McMahon told his readers; simply follow my suggestions.

Every spring, he wrote, "city folks yawn and have a hungry look in the eyes. They are restless and discontented, peeved and out of kilter. . . . they are bitten by the bacillicus countrycus, [which] is beneficent to those who live in the country, but . . . torments those who are prisoned in offices and flats." Urbanites should divorce their city jobs and residences to form a more perfect union. Like Howard, McMahon adopts the marriage metaphor. "My argument is that all city folks who can, should marry nature and settle down with her." You don't have to be rich to escape to suburban wedlock, he counsels. All that is needed is "a snug little home in the nearby country and a piece of ground large enough to grow eggs, fruits, and vegetables."

It is amazing how the family will thrive in its new arrangement.

Pale cheeks will grow rosy. Members of the family will get acquainted with one another, finding with relief that they are not "all monotonous Henry James characters" after all. There will be economic rewards as well. The family will raise its own crops for consumption, and avoid paying into the middlemen's profits. In town, the family had lived up to its income and could save little or nothing; on the suburban farm, they "live better and are able to stow away a few hundred dollars annually without feeling it." In bestowing advice, McMahon seasons his overt agrarianism with good, hard, dollar sense.

The first problem is to find a site, and beauty deserves some, but not final, consideration. "Scenery sticks around your habitation a long time and it is wise to pick out a brand that is pleasing and wears well," he writes. "At the same time scenery is not edible and butters no parsnips." [17] The dollar watcher and the philosophical agrarian come together in the same paragraph; the author speaks at once with the voice of Thomas Jefferson, and with that of Benjamin Franklin. Like Franklin, McMahon keeps his eye on the main chance; he is nothing if not practical.

It is the availability of modern tools and materials, in fact, which has made a utopian life on the suburban farm possible. You can achieve your individualism, and be comfortable about it as well. "On a country place you can attain much of the old frontiersman's independence while having comforts and a fullness of life of which he did not dream." There is not even any real risk involved. "Farming," he acknowledges, "is a gamble; suburban gardening should be a lead-pipe cinch." Marry nature and you live happily ever after; spurn her charms and you reject paradise. Attainment of health, happiness, and wealth was easy. It took only a move to the "real up-to-date suburbs, of uncrowded and unfettered Nature, [which] have become the promised land for the city man with limited means but a fair endowment of vim and enterprise. . . ." [18] The world of Thomas Jefferson was not lost. Every man could find agrarian peace and plenty, every man could achieve success on the suburban farm. A rural paradise waited for Americans, just around the corner.

Motivated by this same kind of thinking, Franklin K. Lane, Secretary of the Interior at the end of World War I, backed legislation to return soldiers to health and prosperity on the farm. The solution, once again, was a marriage of town and country, "a new rural life with all the urban advantages." Each family should have enough land to provide for its own needs, Lane believed, but there should also be a central, John Dewey-style local community "having the telephone, and good roads, and the telegraph and the post office, and the good school, and the bank, and the good store all close together, so that the women can talk across the back fence and the man can meet his neighbors." Several soldier settlement bills designed to finance this latest version of the ideal middle landscape were introduced into Congress, but only one, appropriating $200,000 for a preliminary investigation of the public lands available for settlement, was ever passed.[19]

The bills were opposed by the farm lobby, which figured there were enough of nature's noblemen already working the soil. The farmers' position was understandable, especially after the depression of 1921 drove millions out of work and back to the land. By that time, Ralph Borsodi had moved his family out to a subsistence farm, and while others tramped city streets looking for work, the Borsodis cut hay, gathered fruit, made gallons of cider, and "began to enjoy the feeling of plenty which the city dweller never experiences." Borsodi stressed the economic advantages of such a life, particularly if the family produced only for its own consumption. His wife, he concluded, could produce a can of tomatoes "between 20 percent and 30 percent" cheaper than the Campbell Soup Company by eliminating all middlemen. This kind of saving enabled them to be secure in times of economic stress. The farmer was once selfsufficient, producing his own food and clothing, building his own shelter, chopping wood for his own fuel. Borsodi's message was that those days were *not* gone forever; the farm family could still be self-sufficient.[20]

Like McMahon, Borsodi emphasized the part modern machinery played in making his adventure in homesteading a success. But Borsodi viewed success almost exclusively in economic terms. The healthfulness and virtue of country life he may have taken for granted; he did not make much of these beneficial effects in recounting his financial success story. For a century and more, the city had lured people with the promise of economic gain; the country suburb, its adherents now claimed, held even greater promise. An early advertisement for Waleswood, a 220-acre suburban tract outside Minneapolis, paid only token homage to the agrarian myth before hammering home its selling message:

> Instead of buying a quart of blue milk a day, take two gallons of rich milk a day from a cow for practically nothing.
> Instead of paying 19 to 90 cents or more of hardearned money for a dozen eggs only once in a while, pick up dozens of eggs every day laid for you for almost nothing by generous hens.
> Instead of buying one golden egg, buy the goose that laid it for the same money.

Not only was the land fruitful and its creatures generous, but a lot purchased now would be a sound investment for the future. Quite accurately, prospective buyers were reminded that "as the city grows, the value of your property grows. Opportunity knocks but once at every man's door. This is your call." [21] Jefferson would hardly have recognized his agrarian utopia. Base motives threatened to sully the virgin land.

Most intellectuals, however, remained faithful to the Jeffersonian ideal. Twelve southerners, for example, took a famous stand for agrarianism in 1930: the South, they wrote, could—and must—throw off the yoke of industrialism and restore men to cultivation of the soil, "the best and most sensitive of vocations." In a joint opening statement, John Crowe Ransom and Robert Penn Warren and Andrew Nelson Lytle and Allen Tate and the others agreed that to "think that this cannot be done is pusillanimous. And if the whole community, section, race, or age thinks it cannot be done, then it has simply lost its political genius and doomed itself to impotence." Lytle himself took a stand against emphasis on the economic advantages of rural life. Do not industrialize the farm, he advised; ignore those modern tools and methods urged on you by such preachers of the gospel of success as McMahon and Borsodi. "A farm is not a place to grow wealthy; it is a place to grow corn." [22]

The American public generally, despite the dollar appeal of "how to" books and advertisements about generous hens, and despite the inspiring rhetoric of the agrarian ideal, continued to flock to the cities. Then, in the 1920s, suburbanization became a demographic process of magnitude for the first time. (Compared to the flight from the cities after World War II, however, the exodus of the 1920s represented only a minor trend.) Few who migrated to the suburbs were industrious enough to succeed in McMahon's agrarian terms. There was nothing particularly visionary about these new suburbs; they were built to make money for developers. Still, the high hopes inherent in Howard's conception of the town-country magnet and in McMahon's successful suburb-farm refused to fade. In 1925, H. Paul Douglass concluded that a "crowded world must be either suburban or savage." [23] The planners would make sure that it turned out to be suburban. Clarence Stein and Henry Wright, under the financial sponsorship of Alexander Bing, started plans in 1927 for Radburn, New Jersey, which preceded the greenbelt towns of the New Deal as the nation's closest approximation of a Garden City. Other experiments were to follow.

The melodrama of American thought persisted, well into the twentieth century, in assigning the role of the villain to the city slicker. Confronted with his scheming, legalistic ways, the poor farm girl faced Hobson's choice: either sign over the beloved farm or face a fate worse than death. It was the most natural thing in the world, of course, for the American intellectual of the 1920s and 1930s to regard the city with a jaundiced eye; urbanization was steadily destroying the agrarian ideal. In desperation, he turned to the suburbs as the hope of the future, just as the New Deal planners did. That hope, too, ultimately came crashing to earth; when the suburbs turned out to be more citified than countrified, the in-

tellectual of the 1950s relieved his frustrations with a spate of embittered attacks. Suburbia replaced the city as the villain in the
rural-urban melodrama. In the mid-1950s it was almost inconceiv-
able to imagine that the suburb, in the dim days before World War
II, had been regarded as the *hero* of the piece, the one to rescue the
farmer's daughter from the clutches of the city villain. The record
of New Deal legislation, however, makes it unmistakably clear that
this was the case.

One of the more interesting and ambitious New Deal programs
involved the construction of new communities. The 100 communities
begun by the federal government in the 1930s, historian Paul K.
Conkin points out, "remain vivid reminders of a time, not so long
past, when Americans still could dream of a better, more perfect
world and could so believe in that dream that they dared set forth
to realize it, unashamed of their zeal." [24] Almost all of the 100 communities were made up of subsistence homesteads.

With the backing of President Roosevelt and Congress, $25 million
was appropriated in 1933 to establish and put into working order
the Division of Subsistence Homesteads, under Harold L. Ickes and
his Department of the Interior. Ickes chose M. L. Wilson to take
charge of the program. Wilson did not have his head buried in the
land: he earnestly hoped to restore "certain moral and spiritual
values . . . coming from . . . contact with the soil" by making use of
more and more technology and efficiency. The public response to
the subsistence homesteads appropriation was immediate and overwhelming. Wilson's division had $25 million to spend; by February
1934, requests for loans amounted to more than $4.5 *billion*. Wilson
had a real problem in deciding how best to spend his appropriation,
but he had made his basic decisions late in 1933. The typical community would contain "from 25 to 100 families living on individual
homesteads of from one to five acres, which would accommodate an
orchard, a vegetable garden, poultry, a pig, and, in some cases, a
cow. Eventual ownership was promised for most colonists. . . ."
Representative Ernest W. Marland of Oklahoma described the individual family's homestead somewhat more romantically:

A small farm with a wood lot for fuel, a pasture for cows, an orchard with hives of bees, a dozen acres or so of plow land, and a garden for berries and annual vegetable crops.

There is always plenty on a farm such as this.

In winter a fat hog hangs in the smokehouse and from the cellar come jellies and jams and preserves, canned fruits, and dried vegetables. In the summer there is a succession of fresh fruits from the orchard and fresh vegetables from the garden.

Heaven, indeed, was to be the destination of subsistence farmers. But dissension within Wilson's division kept the program from growing, and as the economy turned upward, the back-to-the-land movement, which "had been motivated largely by the hopelessness and despair of the depression," began to lose its appeal.[25]

The subsistence homesteads program faded into insignificance, but the community building program of the New Deal was far from dead. Rexford Tugwell spearheaded the second, final, and most significant phase of the program. Tugwell, whose enormous ability was matched by his self-confidence, set about "rearranging the physical face of America." He spurned the emotional attractions of the family homestead, and thought instead in terms of the planning process. For example, he saw that farmers trying and failing to eke out a living on submarginal land would have to be resettled on better land. But there was not enough good land to go around, and the surplus farm population would find its way to the cities, where millions were already trapped in slums. The solution to both problems, "the inevitable movement from farm to city" and the barren poverty of urban slum dwellers, Tugwell found in the suburban town or garden city, in a middle landscape planned in hard, cold, pragmatic terms by the hardest, coldest, most pragmatic of planners. Surplus farm families could resettle in these suburban garden cities, and so could slum families. The federal government, in the person of Rexford Tugwell, set about in 1934 to plan and build these modern "middle settlements."

As head of the Resettlement Administration, Tugwell had originally sketched out a program for twenty-five communities. But the courts and the reluctance of Congress to finance projects that the

Republican National Committee soon characterized as "communist farms" limited the number of such communities. Only three were actually constructed: Greenbelt, Maryland, near Washington, D.C., the most famous; Greenhills, Ohio, near Cincinnati; and Greendale, Wisconsin, outside Milwaukee. Consciously working on behalf of collectivist goals, Tugwell's Resettlement Administration was chewed up in the meat grinder of American politics. By June 1937, the agency was no more.

In the greenbelt towns, however, Tugwell had created the "three largest, most ambitious, and most significant communities of the New Deal." As Conkin comments, they "represented, and still do represent, the most daring, original, and ambitious experiments in public housing in the history of the United States." The three communities relocated low-income families, both from farm and from city, in a suburban environment which combined the advantages of country and city life. The suburbs, clearly, were the hope of the future for Tugwell, who believed there should be 3,000 greenbelt cities, not three. In suburbia, still a relatively unexploited frontier in the mid-1930s, was to be found "the best chance ever offered for the governmental planning of a favorable working and living environment. Past opportunities for federal planning had been ignored, with urban slums and rural poverty the results. This new area offered a last chance." The city had turned out badly, and so had the farm. The suburb was the last possible place to plan for a viable environment, and Tugwell, his idealism showing beneath the pragmatic exterior, was determined not to let the chance go by.

The greenbelt city, as he conceived it, was to be a complete community, with its area and population strictly limited in size, surrounded by a greenbelt of farms. There was to be plenty of light, air, and space, with safety assured for the children, many gardens, and good schools and playgrounds. Jobs were either to be available within the community or close at hand, and the town and its utilities were to be owned collectively, not individually. Planning for the three greenbelt towns began in 1935, and construction was underway during the following three years. When completed the three projects contained 2,267 family units and complete community facilities. In many respects, the towns were successful: residents flocked to occupy the comfortable single- and multiple-family dwellings in all three communities, and visitors from overseas were lavish in their praise. But the greenbelt towns never worked out economically. At the low rents charged, it would have taken over 300 years for Greenbelt, Maryland to pay for itself. In 1949, Congress authorized the administration to sell the greenbelt towns at negotiated sale. By 1954, all three cities had been liquidated for $19.5 million, just over half the total cost to the federal government of $36 million, not taking interest or the devaluation of the dollar into account.[26]

However impractical they may have been in terms of dollars and cents, the greenbelt towns demonstrated what federal planning could accomplish in providing suburban housing for low-income families. Today, of course, the suburbs contain people of all social classes, from the very wealthy to the nearly indigent. But the working class suburb of the 1960s, conceived for profit and constructed in the same spirit, lacks many of the amenities of the greenbelt towns. Those who looked to the suburbs with stars in their eyes in the 1930s may be excused for being disillusioned with the results of unplanned growth. Given enough money and time and the right political climate, Rexford Tugwell might have built a modern utopia in the suburbs of the United States. But there was not enough money or time, and the political climate, with its worship of individualism, was decidedly unfriendly. Tugwell's dream, like most, did not come true.

After World War II, of course, came the deluge. The boys came marching home in 1945 and 1946, produced babies, and looked for homes to house their families. Instant suburbs, thrown up by developers, without professional planning or architectural assistance, supplied the homes, and the GI's moved in. To most of them, the new suburban homes, small and neat, seemed entirely adequate. But those intellectuals who, like Tugwell, saw in suburbia the last chance to create an ideal living environment were saddened. There were not enough playgrounds, not enough walkways, not enough trees—

in short, not enough nature. In their disillusionment the intellectuals
turned on the suburbs with a vengeance. Where once they had
attacked the city for robbing America of its agrarian dream, now
they zeroed in on the suburb, which had betrayed their fondest
hopes for a twentieth century restoration of the Jeffersonian ideal.

As the target of abuse shifted from downtown to the fringes of
town, the city gained a respectability, a dignity, which it had never
before enjoyed. Jane Jacobs, in her urban rhapsody, *The Death and
Life of Great American Cities,* perceptively assesses the sentimentali-
zation of nature as a major cause for "the bog of intellectual misconceptions about cities in which orthodox reformers and planners
have mired themselves. . . ." Cities are just as natural as countryside,
she maintains. Are not human beings part of nature? Are not cities
the products of one form of nature, "as are the colonies of prairie
dogs or the beds of oysters?" Of course they are, but Americans
are not sentimental about cities. They are sentimental about the
countryside, but they systematically destroy it in building on it.
Each day, the bulldozers flatten out the hills and tear up the trees;
each day, acres of Grade I agricultural land are covered with pavement; each day, suburbanites kill "the thing they thought they came
to find." Worst of all, it did not have to work out the way it has.
There was no need for suburbs at all. Miss Jacobs would do away
with the middle landscape, leaving only city and country: "Big
cities need real countryside close by. And countryside—from man's
point of view—needs big cities, with all their diverse opportunities
and productivity, so human beings can be in a position to appreciate
the rest of the natural world instead of to curse it." [27]

There is general critical agreement that suburbanization is systematically destroying America's priceless natural heritage. "These
dormitory or bedroom communities displace the forests, the fruit
orchards, and the fields of waving grain which up until a few years
ago covered the countryside," a religious commentator writes.[28] This
accusation makes up only half of the indictment, though. For the
suburbs are not only killing off the country; they are also doing
away with the city. Nathan Glazer argues, for example, that sub-

urbia is invading the city, not vice versa,[29] and political scientists complain that outlying communities are siphoning off the life blood of the city.

The suburbs, in short, have come to be regarded as combining the worst, not the best, of city and country. The dream of an ideal middle landscape has been transformed into the nightmare of a no man's land between two ideal extremes. In their suburbs, Americans have "succeeded in averaging down both the city and the [rural] village." [30]

The flight from the city was entirely predictable in the light of the dominant mythology of American agrarianism. As two sociologists have remarked:

What Suburbia means, then, is a question that can be answered by viewing it more as a continuation of the older values that still exist rather than as a new phenomenon that has somehow taken the worst of all features of American life and encapsulated them within a split-level housing development. Perhaps the fact that Americans are moving in such numbers from the unplanned city to the poorly planned suburb is symbolic that really nothing much has changed except the time and the place.[31]

Nothing much, really, *has* changed. As much as ever, and despite the bitter lessons of history, America remains caught up in the Jeffersonian ideal, in the myth of the sturdy yeoman farmer plowing his own acres in self-sufficient independence, yet somehow part of a rural community. Conrad Knickerbocker has isolated the motivation which continues to produce the exodus to suburbia. The back-to-nature fixation, he writes, "has driven much . . . of the nation into street upon street of meaningless, tiny symbolic 'farms' stretching coast to coast." But these are farms with 60-foot frontages of crab grass, and no front porch on which to simply sit and fan yourself. Robert C. Wood, as Under Secretary of the Department of Housing and Urban Development, also blames "a rustic culture" for creating a decentralized governmental mess around our cities. "The need," he says, "is to develop a metropolitan conscience which demands something more than a rural shopkeeper's values." [32]

It would be reasonable to suppose, from the heat of the tirade

against the suburbs, that the concept of an ideal landscape had disappeared from American thinking. But such a supposition under-
estimates the continuing pull of the country on the imagination of
the urban intellectual. New Deal attempts to plan and construct
the perfect community ended, if not in failure, at least in financial
embarrassment. But the movers and shakers of the Great Society
determined to try once more, feeling again that there must be some
way of happily marrying country and city. Following this goal, the
Johnson administration threw its support behind the New Towns
movement.

New Towns, of course, are really only another name for Garden
Cities or greenbelt cities. Nevertheless, there are some differences between them. The New Towns are being constructed by private developers (often with government loans). And the New Towns will make
a greater effort than was made in the cases of Greenbelt, Greendale,
and Greenhills to attract industry. As Wolf von Eckardt writes, the
greenbelt program was abandoned "partly because . . . these towns
could [not] attract sufficient employment so people could stay put."
The success of the New Towns, he maintains, will depend largely
on "whether they can actually attract employers." [33] For one goal
of the New Towns, like that of Ebenezer Howard's Garden Cities,
is to bring enough jobs out into the middle landscape so that the
tedious commuting from suburb to city can be eliminated. To the
extent that they realize this goal, the communities will be able to
keep "closely accessible the recreative values of Nature." (The cap-
italization is not Ralph Waldo Emerson's, but that of the *Architectural Record*, April 1964.) It is Henry Ford's idea all over again:
men can and should be industrial workers eight hours a day and
nature's noblemen the rest of the time. The New Towns are not to
have any standard population, which can vary from 50,000 to several
hundred thousand, but the limit will be predetermined by planning.
Surrounding land will be purchased and kept essentially open, to
serve as a natural greenbelt. [34]

Perhaps the best known of some 75 American New Towns is
Reston, Virginia, a 10-square-mile site 17 miles from Washington,
D.C., which is planned for a community of 75,000 persons. Robert E.

Simon, Jr., the original developer, was frankly enamored of outdoor life, and instructed his planners to be certain that the growth of Reston did not "destroy the very rural amenities that its residents would seek." As a consequence, apartments and town houses were built to cluster population and preserve more open land.[35]

New Town planners hope that their middle landscape, once created, will be hospitable to all: "We hope to create a community that is economically and racially integrated—that is, contains a substantial range of income and occupation, and a substantial number of non-white families." But they lack confidence that such heterogeneous towns can be built, so long as private developers stay in charge. The developer must not only be willing to admit minority families; he must actively seek them, since they are not likely to apply in serious numbers. Besides, if housing is not subsidized, it is unlikely that many minority families could afford to move. The solution, as Albert Mayer and Clarence Stein see it, is to put the government back in the real estate business, a business it was supposed to have given up with the sale of the greenbelt cities twenty years ago. So long as there is a possibility of speculative profit, they state, "large-scale logically related development is not going to take place." What is needed is a philosophy of long-range disinterested planning by a powerful New Town Committee or Commission.[36]

Stein, one of the developers of Radburn, New Jersey, is back where he and Rexford Tugwell and the other planners of the twenties and thirties always were—on the side of centralized government direction and control of new American utopias. Ada Louise Huxtable, the architecture critic for *The New York Times,* is less insistent on federal control as well as less Panglossian:

Inevitably [she writes], New Towns may fall short of their objectives, and even share some of suburbia's sins. But only through professional community planning can the chaos of the country's growth be turned into order. Concern with the total community is a heartening sign of sanity, order, rationality and realism in the American approach to the problem of urban expansion. There may still be hope for the suburban dream.[37]

Serious, intelligent planning, serious, intelligent concern with the total community bodes well for the future. Planning is not going to cure all the ills of our cities and suburbs, Huxtable realizes, whether it is done privately or through government channels. The intellectual must realize, with Huxtable, that New Towns and other ideal utopias will inevitably fall short of their objectives. It is not going to be possible to restore rural America: "The wilderness, the isolated farm, the plantation, the self-contained New England town, the detached neighborhood are things of the American past. All the world's a city now and there is no escaping urbanization, not even in outer space." [38] To the very considerable extent that the modern ideal of the middle landscape looks backward to the Jeffersonian ideal for direction, it is doomed to failure, and its adherents to disillusionment. In any marriage between city and country today the city is going to be the dominant partner.

III. SUBURBS AND SUBURBS

. . . the suburban situation on the whole is one of transition. Nearly all suburbs are either being made or being unmade . . . one cherishes the hope that the suburbs are perhaps to be the salvation of the city, that in them it is to reach self-discovery on new levels and sense fresh possibilities which may affect its whole fabric now and still more largely in the future. He will therefore desire to believe that suburbs have their own permanent character and genius. . . .

—*Harlan Paul Douglass, 1925*

The motion picture camera tours a Long Island estate in the opening footage of *Sabrina Fair.* The narrator's voice calls attention to the "outdoor swimming pool . . . and the indoor swimming pool, the outdoor tennis court . . . and the indoor tennis court." This motion picture, which concentrates on life among the very rich, hardly presents a typical version of suburbia; few suburbanites maintain two swimming pools or two tennis courts or a staff of servants. A contrasting view is presented in *No Down Payment,* a film which examines life in a tract development. The tract dwellers live in a goldfish bowl, lacking even the privacy of their own quarrels because of paper-thin walls and three-foot sideyard setbacks. Here the suburbanites are young families barely making ends meet.

Which is the real suburbia? The elegant Long Island estate or the treeless tract? Neither place fits the image of suburbia which usually springs to American minds. This image sees the suburbs as the habitat of the middle or upper middle class—*not* of the upper class and *not* of the lower class, or the lower middle class either. Such "typical" suburbanites undertake long commutes from home to offices each day; they drink a little too much on weekends; they have no servants (but perhaps a once-a-week cleaning woman), they live, almost inevitably, in Westchester County or in southern Connecticut. This is where Tom Rath, *The Man in the Gray Flannel Suit*, lives; it is where Harry Bannerman, Max Shulman's inept philanderer of *Rally Round the Flag, Boys*, makes his home; it is where A. C. Spectorsky's exurbanites (suburbanites with a longer commute than most) hang their hats.

Bennett M. Berger, whose *Working Class Suburb* effectively disposes of the notions that suburban life produces excessive neighboring, conformity, and Republicanism, perceptively remarks:

The studies that have given rise to the myth of suburbia have been studies of *middle-class suburbs,* that is, suburbs of very large cities populated primarily by people in the occupational groups often thought of as making up the "new middle class"—the engineers, teachers, and organization men. . . . Thus whereas in most minds, Westchester and Nassau counties in New York, and Park Forest, Illinois, are ideal typical representatives of "suburbia," they may, in fact, be representative only of suburbs of great cities and of a way of life lived by metropolis-bred, well-educated people of white-collar status.[1]

Studies of such middle class suburbs as Levittown and Park Forest and Lakewood are certainly valuable, but their value is partly obscured when the authors generalize from a specific suburban community. Historians rightly object to such easy generalization, seeing it as a weakness of sociological methodology. "In *Middletown,* in *Deep South,* in the 'Yankee City Series,' and in *Plainville,* the authors draw their data from specific places, but insist they are dealing with kinds of communities, so that the species in general assumes more importance than the individual town or city."[2] As with Middletown, so with Levittown.

Any significant generalizations about the suburbs will certainly involve an inductive leap, but such a leap should not be essayed on the basis of so small a sample as is now available. The idea that there is only one kind of suburb must be discarded, and more empirical studies undertaken. As Maurice R. Stein observes, "the whole effort of developing a sociological interpretation of suburbia will rest upon the accumulation during the years to come of a series of studies of different kinds of suburbs. . . ." [3]

Arriving at a definition which will fit the landed estates of *Sabrina Fair*, the arid wastes of *No Down Payment*, and the majority of suburbs which lie somewhere between these extremes is not an easy task. Nonetheless, people keep trying to define what they mean by "suburb." Such definitions are attempted in terms of ecology, demography, politics, and psychology.

William M. Dobriner uses an ecological basis in establishing his working definition of suburbs: "those urbanized, residential communities which are outside the corporate limits of a large central city, but which are culturally and economically dependent upon the central city." [4] The commuter becomes the obvious symbol of the dependent suburb, because he must earn his livelihood in the city in order to pay off the mortgage on his suburban home. And commuting is closely associated with the standard image of suburbia. But just how valid is this picture?

As long ago as 1925, Harlan Paul Douglass isolated commuting as a process which was liable to put a severe strain on suburban living. "At least," he wrote in *The Suburban Trend*, "a process which consumes one eighth to one sixth of the waking hours of suburban people cannot go on without involving very serious economic and social results." With optimism, he predicted that greater use of cars would alleviate both the discomfort and the cost of commuting. "A group of working-men jointly using a depreciated flivver in going to and coming from work frequently have both convenient and profitable industrial transportation." [5] Douglass was writing about the suburbs of very large cities, which have substantial systems of public transportation; in the suburbs of most smaller cities, there is no real alternative to driving to work. Commuting, then, clearly poses a problem to the suburbanite. But is the problem unique to the suburbs? Do not most men today, wherever they work, drive to get there? What distinction can be drawn between the man who lives on the outskirts of town and drives to its center and the man who lives beyond the political boundaries and drives to the center in the same amount of time, or even less? And what of the city dweller who commutes to his job in an industrial suburb? These days, almost everybody travels to work, and father is no more likely to be found at home during the day in the city than he is in the suburb. It may be conceded that most suburbanites travel further to work than most city dwellers, but this is "often true only in terms of distance, not travel time." [6] At least one transportation expert, in fact, predicts that "we are rapidly moving to a condition in which differentials in travel time between any two points on the surface of the earth will approach zero." [7]

Such a condition has not yet been achieved, however, and there is one group of commuters who are subjected to substantial strains because of the length and difficulty of their daily trips between home to job. These are the exurbanites of A. C. Spectorsky, whose daily commutation may eat up as much as three to four hours. Such a man gets up earlier than the urbanite or than the closer-in suburbanite; he gulps his breakfast; he fights for a parking place near the railroad station; he rides the dirty train to the city, and still has a subway or a taxi or a bus ride to his place of employment. In the evening the process is reversed, and the nerves are frazzled and the muscles work to an ache by the time he returns home. Ever since Horace Greeley first built his home at Chappaqua, New York, in the middle of the nineteenth century, hardy souls have been struggling through life under the burden of what amounts to a 12- to 14-hour work day. Such physical and mental cruelty is the more remarkable in that it is self-imposed: Greeley did not have to move out of the city, and neither did any of his twentieth century followers.

Exurbanites are willing to put up with their cruel commute because they cherish what Spectorsky calls a "secret dream," a dream of escape from the rat race into a rural utopia. Exurbanites have always been "diligent in search of the rural, and almost never bought or built houses in the center of town. . . ." [8] If they move far enough out, such commuters are able to persuade themselves that they are farmers, men of the soil.

One such exurbanite arises every morning, seven days a week, at five A.M. to supervise the milking of his $30,000 herd of dairy cattle; in addition, he has a hundred sheep and is cultivating a special clover, his own hybrid. His morning work is over by eleven; hastily he dresses and drives to Trenton to catch the 12:35. He is in a radio studio until late afternoon; he must hustle back to get home in time to supervise the evening milking. . . . He is not happy, and can never be happy, unless he is working around the farm.[9]

Such a man, Spectorsky maintains, is not exceptional; most exurban-ites share the urge to work with the land. If only they did not have to make money in the city, they could become full-time farmers, or so their secret dream tells them. But there is an ominous sound in the background, one which will effectively destroy the dream. You get the impression, sitting in a South Mountain Road home, "that maybe you are sitting in on a re-enactment of the third act of *The Cherry Orchard*." The sound which breaks the silence is not that of the axe cutting down cherry trees but that of a bulldozer, flattening out the land for "a fearful crop of suburban homes." [10] The rural exurb will yield to a pseudo-rural suburb, and the secret dream must retreat even further into the country, away from the metropolis and its enveloping suburbs.

Demographers, working with census data, not ideals, have estab-lished certain rules of thumb by which to distinguish the suburb from the city. Otis Dudley Duncan and Albert J. Reiss, Jr., for exam-ple, used figures called from the 1950 census to find that the aver-age suburbanite makes more money, is younger, is more likely to be married, and has had both more children and more education than his city cousin.[11] An examination of 1960 census figures for three communities has been employed to test these conclusions.[12] One is the central city of Minneapolis, and the other two are sub-urbs, Edina and Bloomington. Each community borders on the other two. Minneapolis, of course, is by far the largest in terms of total population—about 500,000 in 1960, as opposed to 50,000 for Bloom-ington and 28,000 for Edina. (See accompanying table.)

Duncan and Reiss found that suburban incomes ran higher than those in the city. There can be no question that Edina fits this test; average family income in this suburb amounts to $12,082 (highest in the state of Minnesota, by the way), as opposed to $6,401 in Minneapolis. Bloomington's family income of $7,201 is also higher than that of Minneapolis, but in terms of spendable per capita income the Bloomington family is somewhat poorer than that of the Minneapolitan. The reason is simple: Bloomington families have

DEMOGRAPHIC DATA ON ONE CITY
AND TWO SUBURBS *

	Minneapolis	Edina	Bloomington
Total Population	482,872	28,501	50,498
Median Family Income (in dollars)	6,401	12,082	7,201
Number Persons per Owner Occupied Unit	2.8	3.6	4.1
Per Capita Income (in dollars, approximate)	2,286	3,356	1,756
Persons under 18	137,379	11,516	24,711
Median School Years Completed	11.7	13.4	12.5
Unrelated Individuals	75,784	741	809

* Final Report PHC (1)-93, *U.S. Censuses of Population and Housing: 1960* (Washington, D.C., 1962).

more children than Minneapolis families. The average number of persons per owner occupied unit comes to 4.1 in Bloomington, versus 2.8 in Minneapolis and 3.6 in Edina. Dividing this figure into average family income produces these more meaningful per capita income figures: a low of $1,756 for each person in Bloomington, $2,286 in Minneapolis, and $3,356 in Edina. Edina families have more money to spend than any others in the state, but Bloomington families, like those of *most* Twin Cities suburbs, have lower per capita incomes than Minneapolis families.

Booming school enrollments in the two suburban communities reflect larger families, and so does the "Persons under 18 Years Old" census category. There are about 137,000 persons under 18 in Minneapolis, or 28 per cent of the total population; Edina's 11,000 below draft age constitute 39 per cent of that community's population, and Bloomington's 24,000 under 18 represent a large percentage—48 per cent, just under half of the total. Here the figures support the demographers' findings; the suburban population is decidedly younger, if not richer, than the city's. Bloomington, in fact, is the youngest city in the nation, according to the 1960 census, with its median age of 19.6. Edina's median is 31 years, that of Minneapolis 33.

Bloomington resembles Minneapolis rather than Edina in terms of income, but Edina is more like Minneapolis than Bloomington in terms of average age. In regard to amount of education, Bloomington stands almost at a midpoint with respect to its two neighbors. Median school years completed came to 11.7 in Minneapolis, 12.5 in Bloomington, and 13.4 in Edina. By way of contrast, Minneapolis stands out with its 75,000 "unrelated individuals," compared with less than 1,000 apiece in the two suburbs.

The suggested conclusion is that demographic attempts to distinguish suburbs from cities tend to collapse when applied to specific examples. If sociologists have been guilty of generalizing about "the suburbs" from one particular example, demographers may be accused of fostering (if not of making) a statistical leap from the general to the particular. Edina is an upper middle class, executive, dormitory suburb; Bloomington is a fast-growing youthful community which seeks a balance between residential, commercial, and industrial growth; and Minneapolis is a sober, steadfast central city. Each place has its own personality, and attempts to place any two of these neighbors in demographic juxtaposition to the third break down hopelessly.

Chicago is hogbutcher to the world, New York is a helluva town, and San Francisco is a place in which you lose your heart. Just as there are cities and cities, so there are suburbs and suburbs. Douglass, in 1925, tried a breakdown of suburbs into residential and industrial, but realized that such a division was incomplete. There were already in evidence, he noted, planned suburbs and unplanned suburbs, race track suburbs and manufacturing suburbs, worker suburbs and manager suburbs, Caucasian suburbs and Negro suburbs, rich suburbs and poor suburbs. The specific character of any given suburb, Douglass suggested, was dictated by a process of *selective decentralization.* The "many elements" which make up city life "show unequal capacity for decentralization." Of those which can be exported to the suburbs, some go to one place, some to another. "Thus different types are created." He concluded that his study "must confess its inability to furnish a satisfying list of the types of suburbs which surround American cities." [13] Forty years after Douglass's conclusion that suburbs could not be easily classified, the popular image of suburbia has been reduced to a single stereotype. But the same bewildering variety persists. As Berger observed in 1960,

one suburb is apt to differ from another not only in the price range of its homes, the income characteristics of its residents, their occupational make-up, and the home-to-work traveling patterns of its breadwinners, but also in the educational levels, the character of the region, the size of the suburb, the social-geographical origin of its residents, and countless more indices—all of which, presumably, may be expected to lead to differences in "way of life." [14]

It is significant that most of the standards of differentiation suggested by Berger are also adaptable to measurements of social class —income, occupation, education, home cost, and so forth. For it is class and age of community which Dobriner isolates as the principal determinants of suburban character. When people say "suburban," they usually mean "middle class," he observes. But with the rapid growth of blue collar suburbs, an equivalence of "suburban" with "middle class" no longer makes much sense. As Berger's book points out, working class people pick their life styles and political candidates on the basis of socio-economic class, not of home location. In addition, because of the widening boundaries of the middle class, the charge of suburban homogeneity does not stand up. Levittown may have been populated entirely by young white-collar families on their way up when it was first settled in the late forties, but it is a different place in the sixties. More lower class and blue collar families have moved in, and so have more Catholics. The suburban zone, Dobriner concludes, "is becoming increasingly heterogeneous

in economic functions and in class, ethnic, and racial characteristics." [15]

One persuasive measure of this increasing heterogeneity of population is conflict, and Levittown has conflict aplenty. The major
source of trouble lies in the schools, where the suburban war between old and new residents is being fought out. The older families,
with children grown up, and the Catholic families, whose children
attend parochial schools, have opposed construction of new public
school facilities, and higher wages and working conditions for teachers. The new, younger families who want to be certain, at whatever
cost, that their Johnny can not only read but get into college, support any proposed improvement in academic plant or teaching conditions.[16] Such conflicts are rare in brand-new suburbs, where the
population is more homogeneous; they are almost inevitable in older
communities which are invaded by large groups of newcomers. The
difference is one of age, the second of Dobriner's two critical defining variables.

It matters enormously, he maintains, whether one lives in a new,
"cornfield" suburb, or whether one moves to an established, going
community. Levittown, a new suburb after World War II, had to
create its own institutions, but an invaded village like Westport is a
going concern, with its own political, religious, and academic institutions. When the invasion begins, a more or less open battle for
control of these institutions occurs. The community "is soon divided
between the pushy, progressive, and plastic world of the newcomers on the one hand, and the accustomed world of the old-timers,
the villagers, on the other." [17] Often, the arena of local politics serves
as a battlefield. This is what happened in Bloomington, Minnesota,
in the middle fifties, when the invaders succeeded for the first time
in wresting control from the old guard.[18] Suburbs, like other places,
change over a period of time. Sometimes, the change comes because
of this process of suburban invasion (a process which drives Spectorsky's exurbanites even further into the country). This process is
by no means unique to the United States, as Peter Willmott and

Michael Young have shown. They write of vanishing villages, such as Woodford, in England, which has become steadily less rural and more suburban as some of its "most respected citizens . . . have been marching northwards after the receding countryside. . . ." [19]

Generalizing about the suburbs, either from an ecological or a demographic point of view, does not promise to be very rewarding. Still, generalize we must, if we are to increase our fund of knowledge. The question remains: what kind of valid and meaningful generalization can be made which will apply both to the lower class tract suburb and the upper class exurban retreat? A clue to the answer may be found in the current assertion that suburbs are becoming steadily more urbanized. David Riesman puts it the other way around: cities are being suburbanized. Most observers, like Dobriner and Gregory Stone of the University of Minnesota, see the suburbs as "a belt of villages and cities peripheral to the political central city [which] are becoming, over a period of time, increasingly like the city." [20] When the city dwellers move to the suburbs, they bring the city with them.

How does the suburbanite react to his steadily urbanizing suburb? Many react with disappointment, for it was basically to escape the city that they moved in the first place. Talking of the exurbs, Bernard De Voto remarks that the "bluestone-drive areas where the second car is an Austin-Healey and people *fireproof their hay* is as organically a part of metropolitan culture as Times Square. Nobody can put aside its values by changing to a T-shirt and a knotted scarf." [21] Many, however, *want* to change values along with shirts; otherwise, they would surely not pay to have the hay fireproofed. The intellectuals and communications men who live in the exurbs rather consciously seek the purity of a rural life lived in natural surroundings. Somewhat less consciously and certainly less ambitiously, the tract suburbanite settles for a little open space and fresh air, removed from the smoke and noise and dirt of the metropolis. Both exurbanite and suburbanite yearn for the middle landscape, though they do not define it in exactly the same way. They want the compromise between wilderness and city which gives them the best of both worlds. But because so many people want it, the sheer magnitude of numbers defeats the vision of the more ambitious. The bulldozers grind away in the distance as the curtain rings down on the dream. Even where the suburb appears to be more country than city, it is only a matter of time before the city will come to predominate:

Out toward the fringes and margins of cities comes a region where they begin to be less themselves than they are at the center, a place where the city looks countryward. No sharp boundary line defines it; there is rather a gradual tapering off from the urban type of civilization toward the rural type. It is the city thinned out. . . . It is the country thickened up. . . . It is the city trying to escape the consequences of being a city. . . .[22]

Total escape is impossible for the secret dreamer who hopes to immerse himself in nature, like Henry David Thoreau, in a Walden of his own. "Nobody who has to work in the city can escape the city." [23] Those who share the more limited dream of a home of their own surrounded by a green lawn are less likely to be disillusioned. So it is that the intellectuals and communications men continue to tell the suburbanite what a horrible life he is leading, and the suburbanite nods his head in agreement while he happily waters his 60-foot lawn.

Perhaps the best way to distinguish the suburbanite from the urbanite is in terms of psychological motivation. The city dweller enjoys the bustle and the wide opportunities and the privacy of urban life; the suburbanite tries to escape from the noisy, dirty city to the lap of nature. Psychology alone does not account for the twentieth century flight to the suburbs, of course. Surely there are other causes. In the nineteenth century, the movement from country to city was explained in economic terms: there was money to be made in the metropolis. And in the twentieth, economic reasons have certainly played a part in the suburban boom. Inexpensive, easily financed suburban housing became available for the first time to millions of people who had previously only dreamed of owning a home of their own. Land speculators made fortunes as the building boom progressed, pushing the price per acre skyward. Building contractors and real estate developers became rich overnight, in the postwar emigration from the city. There are technological and biological reasons for the flight to the suburbs, too. Quite plainly, Robert C. Wood writes, "fifty million of us live in suburbia today because there are more of us than at any time before in our history; because easily available space in the central cities is used up; because advancing technology—most obviously the automobile and less romantically the septic tank—have opened up new spaces at low costs." [24] There is even additional psychological explanation: people move out of the city because suburban residence confers status.

Each of those reasons may operate to spur the flight to the suburbs. Nowadays, there is little status to be gained by living in those suburban communities which are almost universally regarded with scorn by articulate intellectuals. As a consequence, many have predicted that a counter-movement, a return to the city, would soon get underway. To date, this counter-movement shows no signs of developing: the suburban migration continues unabated. Perhaps the thesis that a psychological desire to return to nature is *the* dominant element in the chemistry of suburbanization is not susceptible to empirical proof. But there is considerable evidence in its support.

It is a commonplace for the suburban resident to explain his move from the city in terms of the children. "It's better for the children out here," he says. "There's more room to play and less traffic." In his study of attitude toward residence in and around Indianapolis, for example, Byron E. Munson found that "Better place to raise children," "Cleaner," and "Want larger lot" were the most important reasons given for wanting to live in the suburban areas.[25] This "open space" explanation is only a way of rationalizing the guilt he feels for deserting the city and its problems, the modern critics tell the suburbanite. But it is not merely the voice of guilt which speaks its approval of fresh air and open spaces. It is also the voice of the latter-day agrarian yeoman, proclaiming at once his independence and his desire for community.

Lundberg and associates, in the thirties, concluded that "suburbanites differed psychologically from those who remained in the

city. The suburbanite," they argued, "has a great attachment to
nature and the outdoor life, and is devoted to neighborhood, domestic life, and family." The rural heritage "is a little more recent and
vivid in this type," they said.[26] The exurbanite of today seeks more
independence and less community, the suburbanite more community and less independence, but both expect to find the good life in
nature, where the American agrarian tradition has always located it.
Still, neither the Glen Cove estate owner of *Sabrina Fair* nor the
California tract mortgagee of *No Down Payment* wants to confront
nature in the raw. It is the middle landscape that is desired, and it
has been that way since the first suburbs where the "pattern was
typically an open one: gardens and orchards and shaded walks, not
just gaping space." [27] H. G. Wells, at the turn of the century,
summed up what he regarded as the centrifugal attractions which
would reverse the nineteenth century trend of movement from
country to city:

The first of these is what is known as the passion for nature, that passion
for hill-side, wind, and sea that is evident in so many people nowadays,
either frankly expressed or disguising itself as a passion for golfing, fish-
ing, hunting, yachting, or cycling; and, secondly, there is the allied charm
of cultivation, and especially of gardening, a charm that is partly also the
love of dominion, perhaps, and partly a personal love for the beauty of
trees and flowers and natural things. Through that we come to a third
factor, that craving . . . for a little private *imperium* such as a house or
cottage "in its own grounds" affords; and from that we pass on to the
intense desire so many women feel—and just the women, too, who will
mother the future—their almost instinctive demand, indeed, for a household, a separate sacred and distinctive household, built and ordered after
their own hearts, such as in its fullness only the countryside permits. Add
to these things the healthfulness of the country for young children, and the
wholesome isolation that is possible from much that irritates, stimulates
prematurely, and corrupts in crowded centers, and the chief positive centrifugal inducements are stated. . . .[28]

The passion for nature, the charm of cultivation, the desire for
a sacred and separate home of one's own in the country, the wholesome healthfulness of the life—all would conspire, Wells predicted,
to drive the city dweller back to the more rural suburbs later in the

century. A drive today around the circumference of any large city will testify to the accuracy of his prediction. Douglass, in the epigraph to this chapter, speculated that the suburbs of 1925, then in a state of transition, might be the "salvation of the city" and therefore hoped that the developing suburbs might "have their own permanent character and genius." [29] The permanent character he had in mind resembled that of Wells's prediction: a ruralized retreat where one might achieve both a measure of independence and a sense of community. The ideal, in short, was much the same for Douglass as it was for Thomas Jefferson, whose utopia could be represented as a band of yeoman farmers conducting the business of their community at an open town meeting. To the extent that he is unwilling to compromise this ideal by bending his utopia more toward community and less toward independence, the modern-day Jeffersonian finds disillusion in suburban life. For if suburbs have "a permanent character," it is expressed most clearly in their political configuration, in their governments of limited size and universal access. Political boundaries really do not matter in defining suburbs, most experts argue. But the fact is that they matter enormously. Here one-half of the psychological programme for an ideal suburbia —the half dealing with a transplanted village—very nearly finds realization. In the formation of this community, however, the natural man must give up some of that independence which forms the other half of his paradoxical ideal.

IV. LITTLE BOXES

THE UNIVERSAL SUBURB

Little Boxes on the hillside,
Little Boxes made of ticky tacky
Little Boxes on the hillside,
Little Boxes all the same.
There's a green one and a pink one
And a blue one and a yellow one
And they're all made out of ticky tacky
And they all look just the same.

—Malvina Reynolds, 1963

When folksinger Pete Seeger sings "Little Boxes," [1] people stop and listen and smile in recognition. This is a song they understand; it is about suburbia, and suburbia is silly and pretentious and conformity-ridden and homogeneous, really no place to live at all. But the corners of the mouth turn downward and the smile becomes a smirk when the listeners remember that they too live in the suburbs, except that their home and their way of life and their suburb are, of course, different from the picture the lyrics and the jangling rhythm are painting. Then, they ask themselves, is it so different after all? And finally, what does it matter: isn't everybody in the same boat?

The answer is that yes, everybody is in the same boat, since nearly half the population has moved or is moving to the suburbs, and that it matters very much.

When you talk about home building, nowadays, you're necessarily talking about suburbs. Cities are already overcrowded; there are few lots left for homes. Small towns are dying, many of them, along with the family farms which they have served as market centers. But listen to the radio in any metropolitan community, and you hear the homebuilders of suburbia presenting their messages of "country club communities" and "picture book homes at practical prices" and "streets and utilities in and paid for."

"During the past four years," Lewis Mumford wrote in 1955, "the population of the suburbs and smaller towns around New York has grown four times as fast as the population of the city." [2] And New York is not exceptional. During the decade of 1950 to 1960, Minneapolis declined in population while its suburbs grew at a pace of better than 200 per cent. Whether we like it or not (and the naysayers make it clear that we should not like it), America is becoming steadily suburbanized.

The suburbanization of America began nearly a century ago, and has only speeded up in the last generation. Except for its elegance of style, the following passage might have been written last week: "Upon the mere numerical preponderance of the suburban house in the domestic architecture of the United States there can be no manner of doubt. The majority of middle class Americans live in suburban houses, and it is a majority which will increase." Actually, the sentences come from a 1902 article in *Architectural Record*.[3] But the anonymous writer goes on to reveal in several ways that the middle class he speaks of is decidedly the upper middle class building suburban homes in New Jersey and up the Hudson River from New York; it is not the mass middle class which now inhabits the suburbs.

"When scarcely any but the well-to-do lived in suburbia, a house there was a desirable goal; now it is becoming a social imperative." The population of metropolitan areas increased by some 12 million persons during the half-decade of 1950 to 1955. Only 2.4 million of the growth took place in the cities; the rest in the suburbs, and largely in the new suburbs established for young families on the way up.[4] What has happened, furthermore, is only a pale prediction

of the future. "During the past decade, as every student of population knows by heart, 90 per cent of all United States population
growth in metropolitan areas has occurred in the suburban fringes.
Within twenty years some 50 million more people are expected to
live there." [5] To take a specific city, "in Chicago . . . nearly 55 per
cent of the whole metropolitan area's nine million persons will be
living in the suburbs by 1975, compared with about 40 per cent
today [1961]." [6]

This process of suburbanization is, we are told, robbing the American of his individuality, his privacy, even his soul. Suburbia is pictured by William H. Whyte, Jr. as the residential equivalent of his
stifling, all-embracing business organization. It is deprecated, more
poetically, by H. E. Bates, who reminds us that what is true in
America is also true in England. Only thirty-five years ago, Bates
writes: "We were really rural; we really lived in the country. . . .
Our square-towered village church stood separated from us on the
crown of a little hill among cherry orchards where sheep grazed . . .
and men bore such names as Flannel and Codger." [7] German bombs
removed the church, and suburban homebuilding cut away the
countryside. Now the church is gone, the sheep are gone, and so,
presumably, is lovable old Codger. Mumford, than whom no one
finds suburbia more repellent, comments that, "A universal suburb
is almost as much of a nightmare, humanly speaking, as a universal
megalopolis; yet it is toward this proliferating nonentity that our
present random and misdirected urban growth has been steadily
tending." [8]

Whether they consider their subject from an aesthetic point of
view or from the point of view of the social order, today's intellectuals have tested the suburban home and way of life and found
them wanting. "It is a shocking fact," writes Ada Louise Huxtable,
architecture critic for *The New York Times*, "that more than 90 per
cent of builders' homes are not designed by architects and that
planners are rarely consulted—even when a town-size development
is involved." The resulting damage, she concludes, "is social, cultural, psychological, and emotional, as well as aesthetic." [9] As H. L.

Mencken wrote to his more outraged correspondents, the critics "may be right," [10] but right or wrong, it is certain that they are dealing with a topic of some importance in the universal suburb—a topic this chapter approaches by looking at the history of the suburb, the present suburban home, and the beclouded future.

THE SUBURB IN HISTORY

And the people in the boxes
All went to the university
Where they were put in boxes
And they came out all the same,
And there's doctors and there's lawyers
And there's business executives,
And they're all made out of ticky tacky
And they all look just the same.

There is nothing new, and nothing particularly American, about the flight to the suburbs. As Mumford demonstrates in *The City in History*, the first suburbs popped up on the outskirts of the first cities, and archaeologists have uncovered evidence that traces the suburb back to greater Ur in Mesopotamia, some thirty centuries before Christ.[11]

Later, in Europe, the wealthy did not wait for the concepts of the noble savage and the intuitional truth of nature to hie themselves to the countryside. Why did they move? Partly for reasons of hygiene and survival: "The very life insurance tables established the superiority of the countryside in terms of animal vitality; in England the peasant and the country squire had the highest expectation of life." [12] But there was another reason, too, as articulated by Alberti: "there is a vast deal of satisfaction in a convenient retreat near the town, where a man is at liberty to do just what he pleases" and again, in triple negative, "I, for my part, am not for having a [villa] in a place of such resort that I must never venture to appear at my door without being completely dressed." [13] Here is the true suburban note of informality, uncorrupted by any studied quality.

Alberti's fifteenth century view of the suburban home was pro-

phetic of the ideal still held in the twentieth century by men like
Frank Lloyd Wright:

Nor should there by any want of pleasant landscapes, flowery mead, open
champains, shady groves, or limpid brooks, or streams and lakes for swimming, with all other delights of the same sort. Lastly . . . I would have the
front and whole body of the house perfectly well lighted, and that it be
open to receive a great deal of light and sun, and a sufficient quantity of
wholesome air.

Then Alberti goes on to advocate both round and square rooms,
and all rooms possible on one floor, prompting Mumford to ask "how
much he left for the early twentieth century architect to invent. The
whole suburban domestic program is there." [14]

Shifted to America, Alberti's ideal of individuality and privacy, if
not his more radical (for the time) concept of a rambling one-story
dwelling, was nearly realized by early suburban home building, in
fashionable suburbs. Men like R. M. Hunt and H. H. Richardson
designed attractive country homes. Other architects followed Richardson's lead, and "Hastings, Price, McKim, Stevens, and Emerson
. . . left many fine suburban and country homes . . . [so that] the
American rich came home after work to a dwelling 'eminently private and lordly.'" [15]

But this was the late nineteenth century, and the excellence of
suburban architecture owed much to the fact that its clients were
both few and wealthy. Two elements conspired to change individual excellence into the mass-produced mediocrity of present suburban homes. The first element was psychological. Lower middle
class couples, seeing these fine upper class suburban homes and
their wide expanse of space, longed for the day when that kind of
life would be possible for them, too. In the late nineteenth century,
wealthy Bostonians used to tell their sons, when they reached maturity, that "Boston holds nothing for you except heavy taxes and political misrule. When you marry, pick out a suburb to build your house
in, join the Country Club, and make your life center about your club,
your home, and your children." [16] Not only young Bostonians, but
the scions of New York and Philadelphia millionaires followed the

advice, and the lower middle class city dweller enviously watched the upper class migration. West followed East as the lower class followed the upper. Eastern architects stressed the rural and rustic in their suburban villas, and William LeBaron Jenney, an engineer from the West, accepted their guiding principles in his essay of 1883, "A Reform of Suburban Dwellings." [17]

Two generations later, new forms of transportation made suburban life accessible to more than the rich. The years from 1885 to 1933 saw several attempts at building park-like residential suburbs near large cities, first Garden City and Forest Hills on Long Island and later Radburn, New Jersey, for example. The period also witnessed the development of many of the best-known and fanciest of American suburbs, including Shaker Heights, Lake Forest, Glen Cove, Tuxedo Park, Grosse Pointe, and the Main Line. [18] But in the end, the exclusive and well-manicured life of the early American suburb paid the price of popularity, as the newcomers poured in, bringing "their depressed and respectable environment with them" from the deteriorating cities. [19] Needless to say, a care for the architectural niceties was not part of their baggage.

Popularity helped break down suburbia's class lines. Still, but for Charles Kettering and Henry Ford, the mass migration might not have come at all. The internal combustion engine and mass-produced automobiles rapidly shortened the distance from city to suburb, and new roadways sliced through the greenbelt between railroad stations, throwing up radial eyesores in their wake. The suburbs of 1850–1920 had owed their existence to the railroad line, and commuting was a reasonably dignified, elegant process, as Richardson's station at Chestnut Hill testifies. In addition, the railroad preserved the countryside, with the stations—and the suburbs —properly spaced. Farms and greenbelts continued to occupy the bulk of the land between each five-mile station stop.

With the highway, it was different. In 1902, the anonymous *Architectural Record* author could comment with more than a trace of snobbishness that:

At the present time the land-owners who are developing under careful restrictions, the pleasantest suburbs near New York, rarely sell on plots which are less than an acre, and while such plots are available only for relatively well-to-do people, it is, after all, only the relatively well-to-do who, under present conditions, count at all in the process of architectural improvement.[20]

By the 1920's, the well-to-do had plenty of company:

The concrete road and the automobile multiplied the avenues of escape as the suburban train and the interurban trolley had been unable to do. More and more people found easy exits from the dingy city into the sunshine and open air of the suburb; and the freedom of movement of the automobile made it possible for suburbs to grow up almost anywhere, without roots, without convictions, without permanence. . . .[21]

There were a few, even in these early days before the explosion of suburban population, who tried to find a solution to preserving the charm of the old suburb while making it available to the average wage-earner. In England Ebenezer Howard developed his Garden City concept, which would place more or less self-sufficient and balanced cities of 30,000 at regular intervals from a larger metropolis of 300,000, maintaining open land between the large center and the smaller centers. This solution to the ills of the metropolis Mumford still plumps for, but architects at the turn of the century on either side of the Atlantic paid little attention to Howard. A few—but only a few—garden cities were developed in England, and in America, in the first decade of the twentieth century, Forest Hills and Garden City experimented with scaling down the excellence of some early suburbs to the middle class pocketbook. Unfortunately, these new communities "remained dormitory suburbs serving only the small portion of metropolitan populations who needed service least. . . . Forest Hills aimed at a lower-income group than it reached." [22] The times were not sympathetic to social planning then, and are only slightly more sympathetic now. The bulk of suburban growth in America has occurred through unchecked private development, without any guidance from planners. And the result, almost everyone seems to agree, has been horrendous.

In the years after World War II, suburban homebuilding erupted. Veterans back from the wars, afflicted with a sense of time lost, married and raised families immediately. Aided by liberal FHA and GI loans, these young families emigrated en masse from the over-crowded city to the multitude of new suburbs springing up through-out the country. Suburbia became a national phenomenon, develop-ing not only around New York and Detroit and Boston and Los Angeles ("a collection of suburbs in search of a city") but around many smaller central cities as well. Everyone already owned his own car, and now just about everyone could drive that car to his own suburban home.

According to the accepted sociological view, the crackerbox architecture of the new suburbia was but a symptom of what was wrong with the suburban experience. The real trouble was that the new suburbanites chewed up the countryside and deserted the de-clining city in a sort of cowardly retreat:

While the suburb served only a favored minority, [Mumford writes] it neither spoiled the countryside nor threatened the city. But now that the drift to the outer ring [sparked by the twin elements of popularity and horsepower and spurred by government housing loans] has become a mass movement, it tends to destroy the value of both environments without producing anything but a dreary substitute, devoid of form and even more devoid of the original suburban values.[23]

The classic reasons for the move to suburbia, derived from pre-eighteenth century sources, had been health and privacy. And if you asked the young couples with their war babies why they moved, you still found that the majority purpose was to "live in a cleaner, health-ier neighborhood."[24] But real-estate developers jammed houses as close together as the law would allow, and equipped them each with well and cesspool, and it would not be many years until the fluids from these cesspools intermingled with shallow wells to create a liv-ing environment as unhealthy as in the least pretentious slum. Mean-while, Alberti's motive of privacy, of a place to be oneself, had disappeared. In their study *Crestwood Heights*, Seeley, Sim, and Loosley discovered that most new suburbanites moved to find more

space—not space to be alone in, but space to accommodate others.
The children, for example, "needed a basement recreation room as
a place to entertain friends." [25] In *The Organization Man*, Whyte
speaks of the rare couple who feel oppressed by the overpowering
friendliness of Park Forest life. They would really rather read a book
or listen to the opera than visit. Another woman would like to keep
the curtain drawn across the picture window, but realizes this would
mean ostracism. In time, these mavericks become acclimated to the
norms of the community and even learn to find a kind of enjoyment
in the always-public, overpoweringly "friendly" life of the new suburbia. In Bloomington, Minnesota, all the couples on one block (*not*
a Jewish enclave) decorate their homes and trees with blue lights
for Christmas. The display is a handsome one to the viewer, but one
wonders about the exceptional homeowner who might not believe
in the birth of Christ or who might abhor blue lights, or who really
cannot afford to decorate this year. Clearly this heretical soul is better off keeping his ideas to himself, and decorating his home with
blue lights.

What the sociologists find in suburbia, then, is a deplorable lack
of privacy, along with a norm of gregariousness which may or may
not rub against the grain of the free-thinking individual.

A HOME IN THE COUNTRY

And they all play on the golf course
And drink their martinis dry,
And they all have pretty children,
And the children go to school,
And the children go to summer camp
And then to the university,
Where they are put in boxes
And they come out just the same.

Americans have always loved the frontier, the virgin land "vaguely
realizing westward." Great movements of populations, even now,
aim for the western and southwestern states, and in 1963 California
became the most populous state in the nation. The myth of the

village became a natural corollary to the myth of the frontier, and assumed more prominence as the nation gradually, through generations of expansion, began to run out of virgin land.

There remains today a feeling that great cities are places to visit, not to live, and many midwesterners believe that New York, for example, is not only dirty and crowded and hectic (and it is all these things) but also, somehow, evil. So Americans pack up and move to the suburbs, living by the village myth, preferring to travel several hours a day to avoid the great city. In the beginning, a century ago, the architectural consequences of this flight to the suburbs were happy ones, resulting in some great domestic buildings. But the mass movement of the middle twentieth century has had different consequences. The exodus led to the modern suburb which, according to Burchard and Bush-Brown, was but a collection of anonymous buildings called homes. For the first time, the low to medium income family could own a suburban home, without a down payment and with monthly installments less than rent, but they did not get much for their money.

What was this new suburban home like? Typically, it was set in a row of other houses very much like itself. Often, there was no garage; providing such an amenity was left to the homeowner himself. Usually, all these row houses were boxes, stark rectilinear structures unaccompanied by ornament. Frequently, there was no professional architecture involved: the post-World War II package builders tended to regard architects as a luxury they could ill afford. The builder's task was to put up as many reasonably sound structures as cheaply and as quickly as he could in order to get them sold and start on the next subdivision. Under the circumstances, hiring a professional architect would have amounted to a luxury both in terms of commissions and, just as important, in terms of time. Besides, there were plenty of simple, foolproof plans available. And, it should be added, the professional architects did not cry in outrage; in 1950, as in 1900, it seemed generally true that only the well-to-do client could command the full attention of the profession.

There were a few architects, of course, who did bend their

thoughts to the problem of the average citizen's home. The most notable was Frank Lloyd Wright, whose concepts of domestic "Usonian" architecture were systematically polluted by the builders who were willing to follow the letter of his ideas, so long as they did not interfere with the most rapid and efficient possible construction, but who never could be interested in the spirit behind them. It is ironic that by following Wright's basic concepts, these builders produced a new suburbia made up of cardboard boxes, the same boxes Wright deplored as the symbols of fascism. "What is this square package of containment? You see? Something not fit for our liberal profession of democratic government, a thing essentially anti-individual." [26]

Wright had proclaimed with Le Corbusier that, "A home is a machine to live in," and added that this idea should thrill the reader; he had announced that "Ornament can never be applied to architecture . . . [and that] all ornament, if not developed within the nature of architecture and as organic part of such expression, vitiates the whole fabric, no matter how clever or beautiful it may be as something in itself"; [27] and he presented the world with the open plan. Mid-twentieth century suburban builders swallowed each of these concepts, digested them, and spewed forth—little boxes.

It should be remembered that Wright was fighting an architectural war against eclecticism, and that his particular brand of patriotism made this war a holy war. Post-World War II real estate developers and construction firms were not inhibited by abstract motivations: the veterans were waiting, and the builders' task as they saw it was to provide reasonably cheap, reasonably livable homes rapidly, so they selected from among Wright's beliefs those which they could fit most conveniently into their crash building program.

"A home is a machine to live in," Wright had told them.[28] From here it was but an easy step in logic to "a home is a machine," and the homes of the new suburbia demonstrate that the step was taken. Labor was expensive, time was short, capital was the greatest problem of all, and efficiency and economy were the bywords of the builders. Clearly, the best way to achieve efficiency was to let the machine do most of the work, to find a home plan and stick to it, with machined parts slapped together at the site by workmen who did not need to be skilled. The result was a glut of identical or near-identical crackerbox structures lined up neatly in rows. As Wright himself commented late in life, "most new 'modernistic' houses manage to look as though cut from cardboard with scissors, the sheets of cardboard folded or bent in relief. The cardboard forms thus made are glued together in boxlike forms. . . ." [29] Mumford, far more oriented to the needs of society than the individualist Wright, saw much the same picture. There had sprung up in the mass movement into suburban areas:

. . . a multitude of uniform, unidentifiable houses, lined up inflexibly, at uniform distances, on uniform roads, in a treeless communal waste, inhabited by people of the same class, the same income, the same age group, witnessing the same television performances, eating the same tasteless pre-fabricated foods, from the same freezers, conforming in every outward and inward respect to a common mold. . . .[30]

Examples of this new housing abound throughout the land. Crackerbox homes went up and sold in astonishing numbers and with incredible speed. Mostly, the previously sleepy suburbs welcomed the growth; the equivalence of growth with progress is part of the folklore of America. An extreme example is the tract suburb of Irving, Texas, located on the main highway between the boom cities of Dallas and Fort Worth. In 1950, Irving's population was 2,621; in 1960 it was 45,489. The results have been less than satisfactory from an aesthetic point of view. "In its pattern of scatteration and, probably, in its built-in decay, Irving tragically represents too many other galloping suburbs across the United States, suburbs which have inflated the worst possibilities of their native landscapes." Part of the tragedy lies in the ugliness of the development tract homes and in the suburb's "homogeneous, tasteless architecture . . ." But Irving is also tragic in its seeming acceptance of growth for growth's sake, without planning, without leaving space for parks, to provide amenities, or for industry, to provide a tax base.[31]

Ornament, Wright had written, had no place in modern architecture. The word must have come as a relief to the developers who were far more concerned with efficiency than aesthetics: if ornament were not necessary, if ornament were in fact undesirable, why should they be troubled with niceties on the exterior of the box? Some distance away from the central city, one universal ornament, the television aerial on the roof, sprouted on suburban roofs; otherwise the outline of the new suburban homes was as plain and retangular and predictable as a box of Saltines.

Still, though the facade of the house bore no decoration, and the trees had been removed as a hindrance to construction, the suburban homeowner retained the greatest outside ornament of all, the front lawn. This sacrosanct strip of greenery, facing squarely toward the street, performs no function other than decoration. Suburbanites do not put up "keep off the grass" signs because there is no need: visitors who have their own decorative greenswards know automatically that the front lawn is to look at, not to step on. (Dogs are less cultivated: they may relieve themselves on the neighbor's front lawn, and when they do, they create a real community crisis that is invariably resolved by passage of a leashing law to keep the dogs, like the people in the homes, under strict control.) Time was, Bernard Rudofsky reminds us, when "cows used to be rented out [on Long Island] for the duration of a garden party to lend a pastoral note to an otherwise bleak countryside. Since then, cows and pastures have given way to interminable rows of what the newspapers hailed as 'lovely brick and hand split shingle colonial type split level homes.' " [32]

Americans might like to persuade themselves that in caring for their front lawn, they were satisfying some kind of primeval urge to return to the good agrarian life. Is there really no parallel? No crop ever had the loving and fussy care—watering, weeding, and cutting—that is lavished on the average suburban front lawn. This vast waste space, sometimes occupying more area than the house itself, stands inviolate, accompanied by three small and banal shrubs, two around the front door, one at the left corner of the house. The mod-

ern suburbanite may chuckle good-naturedly at the Long Island garden party with the rented cows, but at least it was an outdoor party
and the cows were there. (The mind reels at the thought of the
damage one cow might inflict on the front lawns of today's suburbia.)

"In its present state," Rudofsky writes, "the front lawn does not
invite play or rest. It is not a place where one might want to read a
book. There is no question that it belongs to the street rather than
to the house." [33] This, of course, need not be so. "Even the average
front lawn has enough room for a sunny place which, on bright
mornings, may serve as a breakfast nook; a shaded corner for discovering the therapeutic value of a siesta; a well-screened patch of
grass for sunbathing; perhaps a sand pile for the youngest or even
a shallow wading pool. . . . The habitable garden could thus become
additional living space . . ." [34] None of these things can happen, of
course, until suburbanites learn to put up at least a fence and probably a wall. There is no need to dwell on the probable neighborhood reaction to such a show of independence; in some suburbs,
ordinances regulate against so-called "spite fences" or walls.

Whatever outdoor living the suburban family does is done in the
back yard, where the smell of charcoal dominates the still air of a
July night. Here, then, is the real suburban living, and if one is
tempted to doubt it, he need only look on every side to discover that
his neighbors, every one, are proclaiming their devotion to fresh air
and the suburban, even *American* way of life by eating burnt steak
in the dark. Rudofsky concludes that ". . . probably no other civilization has produced gardens as melancholy as ours; aesthetics apart,
our suburban front lawns and backyards are a gigantic waste of
potential outdoor living space." [35] And if space is systematically
wasted outdoors, what happens inside? Here Wright's third concept,
that of the open plan based on a sense of greater space, has been
corrupted into some of the most cramped and cluttered living conditions imaginable. The open plan, as the great architect expounded
it, was supposed to widen the sense of space: "instead of a building
being a series of boxes and boxes inside boxes it became more and
more open—more and more aware of space—the outside gradually

came in more and more and the inside went outside more." [36] Again, the package builders took the concept and decided it meant they need not build any interior walls, or as few as possible, anyway. The modern box, they charmingly tell us in their ads, rambles; what really happens is that the modern house clutters.

By and large, post-World War II suburban homes are small, even tiny by prewar standards. The open plan presented the illusion of space, but it also created homes which were almost impossible to keep neat. But the blame does not attach solely to the builder: the occupants have more than a little to do with the customary clutter of the new suburban home. As a rule, the home buyer aims at a maximum of enclosed space with a minimum of expense. There may be long haggling sessions over cost per square foot. Yet

by the time the owner moves into his house and unloads his belongings, he seems to have forgotten all about it. In fact, he never stops adding more furnishings. The precious breathing space of the house leaks out of its pores under the pressure of forces from within and without—from the outside the crushing weight of confinement by a skimpy lot and looming neighbors, from the inside the cancerous growth of household equipment.

Steadily, the suburbanite fills every inch of available space with the "latest" in furnishings and equipment, and the overall impression is one of cramped clutter. He forgets that "Pure space, or, as we glibly call it, 'useless' space is something of a necessity for man to keep sane and to live a dignified life. 'It is the unoccupied space which makes a room inhabitable,' says Lin Yutang. Unfortunately, the implications are largely lost upon us." [37]

The clutter, some sociologists feel, is indicative of a change in ways of thinking about the house. Seeley, Sim, and Loosley view the Crestwood Heights suburban house as a center for consumption, just as they, and most sociologists, view the suburbs in general as the site of a consumption-oriented society. From this point of view, it is almost inevitable that the suburban house becomes

little more than a repository of an exceedingly wide range of artifacts. It contains the traditional bed, stove, table, and chairs, of course; but it also contains (among other things) freezers and furnaces, Mixmasters, medi-

cines, bed-side lights, rugs, lamps, thermostats, letter boxes, radios, door
bells, television sets, telephones, automobiles, foods of all kinds, lead
pencils, address and engagement books, pots and pans, mousetraps, family
treasures, pictures, contraceptives, bank books, fountain pens, and the
most recent journalistic proliferations.[38]

Attempts are made to organize all these objects as neatly as possible, but this can be done only at the expense of training children
never to touch *anything*. The objects become the house; it is a
museum, not a home, and one wonders during inspection just where
it is that the people live.

This suburban house is a museum in more than one sense. Not
only does it serve to display the latest in technological products,
such as electric toothbrushes, Exercycles, and self-rotating chairs,
but it also shows off the most up-to-date in mass cultural products.
The suburbanite is as much a consumer of culture as of cars and
household furnishings. The budget may be tight, but Johnny still
gets his piano lessons and Susie her ballet. Reproductions of third-
rate paintings adorn the walls, and the *Reader's Digest Condensed
Books* are displayed on the end-tables. There is great consumption
of culture, but, the intellectuals maintain, the suburbs are not an
environment likely to *produce* much culture. What's more, a national
communion in culture may not be a healthy thing; "the danger is
that communion will come to be valued irrespective of the quality
of the works that provide it. [We all share Lassie.] When this happens, the distinction lost is the kind of distinction one perceives
between the bells that make Pavlov's dogs slaver and the bells that
constitute a carillon." [39]

A natural consequence of this proliferation of objects, when allied
with the builder's perverted version of Wright's open plan, is that
each room does double duty. The "family room" is the perfect example; here is a no man's land where all may enter and no one, parent
or child, feels comfortable. (Marcel Breuer's bi-nuclear homes, with
their separation of parents' from children's living quarters, are apparently considered unwholesome in a child-oriented culture.) The

kitchen, to take another example, is no longer simply a place to cook but an all-purpose room:

It often serves as nursery, laundry, and, of course, as pantry. Under duress, its usefulness seems to increase and it becomes, if not exactly a dining room or living room, something like a domestic picnic area. . . . Even in the open country where space is cheap and plentiful, life at home is crowded and not much different from that in a city apartment.[40]

"Bedroom" has also become a misnomer. Ours is a culture which does not get to sleep easily, and so we have improved the bed. "Improved within and without, crammed with occupational devices that would have paralyzed Casanova, some beds resemble a shooting gallery rather than a bed." [41] Still, the bedroom does not seem functional enough for us, considering the cramped quarters and the need for a place for all our artifacts. So we move in ironing tables and desks. "The master bedroom, once the perfect retreat, has acquired something of the vapidity of rented rooms. No longer is it out of bounds for children and strangers. . . . The bed is charged with eroticism no more than a refrigerator. Above all, it lacks privacy. . . . [42] For a place to think, for the semblance of privacy, the modern suburban adult is driven to the bathroom. As Martin Gumpert remarked, "The time spent in the bathroom has become for many people in our civilization the only time which they spend in complete privacy and isolation." It is here that columnist Cedric Adams of the *Minneapolis Star* had his "Thoughts While Shaving." Rudofsky adds his usual pungent comment: "Things have come to a pretty pass: for lack of privacy, we take our thoughts to the privy." [43]

The *public* atmosphere of the contemporary suburban home is unmistakable. One does not even need to go inside to discover it: the picture window advertises the home as patently as the high-windowed store front. Here it is, the picture window proclaims, our modest little home—but see the new couch or the new lamp. The open plan, bringing the outside inside and taking the inside outside, has become the excuse for a style of home that prevents any privacy.

Stone walls do not a prison make; in fact, they serve the function of keeping the merely curious out, as well as keeping the prisoners in. The modern suburban homeowner has no such protection from the outside world: "Glass walls have taken out of life at home its last secret wrinkles and make it as transparent as life in a fish bowl." [44]

The picture window resembles the kind of window used in psychological testing programs, in that it has become a one-way window, with those on the outside looking in. Those inside seldom have a view of anything more exciting than the street or the picture window of the house opposite. In a belaboring of the obvious, Seeley and his fellow researchers tell us that the suburban Crestwood Heights picture window is "most frequently located in the front of the house overlooking the street—rather than in the back where [it] would afford a view of the garden. The purpose seems less to give the occupants a view of the outside . . . and more to extend an invitation to the outsider to look in . . . [at] a grand piano, a valuable crystal chandelier, or a striking red brocade chair. . . ." [45] And, incidentally, the expanse of glass makes of modern houses "some of the most intolerable hothouses and cold frames that have ever been offered as permanent homes for human beings." [46]

Again, a caution must be issued: if the picture window destroys the suburbanite's privacy, there is every indication that he likes it that way, a point we shall return to later. The *Architectural Record* writer noted in 1902 that, "The American suburban resident of the present day not only likes to expose himself and his family to public view, but he has a much less commendable want of reticence about some of his domestic arrangements. . . ." [47] The author hopes that fences and walls will spring up to arrest this deplorable trend; obviously, his hopes have been in vain. For the function of the suburban home, as Seeley and his colleagues demonstrate, is display. It is psychologically important (one is tempted to say, fatalistically, that it is psychologically *necessary*) to display the house and the articles in it, and this remains true of both high income suburbs and the new, imitative suburbia of the last two decades. "The rug, or the painting, or the drapes are 'shelter,' not at the margin between bodily exposure and survival, but on the dividing line between discomfort and psychological well-being." The latest purchase is not validated or "fully integrated" until it has been displayed as property and earned the stamp of approval.[48]

So we come to the suburban paradox. The escape to the wide open spaces of the countryside leads to a homogeneous life lived in homogeneous homes, every bit as confining as the most crowded city existence. "Not the least factor in this [suburban] development," as Mumford comments, "is the persistent residue of the curious pioneer belief in space and mobility as a panacea for the ills of social life . . . [but] this spatial openness, on close examination, proves to be social enclosure and construction." [49] The avowed quest for space becomes a search for companionship and acceptance and approval, at whatever cost in conformity. And part of the cost is living in a house with a tasteless and unornamented box-like exterior, a yard cruelly split between a display front lawn and a smaller, overused back yard, and an interior that serves as a cluttered public museum. Or so, at least, we are told.

V. FUTURE UTOPIAS

It will certainly be a curious and varied region, far less monotonous than our present English world, still in its thinner regions, at any rate, wooded, perhaps rather more abundantly wooded, breaking continually into park and garden, and with everywhere a scattering of houses. These will not, as a rule, I should fancy, follow the fashion of the vulgar ready-built villas of the existing suburb, because the freedom people will be able to exercise in the choice of a site will rob the 'building-estate' promoter of his local advantage; in many cases the houses may very probably be personal homes, built for themselves as much as the Tudor manor-houses were, and even in some cases, as aesthetically right. Each district, I am inclined to think, will develop its own differences of type and style.

—H. G. Wells, 1901

Critics of modern suburbia are legion, but a critic with a constructive and workable plan has not yet appeared. Such giants of modern architecture as Wright and Le Corbusier have advanced plans for a happier urban and suburban atmosphere, but their solutions make little sense, and Wright's are patently unworkable.

Plans for reinvigoration of the deteriorating architectural landscape fall roughly into two categories. First is the anti-city, exemplified by Wright's thinking on the subject; the other is the city in a parking lot, characterized in Le Corbusier's ideas. In Broadacre City, Wright sketched out a community made up of homes on full-acre lots; as a gesture in the direction of democracy, there were to be all kinds of homes—big ones, little ones, cheap ones, expensive ones. No matter what the size of the house, however, each "was to stand on a large lot of landscaped ground." [1] But such a concept would only worsen the present tendency toward unplanned and dysfunctional decentralization, in Mumford's view. Like Wright's buildings, his concept of Broadacre City is essentially a "solo performance" and "he has never faced the paramount problem of modern architecture —to translate its great individual accomplishments into an appropriate common form in which, by pooling economic and social resources and cooperatively integrating designs, advantages that are now open only to a wealthy few will accrue to a great many. . . ." [2]

Broadacre City is no city at all, but an anti-city; Wright "believes that cities should be abolished and that everyone should have at least an acre of land to live on." [3] Wright never did like cities much, and used to quote Ralph Waldo Emerson's remark about cities making men artificial. So it is not surprising that Broadacre is decentralized, horizontal (the horizontal is the line of man in love with nature, Wright wrote, the vertical the line of man against nature), low in population density, self-contained, and self-sufficient—a Jeffersonian community put down in the twentieth century. "What Wright was really trying to say with Broadacre City is that the modern metropolis . . . should be destroyed and that the only way to save America from 'mobocracy' (his term) was to give everyone enough land and air and light to enable him to live as an individual, rather than a cipher." [4]

Many upper class residential suburbs today follow Wright's lead, insisting on one-acre and sometimes two-acre lots before approving building permits. These suburbs are usually the older, more established suburbs, and the ones whose names are well known—Westport, Greenwich, Shaker Heights, Grosse Pointe, Whitefish Bay, Wayzata. Communities like these are truly "genteel dormitories" of high-toned residences, with little commerce and no industry allowed. Because of their prominence, traditional suburbs like these are often taken to be typical of modern-day suburbia. But the typicality is spurious: a very small percentage of the nation's suburbanites live here. These communities, and the people in them, form the subject of innumerable novels and short stories; movies, when they look at suburbia, almost always focus on upper middle class suburbia. But the general public cannot long be persuaded of their typicality, for the general public lives in the real, dominant suburbia of split levels and ramblers.

Contrasting with Wright's Broadacre City is Le Corbusier's La Ville Radieuse, or City in a Park concept. Here, the population is concentrated in tall towers with plenty of open land surrounding them. The idea heads in the right direction, Mumford agrees, but offers the wrong solution. Something must be done to stop the scattering buckshot development of the suburbs. We must, Mumford tells us, get higher densities on suburban land. But we need not throw up "the sterile, space-mangling high-rise slabs that now grimly parade, in both Europe and America, as the ultimate contribution of 'modern' architecture." This would only lead to a congested suburbia.[5] In short, there seems no good reason why a village should be a skyscraper on stilts. Additionally, the City in a Park, in modern terms, becomes a City in a Parking Lot, dominated by the acres of parked cars housing the cliffdwellers.

Having dispensed with Wright and Le Corbusier, Mumford offers his own solution—or rather that of Ebenezer Howard, who spelled it out in *Garden Cities of Tomorrow* in 1898. Howard propounds two basic principles. One is that cities should be limited in size. Population should close off at the 30,000 mark, and area should be limited as well to prevent scatteration. Secondly, Howard proposes that these cities—the suburbs of the future, as he saw them—be located at some distance from a larger, 300,000-population central city, with careful attention to preserving the green patches between metropolis and regional city.[6] Eliel Saarinen, writing in 1943, proposed much the same arrangement of the urban-suburban population mass. His concept, labeled "organic decentralization," would transfer activities from decayed areas to those locations which are functionally suitable. The basic plan would be to collect ill-located but functional operations in new, better-suited townships around the central city. The abandoned areas would be rehabilitated, but the "most conspicuous characteristic of organic decentralization is the fact that the former urban compactness will be split by it into individual townships, separated one from another by protective zones of green land." [7] Such regional towns would presumably be more distinct from the city than today's suburbia. "Clean and manageable, each would have an optimum balance of activities, would be nourished by its own industry and have an amateur culture of symphony orchestras, art schools, and little theatres, all its own."

This dream will never come to pass, according to William H. Whyte, Jr. Instead, "the result will be more scatteration—no nice clean regional towns, but a vast sprawl of subdivisions, neither country nor city." [8] Whyte concludes that explosion outward, as Wright advocated, or explosion upward, as Le Corbusier proposed, are both undesirable, and that Howard's regional towns may lead to scattered suburban chaos.

No matter whose scheme is adopted, however, none is workable without a basic change in the governmental structure of metropolitan America. The profession of planning is one of the fastest growing in the land, but most planners today are empowered only to draw up plans for development of the cities and suburbs of tomorrow. Their role is advisory, and that is as it should be in a demoocratic country. But if planners have little or no power of implementation, neither do those they are advising—the legislative and executive leaders of the great metropolitan areas. The fragmentation of governmental units effectively stands in the way of any planning that can produce concrete results.

For example, the New York Regional Plan Association is wrestling with the problem of population growth in an area that includes more than a thousand municipal subdivisions. Its planners have predicted that economic expansion will lead to enough jobs to take care of the expected natural population increase (through more births than deaths) during the next fifteen to twenty years. But there will not be enough jobs for in-migrants, too. Unless something is done, there are going to be a great many more people than jobs in the New York region by 1985. But what can be done? The regional planners are unsure, but their questionnaire to citizens of the area indicate the direction of their thinking. Do you, they ask the resident of South Orange, New Jersey, believe that population growth should be controlled? Does industry, they ask the man in Yonkers, have a responsibility to provide housing for its workers when it locates plants in the suburbs, as more and more industrial firms are doing? Should laws be passed, the Manhattanite is queried, to establish quotas on those moving to New York from other parts of the country, especially if they have no job waiting? [9]

Most such actions would do considerable damage to the American democratic ideal, as expounded by the stream of political thought stemming from Thomas Paine and Thomas Jefferson. In the United States, a man can live anywhere, pull up stakes anytime, have as many children as he wishes, change jobs at will. He is, in short, free to make most of his own important decisions. And he likes it that way: "The average middle class American does not understand and positively dislikes planning. . . ." [10] Any implemented planning would require that he be deprived of at least some of these important decisions, that they be made for him on the basis of the general welfare. Such is one dilemma of the planning process.

Another dilemma is more concrete, but just as puzzling, and it inheres in the multitude of governmental subdivisions surrounding every American metropolis. As has been said, neither the planners nor those they advise have any real power to initiate proposals suggested in their questions to the public. The very planning concept is almost never accepted until it is too late to do any real planning, Clarence Stein maintains. There is no real city planning, only city *patching*. His model community of Radburn, New Jersey, on the other hand, *was* planned, with a conscious goal in mind: "We have sought ways of bringing peaceful life in spacious green surroundings to ordinary people in this mechanical age." [11] If the goal was not entirely reached, it may perhaps be attributed to the perversity of animate beings. There are handsome play areas in Radburn, but the children play in the paved cul-de-sacs; greenways stretch from home to school, but the youngsters walk on the road. Even the most careful planning "does not perforce create a community." [12]

Such perverse behavior underlines and supports the conclusion reached by Gans in his exhaustive study of Levittowners. He set out to find to "what extent a community is made by its residents and to what extent by leaders, planners, and other experts who want to stimulate innovation and change" and concluded that "what happens in a community is almost always a reflection of the people who live in it, especially the numerical and cultural majority." [13] Communities are made by people, not planners. And left to itself, the numerical and cultural majority seems unlikely to recreate agrarian utopias on the face of the land. The town of Reston, Virginia, outside Washington, ran into financial difficulty largely because its developer thought the public would be willing to pay for more of the amenities of open space and fresh air than were available in more conventional, less ambitiously planned suburbs. He overestimated the market of latter-day Jeffersonians.

In short, it does not look as if any planned utopia will solve what the sociologists maintain is a socially and architecturally intolerable way of life. Perhaps it is just as well; perhaps the suburbs are already travelling in the right direction; possibly the new suburbia has awakened to its own problems and is solving them. The suburban picture may not be nearly so dark as it has been painted, as the following suggests.

The new suburbs, most of them, have learned their economic lessons, and are developing into balanced communities. There are still some content to remain mere dormitories for the central city business elite, but most have realized that they must bring in commercial and industrial development to alleviate the heavy tax load on their residents. The economic facts of life came hard to the new suburbia. The package builders surely had no intention of creating self-sufficient, balanced communities when they threw up a plethora of boxlike single-family dwellings after World War II. And, for the first decade or so, local suburban governments were largely content to watch themselves grow. But then the influx sent school taxes skyrocketing, and most suburban town boards and village councils called a halt to unchecked residential growth and started to try to attract industrial development. For its part, industry was happy to be lured; sites were few and far between in the overcrowded central city and the new circumferential highways, such as Route 128 around Boston and 494 around the Twin Cities, made the suburbs attractive from the point of view of transportation, both of goods and employees.

Sometime during the past decade, these new suburbs have asked themselves the question: "Shall we attract some industrial plants to help ease school taxes?" Except in the rare case of the wealthy suburb, the answer has been a resounding yes. In the Minneapolis area, two suburbs, Hopkins and Golden Valley, boast industries which supply more jobs than the total population of the suburb could fill. Another, much larger suburb, Bloomington, has reached a state of equilibrium between jobs and job holders living in the community.

Such old-line suburbs as Westport, Connecticut and Palo Alto, California have also sought clean, modern industrial plants to spread the tax load. In Westport, the classic battle between oldtimers and newcomers has been fought with the newcomers apparently victorious.

While population continued to mount, and the newcomers clung [at first] to their white-clapboard dreams, an old-time Yankee government kept the tax rate down, let community obligations quietly build up. Also building up, however, were the tempers of some of the city folk, who had once come from pretty nice small towns themselves and were damned if they were going to spend three hours a day commuting to and from a slum.

And so the battle began, with the newcomers lobbying for more public services and better schools as well as the industrial and commercial base to help pay for them. "Like many towns, Westport is trying to strike its balance, to build ambitiously without going broke, and yet to conserve a nostalgic 'character' that persists in changing every day." [14] The citizens of Palo Alto, which houses Stanford University, cheerfully consigned part of the open land once reserved for university expansion to smokeless research plants. "In their efforts to achieve a 'balanced,' largely self-sustaining community—efforts which are being duplicated less dramatically in other strong American suburbs such as Pasadena and Princeton—can be seen one of the crucial struggles of the present urban revolution." [15]

But when industry opts for the suburbs, it rejects the central city, and that rejection accounts for much of the present conflict between suburb and city, and, suburbanites suspect, most of the lobbying for metropolitan government on the part of central city leaders. "The old city-suburb reciprocal relationship is breaking up. For quite a while it has been degenerating into a battle." The battle involves competition for leaders, who have been moving to the suburbs; for better schools, which are being built and staffed in the suburbs; for shopping centers, which are moving out to serve the outward ring of population and threatening downtown stores, and finally for industrial growth, an encounter the suburbs also appear to be winning.

Suburbanites have seen the folly of haphazard, unchecked growth and are taking steps to halt scatteration. Builders who once needed only a rough diagram of a housing subdivision to get approval now must bring in carefully worked out plans. Often as not, they must also post bond for sewers, water, and permanent streets before they are allowed to break ground. The suburbs are tired of tearing up their streets every few years to add one more utility that was unhappily omitted at the time of original construction. They are making sure there will be no repetitions of the mistakes made in the hasty building of the late 1940s and early 1950s. Almost always, today's builders must deed part of their subdivision to the city for park purposes.

In addition, many suburban governing bodies have viewed with distress their regular rows of boxes surrounded by small lots. As a consequence, the standards of building ordinances have risen, and lot sizes, too, have gone up. There is now a far friendlier feeling than before toward plans which "cluster" dwellings in order to provide more open space. A development outside New Haven, Connecticut, serves as an example. Here,

row houses and apartments . . . demonstrate a pattern for suburban living far different from that found in most speculative developments: in place of scattering individual, dinky little houses on dinky little lots, the architects concentrated all dwelling units . . . and freed the rest of the site for a private park. By concentrating the 74 dwelling units in this development, the architects managed to keep 92 per cent of the site entirely open.[16]

Happily, this was not a project for only the well-to-do; the dwelling units were designed to sell to a middle class market for about $20,000 apiece (in 1961).

Such clustering not only preserves open space, but may be necessary to ensure the survival of the suburbs in the continuing emigration. "If, as seems likely, most of the 17 million new households to be settled in America by 1975 must be in the suburbs, the suburbs must find a new kind of housing or run out of space." [17] One-acre lots won't house all the people. Another pioneering example of clustering has been proposed on Long Island, with "town houses" occupying only 6 per cent of the available land, "the remainder to be devoted to golf courses, woodlands, and recreational space of other kinds." [18] One advantage of clustering is that it would put at the disposal of the suburbanite not merely one acre of his own, but all the greenery and recreational facilities in hundreds of acres of a combined nature preserve and country club. Another advantage is economic: clustering, with its row houses and apartments, should produce more taxes and fewer demands for service than single-family dwellings. Tenants of the average apartment, one study has shown, annually "gave $35 more in taxes to the public schools than they received in school services." [19] At the same time, the Long Island cluster, for example, would house slightly more people than present one-acre lot zoning laws would allow. The designers have sought in addition to eliminate the City in a Parking Lot danger with a huge central underground garage, from which scooters carry the traveler to his individual town house.

The clustering principle is one that more and more suburbs are considering, as a way of combining reasonably high population densities with the amenities of natural surroundings. The projects in Connecticut and Long Island have demonstrated that the expected influx of suburban homeowners can be accommodated without inevitably leading to the paradox that as suburbia grows, its attractions diminish. Happily, the public seems to be taken with the idea of clusters. "One cluster, Village Green, in Hillsboro, New Jersey, was completely sold out in six months while conventional housing in the same neighborhood, by the same builders, went begging." [20]

At their worst, today's suburbs may still be functional tomorrow. The *worst* assumes that the suburbs have not wakened to their economic and social possibilities, and will remain psychological and architectural wastelands, rows of homogeneous, dull structures occupied by people driven to conform. It further assumes that no steps will be taken to avoid scatteration and no action initiated to create a balanced community rather than a dormitory. It focuses on the very worst in post-World War II housing—cheap, quick, and barely habitable—and proclaims solemnly that the suburbs will become the "slums of tomorrow." In spite of the fact that these slums of tomorrow have been expected for some years now but have not yet materialized, there is undoubtedly some justification for the assertion that homes as small and cramped as those thrown up by the package builders must inevitably deteriorate.

But even these suburban slums may serve a vital social purpose. There are two good things about these crackerbox homes. The first is that they may well serve as vastly improved housing for those moving out from city tenements. If the central city is going to better its lot, it must tear down the long-established tenements that litter its urban landscape. And the people so displaced must find some place to go: why not to the $10,000 or less tiny bedroom boxes of the package builders? The problem here is that the suburbs may do their best, as they have so far done, to keep out the tenement dwellers through fear of differences in race and/or religion.

The second reason these hastily put up crackerboxes may be useful is this: *If they were built in a hurry, they also can come down in a hurry.* Certainly, they can be wrecked far more easily than the brownstones or Tudor mansions of a century or half-century ago, and in a culture whose only certain direction is change, this is a valuable quality. There is persuasive precedent for this point of view. Montgomery Schuyler, the nation's foremost architectural

critic in the nineteenth century, applauded the rapid, shoddy building which followed Chicago's great fire of 1871. Such hastily thrown-
up buildings could later be torn down to make way for architectural
achievements of real merit.[21]

Today, we build not for general purposes but for specific ones.
Buildings, as a result, cannot easily be converted from one use to
another; an industrial research plant will make a hopeless department store, a totally inadequate warehouse. In the same way, the
Jack Robinson-quick homes that went up in the new suburbia will
be difficult to force into any other use than that for which they were
built: as temporary dwelling places of young families desperate for
cheap, reasonably sound housing. This is a need that is not likely to
disappear, but should it fade away, the houses can rapidly be leveled and the slate wiped clean.

Rapid obsolescence is a way of life in America, and so is frequent
change of residence. Time was when one family might live in the
same house for several generations, and this is still the habit in
Europe, even today. In America, however, there has always been a
certain restlessness about living in the old family mansion, a feeling
which may derive from Jefferson and Emerson and their shared
belief that each generation must write its own laws and its own
books. The decentralization of American business now requires frequent moves; in a big company (and most people work for big
companies) the only way to get ahead is to be ready to move to the
next town whenever the organization suggests. "We never make a
man plan to transfer," a company president slyly remarks, "and we
never make a man move. Of course, he kills his career if he doesn't.
But we never *make* him do it." [22]

Frequent change of residence is not solely job-related, of course.
Rudofsky suggests in fact that the modern American's habit of moving often and rapidly is an attempt to "escape from the boredom of
his environment." Change, in his world, is "a promissory note on
happiness, and, because of its short term nature, fits ideally into our
fast-moving world." [23] Whatever the motive, it is abundantly clear
that the three-generation house is a thing of the past. But we need
not despair: obsolescence may be at least as useful in building

houses as in building cars. The one thing that appears certain about
our way of life in the next century is that it will change rapidly. The
best policy when contemplating the inevitably changing future is a
policy of flexibility, and the simple suburban box, easy to build, easy
to tear down, provides this flexibility.

People like to live in the suburbs. It may seem perverse of them,
but most suburbanites are more than content with their lot. It is for
this reason, perhaps, that they tend to look toward the next suburb
or even the next block as an example when wryly regarding the
critical voice of Pete Seeger on "Little Boxes." The average suburban resident is exposed to such a torrential variety of criticism that
he builds up a defense mechanism, preferring to believe (and in his
belief, helping to make it true) that the criticism cannot possibly
apply to him, no matter how well it applies to others.

If suburbanites did *not* like suburbia, they *could* stay in the city.
Nobody makes the middle class office worker commute for the privi-
lege of paying higher taxes in the suburbs. The attendant worry and
fatigue are a high price to pay. But this is a price "millions of parents have elected to pay, and their reason almost invariably is: 'the
city is no place to bring up kids.' " [24]

The suburb is no longer an idyllic retreat for the wealthy few, but
a much less idyllic one for the middle class mass. In this process of
democratization, the suburbs have lost many of the qualities that
made them most desirable. But other qualities remain, and it is still
true that the suburbs "come a lot closer than cities to the idyllic
open country which, a half-century and more after the western
frontier disappeared, still haunts Americans as the desired land for
pure living." [25] Even in Long Island's Levittown, former city dwellers cultivate a sense of compatibility with nature. "From under their
spreading trees they look out of their remodeled houses on a landscape that represents a giant stride from the dreary apartments and
drearier streets of the cities from which most of them escaped. 'This
is where I want my children to grow up,' they say, and mean it so
firmly that many of them do not move away when, economically,
they are able to." [26]

And it *is* better for children. There is more room to play with less danger, and there are better schools and parks than back in the city. "Suburbanites themselves say proudly that it is the best life in the world, the American dream in its flowering, especially for kids, and no one can argue with them. . . ." [27]

But what of the ugliness of the architectural landscape? What of the terrible ticky tacky houses? How can people abide them? The fact seems to be that people abide them very well. On a trip to England, Frank Lloyd Wright delivered a scorching diatribe on the inadequacy of domestic housing in the London suburbs. This prompted an English architect in the audience to ask:

Much as we might despise and condemn most of the buildings in the suburbs of London, the people living in them think that they are wonderful: they love their houses. Do you suggest that we should take the liberty, the burden, and the responsibility of advising them that they are quite wrong, to satisfy our own ideals of what a house should be like?

If I thought the houses were quite wrong [Wright replied] I should certainly tell the people living in them so, if they asked for my opinion. But I do not think I would walk in on them, just to tell them so.[28]

It was a reply oddly just for a man who rarely hesitated to rush in where angels fear to tread. There can be little doubt that "the future of architecture lies eventually in what kind of buildings people demand," [29] and the American middle class seems quite content to demand no more than they are getting in their little suburban boxes.

Intellectuals who predicted a sort of agrarian utopia in the suburbs, as H. G. Wells did in the epigraph, have been disillusioned by what has happened, on both sides of the Atlantic. Those who once shared or who continue to share Wells's idealistic expectations must inevitably face disappointment. But the overwhelming majority of people who *live* in rows of identical little boxes brought a more limited dream with them from the city: a little open country, a little fresh air, at a price they could afford. It is a dream they think they have realized. Whose duty is it to disillusion them?

VI. THE TERRITORY BEHIND

For more than a century, the territory ahead has been the world that lies somewhere behind us, a world that has become, in the last few decades, a nostalgic myth. On the evidence, which is impressive, it is the myth that now cripples the imagination, rather than the dark and brooding immensity of the continent. It is the territory behind which defeats our writers of genius, not America.

—*Wright Morris,* 1957

In its consistent emphasis on looking backward, in its continuing celebration of an innocent life that will return no more, in its persistent evocation of the ideal middle landscape, American literature accurately reflects American thought. Or it may be the other way around: it may be that American thought is shaped by American literature. A third possibility, that there is simply an interaction between literature and cultural ideas, is most likely of all.

The relation of literature to intellectual history is undoubtedly a complicated one, but that there *is* such a relation seems beyond dispute. Thomas Jefferson and James Fenimore Cooper, Ralph Waldo Emerson and Henry David Thoreau, Henry George and William Dean Howells, John Dewey and F. Scott Fitzgerald: there is a world of difference between the first named public philosophers and second mentioned literary artists who make up each of these roughly chronological pairings, but *all* these men share a heritage: they are Americans affected by the myth of pastoralism. The writers provide both a more complicated and a more immediately compelling reaction to this myth than do the thinkers. For, in examining American literature, as R. W. B. Lewis points out, the student can find dramatized "as human conflict what is elsewhere a [mere] thoughtful exchange of ideas . . ." [1]

Popular fiction usually serves as a mirror-image of the culture, whereas more serious literature often creates fresh ideas which have a lasting effect on the cultural imagination. As William H. Whyte, Jr. has observed: "The very fact that fiction does tell people what they want to hear . . . does make it a fairly serviceable barometer. Whether fiction leads people or merely reflects them, it is an index of change in popular belief that might be imperceptible at closer range.[2] It is as an index of *changing* ideas that Whyte is most interested in analyzing literature, but it is as an index of the *persistence* of a dominant idea that American fiction is inspected here.

The pastoral tradition is one of the oldest of Western literary traditions. The Romans and the Greeks celebrated the wonders of nature even before the authors of the Bible did so. The abundance of Arcadias in English literature testifies to the continuing vitality of the pastoral as a literary convention. In American literature, however, pastoralism is more than a convention. Characteristically, the Virgilian pastoral has been placed in what Leo Marx calls the middle landscape, midway between the wilderness and the city.[3] In England, this middle landscape is regarded as a utopian ideal, pleasant to dream upon and write about but never to be realized, never to be taken seriously. In America, the land of milk and honey and nature undefiled, it is believed that the pastoral ideal will be realized, not merely imagined. Such, at least, has been the conviction of most American public philosophers, and of most American writers.

For these men, the ideal middle landscape lies somewhere in the past, in a Jeffersonian world of virtuous yeomen tilling their acres in harmony with benevolent nature. This is "the territory behind" which Morris finds so crippling [4] to the nation's present writers, as it has been crippling to its creative men of whatever intellectual bent, whether politicians or philosophers or artists. A dead-serious and persistent pastoralism infects our thinking. Leo Marx writes:

There can be little doubt that it [pastoralism] affects the nation's taste in serious literature, reinforcing the legitimate respect enjoyed by such writers as Mark Twain, Ernest Hemingway, and Robert Frost. But on the lower plane of our collective fantasy life the power of this sentiment is even more obvious. The mass media cater to a mawkish taste for retreat into the primitive or rural felicity exemplified by TV westerns and Norman Rockwell magazine covers.[5]

Having demonstrated the attraction of the pastoral, Marx paints a word-picture of its ideal landscape reminiscent of a George Inness painting:

Beginning in Jefferson's time, the cardinal image of American aspirations was a rural landscape, a well-ordered green garden magnified to continental size. Although it probably shows a farmhouse or a neat white village, the scene usually is dominated by natural objects: in the foreground a pasture, a twisting brook with cattle grazing nearby, then a clump of elms on a rise in the middle distance and beyond that, way off on the western horizon, a line of dark hills.[6]

This cardinal image is repeated, time and again, in American fiction as in American art. There is a harmony with nature in this golden land by which the noble savage is instinctively guided. It does not matter if the American, like Leatherstocking, lacks educational training. "This book I can read," Natty Bumppo says of the book of nature, "and I find it full of wisdom and knowledge." The English novelist George Walker portrayed natural man as a liar and stealer and murderer in his novel of Kentucky, *Vagabond,* written in 1799.[7] But this approach must have rubbed American readers the wrong way in the early days of the nineteenth century. Instead of such myth debunkings, they were reading the novels of Sarah Hale, where the "surest way to work out your salvation . . . was to keep your hand on the plow and stay in the provinces" and those of Cooper and John Pendleton Kennedy, the continued popularity of whose *Swallow Barn* revealed "a growing need . . . to sentimentalize country life" as the nation began its drift toward urbanization and industrialization.[8] It was inevitable, as Henry Steele Commager remarked, "that the American should choose rural heroes, for his ideas and ideals were formed by country living; his poetry and song were unfailingly rural. Of all the writers whose countenances shone benignly on playing cards of 'Authors' only Holmes could be called urban. . . ." [9]

Speaking in Chicago on December 28, 1965, novelist Norman Mailer, one of the most urban of modern writers, accused his fellow countrymen of spreading "suburbs like blight upon the land." Later in his address, he spoke of "suburbs and caves." [10] The attitude betrayed in these offhand denigrations of suburbia is a common one among modern writers. It is an attitude of disillusionment which can be traced directly to the persistence of the pastoral ideal in American thought, and to the literature that has shaped and reflected this ideal.

In his retreat to Walden Pond, Henry David Thoreau became the first American to reject the life of the suburb. The suburb, of course, was Concord, a community less suburban in 1850 than it is now, but a community whose vitality even then depended in good measure on its proximity to Boston. In Concord, Thoreau observed men leading lives of quiet desparation; as an alternative to leading such a life, he went to the woods. "Let me live where I will," he wrote, "on this side is the city, on that the wilderness, and ever I am leaving the city more and more and withdrawing into the wilderness." Thus can be seen the pull nature exerts on the imagination of our serious writers like Thoreau. For nature, as Thoreau went on to observe, casts its magnetic spell everywhere. "I should not lay so much stress on this fact if I did not believe that something like this [withdrawal into the wilderness] is the prevailing tendency of my countrymen." [11] Having built cities, Americans fly from them as from the plague. Morris elaborates the point: "Turn your back on the city, the civilized inessential, and withdraw into the wilderness. Turn your back on those things built with hands, and withdraw into a world not made with hands. The territory ahead lies behind you. *Allons donc!* Take to the woods." [12]

Thoreau, of course, does not really go to the wilderness (Walden Pond is too tame for that). What he seeks is "an integrating midpoint." The mirror of wild nature, like the placid, pure depths of the pond, is to serve as an instrument of self discovery. But Walden itself is not wild; it symbolizes a landscape "moored midway between the wild and the civilized, preserving the best in each mode of life—simplicity without brutishness, refinement without affectation, learning without depravity." [13] It symbolizes, in short, the classical American version of the pastoral ideal, not an ideal to be expressed as a literary convention but an ideal which is available to all Americans, in the world of nature that lies a few miles outside of town. Thoreau speaks of the virtues of the middle landscape, and his countrymen have been trying, ever since, to follow his directions, retrace his steps. The Bosky Dell of the twentieth century developer's advertisements, with its emphasis on fresh air and open space and glorious greenery, is but a pale replica of Walden Pond, and those who wish it were an exact copy will be disillusioned.

In an unmistakable echo of Thoreau, Ada Louise Huxtable of *The New York Times* attacks a world she never made. "Suburban spring is not a walk in the awakening woods, but mud in the poorly built roads. Suburban life is no voyage of discovery or private exploration of the world's wonders natural and man-made; it is cliché conformity as far as the eye can see, with no stimulation of the spirit through quality of environment." [14] The modern suburb is not Walden, after all; it is, in fact, rather more like Concord. But only the idealistic would state a strong case against Concord as a place of residence, and even Thoreau, the most idealistic of writers, lived there all the years of his life save the two he spent in relative seclusion at the nearby pond.

The trouble with Concord, as with almost all modern suburbs, is that the promise of communion with nature is not totally fulfilled. Instead, houses crowd in upon each other, and the residents lack that feeling of spaciousness that is part of the pastoral ideal. The suburbs originally gained popularity as retreats from the city, but the city followed hard on the heels of the emigration. That there is nothing new about this process is demonstrated by the letter Edgar Allen Poe wrote to the newspaper *The Columbian Spy*, in 1844, protesting the heedless growth of the borough of Manhattan. Angrily, he complained that "the most picturesque sites for villas to be found within the limits of Christendom [are] doomed. The spirit of Improvement has withered them with its acrid breath. Streets are already 'mapped' through them, and they are no longer suburban residences, but 'town-lots.'" Prophetically, Poe predicted that in thirty years "the whole island will be densely desecrated by buildings of brick, with portentous facades of brownstone." [15] He assumed, as did Nathaniel Hawthorne, that suburban life was better and healthier than city life. In *The House of the Seven Gables*, Hawthorne writes that "we should soon have beheld our poor Phoebe grow thin and put on a bleached, unwholesome aspect, and assume strange, shy ways . . . [had she not] now and then indulged her brisk impulses, and breathed rural air in a suburban walk, or ocean breezes along the shore" away from the center of Salem.[16]

Harriet Beecher Stowe, in her stories of Oldtown, or Natick, Massachusetts, a mere twelve miles from Boston, looks back on the glories of the rural past when the children would listen to Sam Lawson spinning yarns as they picked blueberries or clambered up to the loft of the barn, "with a swinging outer door that commanded a view of the old mill, the waterfall, and the distant windings of the river, with its grassy green banks, its graceful elm draperies, and its white flocks of water-lilies. . . ." [17] However idyllic, Mrs. Stowe's natural world is clearly domesticated. The banks of the river are grassy green, and the water-lilies congregate in peaceful, well-ordered flocks. Mark Twain moved his pastoral utopia away from the land, where people were always getting in the way, to the Mississippi River, where Huck Finn and Jim watched the sunrise with their feet curled up happily in the sandy bottom. Twain saw that his watery utopia must end when there was nothing left for Huck but to light out for new territory. He realized that you cannot go home again, and that it would not be the same if you did; Mrs. Stowe sang a lament for a bygone way of life she thought could be restored.

But where was the golden life to be recreated, in a land where progress meant rapid and continuous urbanization? The only possible location for this idyllic life was suburbia, where a man could have the best of both worlds—economic success in the city and the wonders of nature in his back yard. When William Dean Howells came to Boston as a magazine editor, he and his family lived in the suburbs for a period which is recounted in *Suburban Sketches*. About the end of June, he wrote, "Charlesbridge appeared to us a kind of Paradise. The wind blew all day from the southwest, and all day in the grove across the way the orioles sang to their nestlings. . . . We were living in the country with the conveniences and luxuries of the city about us. . . ."[18] But at other seasons of the year, and as time went on, he saw that there were serpents in this Paradise. The necessity of commuting was one. He watched the train disgorging its passengers, "suburbanly packaged, and bundled, and bagged, and even when empty-handed proclaiming the jaded character of men that hurry their work all day to catch the evening train out, and their dreams all night to catch the morning train in. . . ."[19] The second serpent was the migration of too many people for the natural landscape to support: "The lessening pasturage also reduced the herds which formerly fed in the vicinity, and at last we caught the tinkle of the cow-bells only as the cattle were driven past to remoter meadows." Still, Howells concluded in 1871, his suburb had "not yet been quite stripped of the characteristic charms which first took our hearts. . . ."[20] By his clear implication, though, it was only a matter of time until the stripping process should have denuded suburbia of all its agrarian charms.

The suburb still beckoned to the young family as the ideal place of residence, however, and to no one more than to poor Marcia Hubbard, wife of Howells' amoral journalist, Bartley Hubbard, in *A Modern Instance* (1882):

She did not like being in lodgings or dining at restaurants; on their horse-car excursions to the suburbs, when the spring opened, she was always choosing this or that little house as the place where she would like to live, and wondering if it were within their means. She said she would gladly do all the work herself; she hated to be idle so much as she now must. . . .[21]

Transplanted from the farm to the city, Marcia sought communion with the middle landscape, especially when "the spring opened" in all its beauty. A great many others felt much the same way as Marcia Hubbard, enough others, in fact, so that real estate developers began to take advantage of the pull of the pastoral ideal. The promoter McDowell in Henry B. Fuller's fine novel, *The Cliff-Dwellers* (1893), for example, launched a new subdivision ". . . out beyond the South Parks. He had bought up a ten-acre tract, which he himself acknowledged to be rather low-lying, and which his rivals, with an unusual disregard of the courtesies of the profession, did not hesitate to call an out-and-out swamp." Having drained off some of the moisture, he posted his banner, and "on bright Sunday afternoons, folly and credulity, in the shape of young married couples . . . would come out and would go over the ground—or would try to." [22] The novelists' warnings were in vain, however, as the Americans of 1900 first began the suburbanward trickle which was to become a river in the 1920s and a flood in the 1950s.

Fuller and Howells saw that life in the suburbs did not measure up to the pastoral ideal, but it remained for twentieth century writers to examine the corruption of the potential Garden of Eden in detail. As Charles Sanford has observed, the "main theme in American literature during the twentieth century has been dispossession from paradise, America's abandonment of the security and innocence of an earlier day through some essentially sinful act, an act most frequently associated with industrialism and the commercial ethic." [23] The besetting sin is materialism, and American writers have chosen to locate materialism squarely at the center of the would-be middle landscape of suburbia. No one, perhaps, has more virulently expressed this point of view than Ring Lardner, who was Scott Fitzgerald's neighbor in Great Neck, Long Island, during the early 1920s.

Lardner wrote of ballplayers and businessmen, actors and newspapermen, and he saw them all as ignoramuses. "The ultimate paradise for all these typical Lardnerian figures was suburban life. They came from the sticks and the small western towns [as did their creator himself, a native of Niles, Michigan]; they came to Chicago and New York to make their fortune and get somewhere in 'society'; to lead the dream-life of American success." To give notice of their status, financially insecure as it almost always was, they moved, like Fitzgerald and Lardner, to the Long Island or Connecticut mansion. The quest for a bucolic retreat from the city had turned into a materialistic straining after status. The spectacle appalled Ring Lardner, and he excoriated suburbia in a number of stories.[24]

Perhaps the best of these stories, and one of the very best stories he ever wrote, is "A Caddy's Diary," a tale of morality in business and on the golf course. One of the country club's members has embezzled money, and it is said that he has sold his soul. But the caddy and his pal wonder if Mr. Thomas, who is vice president of the bank but who lied about his golf score "so as he would win 9 golf balls instead of a ½ a dozen," or Mrs. Doane "that made me move her ball out of a rut to help her beat Miss Rennie out of a party dress," have not sold their souls even more cheaply than the embezzler. As for the caddy who is willing to cooperate in Mr. Thomas's lie in order to get a $1 tip or to improve the pretty Mrs. Doane's lie in order to get a smile of reward—for what has he sold his soul? [25]

If the morality of suburbia is polluted by materialistic considerations, its social life ranks as so dull that one of Lardner's fictional playwrights must leave standing orders for an emergency telegram to be sent to him twenty-four hours after the start of weekend visits to the "country." Another suburban enthusiasm, the remodeled farmhouse, comes in for heavy satiric comment in "Ex Parte," when hubby is asked to admire a "simply gorgeous old barn" with handhewn beams. Under penalty of wifely ostracism, the husband keeps his peace while looking at "some dirty old rotten beams that ran across the living-room ceiling and looked as if five or six generations of rats had used them for gnawing practice." [26] The barn is no place for people to live, as a country boy like Lardner could see. The potential Garden of Eden in suburbia had degenerated into a ruralized playground for middle-aged, upper middle-class status seekers.

The West Egg of F. Scott Fitzgerald's *The Great Gatsby*, where James Gatz throws his fantastic parties in his fantastic mansion, is a phony world, as phony as the name of Jay Gatsby itself. Behind

the facade of the assumed name lies the boy from Duluth with the
Benjamin Franklin dreams of success. Success, Gatsby felt, would
be paradise and so he achieved (albeit crookedly) great financial
success. He buys the Long Island mansion and gives parties in the
hope that a golden girl who lives across the sound will some day
come to one of them. The golden girl, Daisy, lives in East Egg (obviously the more exclusive North Shore as opposed to the South
Shore of Long Island) where her beacon for the love-struck Gatsby
is a glowing green light. But Daisy turns out not to be a real golden
girl after all; nothing turns out to be real after all, save the dream
itself. "From the beginning," as Leo Marx comments, "Nick [Carra-
way] is aware of something odd about the elegant green lawns of
suburban Long Island. They are green enough, but somehow syn-
thetic and delusive." [27]

Daisy's green light comes to represent Gatsby's dream of an orgi-
astic future that "year by year recedes before us." Note the "us," for
by switching from the third person singular "Gatsby" to the first
person plural pronoun, Fitzgerald has implicated all Americans in
Gatsby's dream:

It eluded us then, but that's no matter—tomorrow we will run faster,
stretch out our arms farther. . . . And one fine morning . . .
So we beat on, boats against the current, borne back ceaselessly into
the past.

For Gatsby's dream—America's dream—is not merely a dream of
material success: that can be achieved. It is the agrarian dream of
virtue and beauty and the land that has slipped "behind him, somewhere back in that vast obscurity beyond the city, where the dark
fields of the republic rolled on under the night." [28]

What is wrong with this dream? Nothing at all, so long as it is
recognized for what it is, as a dream that will not come true and
cannot, because it asks history to turn around and run backward
toward a mythic past. What is wrong with having this dream?
A great deal, if it continues to hold its grip on the American imagination. Among other things, its persistence has led to orgies of
meaningless vituperation directed at a suburban landscape which

was never meant to be the place in which the pastoral dream would come true. This kind of overstated attack ignores the real problems that presently beset the nation's suburbs and cities. "Imperceptibly," as Wright Morris writes, "the function of nostalgia reduces the ability to function." [29]

VII. LIFE STYLES: CONFORMITY, NEIGHBORING, AND HYPERACTIVITY

Because they constitute an unscrambling of an overcomplex situation, because they are largely composed of like-minded people to whom cooperation should not be difficult, and because of the environmental advantages of roominess, the suburbs, in spite of their limitations, are the most promising aspect of urban civilization. . . . They reflect the unspoiled and youthful aspect of urban civilization, the adolescent and not yet disillusionized part of the city, where, if at all, happiness and worthy living may be achieved, as well as material well being.

—*Harlan Paul Douglass, 1925*

A real estate development outside Detroit, Michigan bills itself as "The Land that Time Forgot," a Shangri-La where suburban housewives can, presumably, stay forever beautiful, as did June Lang in *Lost Horizon*.[1] But time has not forgotten the suburbs, and they have been withered by decrepitude when exposed to the judgment of the last few decades. Here, like June Lang when she *leaves* Shangri-La, "the most promising aspect of urban civilization"[2] went bust; here the once optimistic communities formed of the city's embers turned to ashes. Disillusionment set in, and the suburb, a potential paradise for Douglass in 1925, became an actual hell for the intellectual of the 1950s. "In the suburb, in the opinion of its prominent investigators, the modern American exchanges individuality, privacy, the certain satisfactions of pride of craftsmanship and work well done, for something obscurely defined as the social ethic, being a good fellow, and group cooperation." [3] The stereotype "is that of a continuous *Kaffeeklatsch* between wives in an ecologically determined common ground, and a gardening-*klatsch* between husbands in the local hardware store." [4] The suburban way of life, according to the critics, is one of social, intellectual, political, financial, and, frequently, emotional bankruptcy. Above all, there is "too much socializing, too much organized activity, and that scourge of the suburbs, [too much] enforced conformity." [5]

This excessive neighboring, this dominant hyperactivity, and this dreadful conformity all stem from the same root, as the critics see it. The cause is homogeneity. Nothing is easier than to assume solely on the basis of the architectural evidence that suburbia is homogeneous. All the homes are alike; ergo, all the people who live in the homes are alike. John Keats makes this generalization without pausing for breath. The dwelling, he states, shapes the dweller, and when "all dwellings are the same shape, all dwellers are squeezed into the same shape." [6]

This radically deterministic point of view gets partial—but only partial—support from the facts. It has already been demonstrated that suburbs vary widely in the socio-economic characteristics measured by the census. But *within themselves,* many suburbs are remarkably homogeneous. In fact, there is evidence that the make-up of most suburbs is shaped by their original character, even though they may later go through periods of intensive growth. Reynolds Farley calls this phenomenon "suburban persistence," and uses as examples Hammond, Indiana, and Evanston, Illinois, two Chicago suburbs approximately equal in size. The original attraction of Hammond, an industrial suburb, was a meat packing plant; that of Evanston, a residential suburb with an unusually high number of older residents, consisted of several Methodist centers, including Northwestern University. Obviously, industrial workers moved to Hammond, Methodist churchmen to Evanston. Once a suburb is established, he concludes, "the population that moves into that suburb tends to resemble the population already living there." [7]

The critical argument takes this relatively mild dash of demographic evidence and adds ingredients freely, until it is transformed into a different composition entirely: a hopelessly homogenized, totally unpalatable dose called suburbia. In this environment, there is little or no diversity, and hence little chance for self-realization or creativity. The suburbs, in fact, even posed a threat to the liberal tradition, as historian Arthur Schlesinger, Jr. saw it in the 1950s. People in the suburbs don't think for themselves, he complained. This must be so because they "vote the straight Republican ticket even though they have been Democrats in the big city." These suburbanites are other-directed and do and say those things that are expected of them, in lawn care and backyard barbecues, PTA attendance and Republican registration. "What liberalism must resist is the tendency to turn America into one great and genuinely benevolent company town—the bland leading the bland. It must oppose the drift into the homogenized society." [8]

The major problem with this accusation lies in the terminology. Notice the ease with which Schlesinger's argument shifts from "homogeneous," which is undefined here (and for almost 100 per cent of the critics) to the more damning term, "homogenized." Homogeneity usually measures certain social characteristics, such as percentage of home ownership and proportion of young families with children, to select two tests on which most suburbs would score high. But the more variables you add, the less likely you are to find continuing homogeneity. "In any new development," as a recent study points out, "the families have almost nothing in common but the price of the houses and the ages of their children." There is economic homogeneity, but not necessarily educational or social homogeneity, except as money is a measure of social class. The university professor lives beside the plumber, the factory foreman next door to the aspiring lawyer. Generally, when the critics talk about homogeneity, what they mean is homogeneity in terms of spendable income and average number of children, and though these

indices may correlate with certain behavior patterns, they do not
determine everything that is to be determined about the way people
live and act and think. Homogeneous, in other words, does not mean
homogenized.[9]

Henry David Thoreau, a premier individualist and a man who
was not born to be forced, once told his fellow citizens that he did
"not wish to be regarded as a member of any incorporated society
which I have not joined." [10] Once he had so stated, the local con-
stabulary left him alone as he continued to refuse allegiance to his
state and nation. The position Thoreau took was a courageous, if
not a particularly constructive, position in the mid-nineteenth
century. It is a position almost impossible for the suburbanite living
in the middle of the twentieth century to take, according to the
myth of suburbia. The suburbs "do not easily permit one to remain
anonymous or irresponsible. There is something in them which says,
'Be a full member or nothing.'" and the "nothing" means social
ostracism.[11]

Conformity is the scourge of the suburbs, the critical indictment
claims. The suburbs are peopled by automata who do not think
because they have never had to think. Early in life, they learn how
to adjust to others, to become "full members," and degree of adjustment constitutes the measure of success. Robert Hutchins has written that a moron is a person who cannot think, and that the industrial revolution has made it possible for morons to be successful.
Rabbi Albert I. Gordon, in his book on *Jews in Suburbia,* comments
that "Hutchins might just as well have been talking about the people of suburbia. They fear criticism and they seek to avoid controversy. They generally refrain from participation in any situation
which makes one appear different. Acceptance by the larger group
requires that one conform to its standards." [12] The suburbs, then,
are a vast wasteland of moronic humans, each trying desperately to
conform to the dominant standards of the group, each unwilling
and perhaps unable to think for himself. That, in essence, is the
argument the critics of the 1950s brought to bear.

One may justifiably object that the trend toward conformity, and objections to that trend, stretch back to the beginnings of American history. The Puritans imposed severe restrictions on the inhabitants of the early villages of Massachusetts Bay. "Your work is needed in the community and you have a Christian calling," John Cotton told these first settlers. "There is more than one kind of liberty," John Winthrop explained, "and those who pursue natural liberty are corrupt, while those who abide by the laws which define civil liberty follow the path of godliness." Two centuries later, when Emerson and Thoreau preached their secular heresy that each man must realize his own potential in solitary communion with nature and the oversoul, they were reacting against what seemed to them to be the same kind of pressures exerted by Governor Winthrop. Roger Williams and Anne Hutchinson were the seventeenth century counterparts of the transcendental non-conformists of the nineteenth century.

Is it truly more difficult to be a non-conformist today than in the time of Emerson or the time of Williams? The intellectuals see individualism submerged by the waves of the industrial and technological revolutions which in standardizing products have supposedly standardized ways of life and thought. As long ago as 1902, Josiah Royce was troubled by the standardization of modern industrial civilization. With the spread of popular education and the centralization and consolidation of industry and of society, he wrote, "we tend all over the nation . . . to read the same daily news, to share the same general ideas, to submit to the same overmastering forces, to live in the same external fashion, to discourage individuality, and to approach a dead level of harassed mediocrity." Royce's warning voice sounds eerily familiar; it speaks in the same accents as any of a hundred social commentators who have found "a dead level" of mediocre conformity dominating our suburban way of life.

Royce's solution to the problem of national conformity, seen in the light of his later mimics, represents real irony. The solution, Royce said, was provincialism. To achieve non-conformity, Americans must retire to a county, a state, a section of the country which is, geographically and socially, "sufficiently unified to have a true consciousness of its own unity, to feel a pride in its own ideals and customs, and to possess a sense of its distinction from other parts of the country." [13] One must go, in other words, to a place with a sense of community, and though Royce's suggestions are not explicitly agrarian, such provincialism hardly suggests the metropolis. It was under the influence of just such ideas as those of Josiah Royce that the planners and dreamers of the twenties and thirties sketched out their self-sufficient suburban garden cities of the future. Like Royce, these men saw no contradiction between the idea of individualism and the idea of organic community. You could have it both ways, and destroy the stifling atmosphere of conformity into the bargain, simply by going back to the middle landscape of the provinces, or building a new middle landscape of cities in the fields.

Charles Duff, in his satiric *Anthropological Report on a London Suburb,* demonstrates that the charge of conformity in suburbia extends across space as well as time. In his imaginary Hemperley-wood, people try to dispossess themselves of any traces of Cockney in their speech. "The elimination of all such traces, and the acquisition of 'blahness' is the chief object of suburban education." His stuffily scientific narrator, an anthropologist ostensibly named Professor Vladimir Chernichewski, notes a curious initiativeness in the suburb. "They imitate each other in speech, dress, and behaviour. They imitate each other in such habits as the angle of wearing a hat, the colour of a necktie and the kind of flowers grown in this gardens. . . . There seemed to be a lack and even a fear of individual originality everywhere." If one family acquires a cocker spaniel, the others follow, and it is the same with such other household items as babies and sewing machines.[14] In England as in America, the tide of invective crashed against the suburban shores of conformity.

If it is true, as one religious observer maintains, that complacency "distinguishes conformity from community," the American suburb would seem to be in little danger of drowning in conformity. For in the suburb, as everywhere in mid-twentieth century American life, the devil is conformity. Like many devils, this one takes different shapes, making it difficult to determine who is conforming to what.

"*The New Republic* cries that 'hucksters are sugar-coating the culture.' *The National Review*, organ of the 'radical right,' raises the banner of iconoclasm against the domination of opinion-making in our society by 'the liberals.' *Fortune* decries the growth of 'organization man.' Each of these tendencies exist, yet in historical perspective," Daniel Bell writes, "there is probably less conformity to an over-all mode of conduct today than at any time within the last half century." Suburbs are less conformist, for example, than the Main Street of Sinclair Lewis. Daniel Bell goes on to demonstrate that everyone is against conformity, and "probably everyone always was." As Delmore Schwartz has observed, the beatniks fight an imaginary foe, since almost any form of non-conformism is now acceptable. The "new rebel bears a great deal of resemblance to a prize fighter trying to knock out an antagonist who is not in the ring with him." [15]

There is mounting evidence to support the view that conformity is at best a paper tiger. William N. Leonard, in his study of suburban shopping patterns, concluded that "consumption standards reveal a high individuality of taste for what is normally thought to be an area eminently conformist in character." Nearly all buy on credit, but *what* they buy varies widely from family to family.[16] This diversity of tastes is matched by a variety of leisure pursuits, at least in Phyllis McGinley's "Spruce Manor." How is it possible to keep up with the Joneses when some of the Joneses play chamber music, others garden, still others sail, and a few even write books? "So far as I know," she writes, "not one of my friends is doing any of the things that suburban ladies are popularly supposed to be doing," with the exception of gardening.[17]

A number of sociologists have attempted in the past decade to lay misconceptions about suburban life styles to rest. Berger's report on Milpitas, California, helped to clear the air, as did Dobriner's book, *Class in Suburbia*. Gans has made an important contribution also in articles and in *The Levittowners*. Gutman, comparing techniques of socialization in an established suburb and a new tract development, found that the older suburb assimilated newcomers through voluntaristic channels, through friendships formed on the battle lines of

PTA or Girl Scouts, while the new suburb had developed no real norms of assimilation. This lack of clear norms, he concludes, "results in a wide range of tolerance." [18] Where assimilation presents problems, it is likely to be not because of pressures to conform, not because of an abundance of homogeneity, but because of a *lack* of it. As for enforced conformity, Gans reports that the "vast majority of suburbanites are . . . free to live as they please," and frequently acknowledge having more privacy in the suburbs than they had in the city. (Like McGinley with gardening, Gans notes an exception with lawn care: suburbanites do care for their share of the street front greenery, and they are expected to do so.) [19]

In a brief essay published in 1967, Dennis H. Wrong reviews the findings of these men and tries to account for the "myth of suburbia" they have been debunking. Wrong concludes that it was the coincidence of mass suburbanization with such other postwar phenomena as relative affluence, moderation of class conflicts, political timidity, rising marriage and birth rates, religious revivals, and growth in the penetrating power of mass media that created the attack. "Whether described in the neutral language of the sociologists or in the satirical and rejecting epithets of social critics deprived temporarily of their usual target of political attack, the suburbs seemed to exhibit all that was most contemporary and most typical in American life," Wrong writes. "All this seems very passé nowadays," he continues, arguing optimistically that the debunkers have done away with the stereotypes established in the late 1940s and the 1950s.[20] The common sense observations of McGinley and the scientific ones of Gans and others have not yet succeeded, however, in amending the ugly portrait of the suburbs painted so often and convincingly in a host of popular articles, books, novels, and films of the 1950s.

However little conformity may actually exist in the suburbs, there is enough to disillusion the roseate hopes of such early visionaries as Douglass, who described the suburbanites of 1925 as "the more individualistic, people who cannot stand the normal conditions of cities —just as Natty Bumpo [sic] could not stand life within the feeble fringe of pioneer settlement." Such men he saw as twentieth century giants in the earth, men who "cannot fully adjust themselves to the era of urban civilization. . . . *They are the frontiersmen of cities.*" [21] It is reasonable to refer to the suburbs as a frontier of democracy, as shown in Chapter IX, but they decidedly do not represent the kind of frontier Natty Bumppo and Daniel Boone were seeking. That frontier is gone forever.

The Jeffersonian ideal of the selfsufficient yeoman farmer may no longer have a place in urban, industrial America, but that has not prevented keepers of the dream from trying—and necessarily failing —to restore Jefferson's lost world. The idealist assumes an impossible task, and when he does not succeed, looks around for a scapegoat. The most visible scapegoat in the middle of the twentieth century is suburbia, with its admittedly often dreadful architectural sameness. And the choice of this particular scapegoat is made almost inevitable by the hopes the dreamers once held for the suburbs. They were to have been the reincarnation of the agrarian village. So it is, as two social scientists recently understood it, that the suburbs "display a far greater role in the sociological imagination than in American society." [22] The new suburbs are nothing if not *visible*, with their picture windows and backyard living. If the observed life seems to be highly conformist, the reason has to do with the way of life of youngish, middle class Americans, not with place of residence.

But, as has already been suggested, there is nothing new about conformity, nor about violent reactions to it. In a land where the ideal of individualism does eternal and bloody battle with the ideal of community, there will always be fire directed at conformity. There are complaints, for example, about

the decrees of the peer groups to which everyone must adjust—in schools, at home, or in the club. Are they so different from the dictates which church and town fathers early imposed along the Atlantic seaboard? . . . . Is the community construction of a swimming pool so different from a barn-raising? . . . . Modern interdependence among neighbors is not expressed in fighting Indians or gathering crops, but in sharing children's clothes and alternating trips to the supermarket.[23]

The new suburbanite lives a more interdependent life than the city dweller. There is a sense of community, a spirit of cooperation, in the suburbs which he may well have been seeking when he left the city. When he finds it, he is accused of conformity; entertaining such accusations is part of the price he must pay for the limited, achievable dream of fresh air, room for the children to play, and a house of his own.

If the critics view suburbia's supposedly proliferating conformity with genuine alarm, they are less seriously concerned with what they regard as excessive neighborliness. An occasional commentator will lash out bitterly at "savage togetherness" in the suburbs, but most are inclined to view all that suburban socializing with amused intolerance. The *Kaffeeklatsch* symbolizes this attitude of (mock?) friendliness; left to themselves during the day, the neighborhood ladies get in the habit of sitting around drinking coffee and exchanging lies. But it is hard to get really upset about *Kaffeeklatsches* when conformity is a more respectable target. Sober-sided editorials condemn conformity in the suburbs; feature writers deal satirically with neighboring on the inside pages. Irving Tressler, for example, advises his readers to avoid "the neighborly spirit," which will do away with peace and quiet, and observes that:

Some of the finest axe murders of our history have been committed in the small community. Usually the newspapers blame sex or incompatibility or money, but this is absurd. Once one gets into the routine of 'We must have the Andersons over Thursday night,' and 'Saturday we're going to the Yardley's!' And 'Sunday I've invited the Berkoffs over because we've owed them for so long!' there's nothing left but the axe.[24]

Whatever the critical attitude, however, it is widely, and correctly, believed that people in the suburbs make friends with the neighbors more easily than people who live elsewhere. Some will maintain that suburbanites continue the same friendship patterns they previously learned in the city. The woman "who unburdens her family woes to a neighbor out of a third-story window across an apartment court continues to unburden her soul in Levittown." [25] Still, *the* distinctive feature of suburbanism as a way of life, Sylvia Fleis Fava maintains, consists of an unusually high degree of neighboring. Her research discovered that there was considerably more neighboring in Nassau County than in the city of New York and that this

difference persisted when other demographic and economic factors
were held constant. Fava concluded that there was a positive relationship between suburban residence and neighborliness. Other observers argue that it is the newness of some suburban communities
which creates this spirit of friendliness or that learning how to make
friends is a skill most likely to be acquired by middle class (not
working class) families. Age of the suburb and class structure of its
inhabitants are the determinants, according to this view. There may
be a correlation between home ownership in the suburbs and high
levels of neighboring, but the correlation is merely fortuitous and
does not involve a cause-and-effect relationship.[26]

There are two good reasons beyond the research evidence to accept the cause-and-effect idea. The first has to do with that villain,
homogeneity. Maybe, Willmott and Young speculate about the English suburb of Woodford, maybe "uniformity is one of the prices we
have to pay for sociability in a more mobile society." [27] Closer to
home, Gans has carefully traced the effects of homogeneity on
friendship patterns in the suburbs. Propinquity is important in deciding who makes friends with whom, but homogeneity (a broad
homogeneity, not just of age and income, but of taste and education
and behavior patterns) is still more important. "Friendship requires
homogeneity," he writes, and most suburbs, partly due to the pattern
of suburban persistence Farley has isolated, have it.[28] Again, the
distinction between homogeneous and homogenized should be kept
in mind. Suburbanites have enough in common, particularly problems, that they learn to rely on each other as friends. The families
are young and there are plenty of small children around in most
suburbs, for example. So fathers develop a massive athletic program
such as the Bloomington Athletic Association (BAA), which organ-
izes teams in four sports for some 5,000 youngsters. Mother needs to
escape from the children occasionally, but can ill afford to pay the
baby-sitter with her grocery money. So a baby-sitting club is organized, with mothers baby-sitting for each other and piling up credits
they'll need on a big weekend. Or a young mother hemorrhages
badly after delivery, and a blood bank is started in the neighborhood, not just for her but for future emergencies. Such baby-sitting

and blood-giving clubs exist in Bloomington, and in many other suburbs. One observer writes of his nationwide tour of American suburbs:

Socially, the outstanding characteristic of these people is their friendliness, warmth, and lack of pretentious snobbery. Outgoing and buoyant, they are quick to recognize common problems and the need for cooperation. . . . Nothing in these communities . . . is more impressive than this uniform pattern of casual but warm friendliness and cooperation.[29]

The second reason that people are more neighborly in the suburbs is that they come seeking a community which will encourage neighborliness. Those who are willing to neighbor move out to the suburbs from the more or less cold city environment. Thus Gans reports that many "move to the suburbs with the hope of making new friends, and those that come with this purpose are able to do so." [30] In other words, a selection process is operating to keep the suburbs neighborly. And where does this desire for community, this pursuit of a neighborly environment, come from? Its origins lie at least partly in the myth of the farm village. (The myth of the yeoman farmer and the myth of the village run together in American history and thought, as well as here.) [31] Douglass writes of the Villager:

. . . [who] is closely akin to our inner selves, [who] gets released in the suburbs as he rarely does in the city. . . . The block, the little zone of backdoor borrowing, the sphere of American neighborly kindnesses in sickness and in health become a natural unit of group life. Suburban hedges are full of natural gaps where neighborhood comings and goings have broken through. . . . This assertion of innate friendliness, in an environment which partly invites, . . . is in most grateful and creditable contrast to the perhaps necessary anonymousness of the city.[32]

It is a part of the combined myth of the village and the farm that the self-sufficient yeoman farmer should double as the friendliest and most cooperative of neighbors. In its penchant for neighboring, the suburb expresses the cooperative half of this paradox. It is a place "to which one can belong. 'Togetherness' . . . is not merely a fad. It represents modern man's attempt to regain some of the community which his ancestors had in the peasant society of Europe or the frontier society of nineteenth-century America." [33]

In seeking the goal of community, however, the modern subur-

banite has lost sight of the goal of individualism, the critics of the
1950s charged. He would be better off back in the city, where he
could have plenty of privacy to realize his own potential freed of a
constricting conformity and an annoying, if amusing, neighborliness.
So the critics conclude, blissfully unaware how hard they are to
please. Daniel Bell spells it out:

The early theorists of mass society . . . condemned it because in the vast
metropolitan honeycombs people were isolated, transient, anonymous to
each other. Americans, sensitive as they are to the criticism of others,
took the charge to heart and in building the postwar suburbs, sought to
create fraternity, communality, togetherness, only to find themselves accused of conformity.[34]

The critics have assumed that the individual can be both self-reliant
like the yeoman farmer and neighborly like the New England villagers of *The Country of the Pointed Firs,* both John Brown and American Gothic. Short of rampant schizophrenia, the two ideals cannot
be resolved in any one person or place or institution.

America was known as a nation of joiners before the suburban
trend was fairly underway; and in the English suburb of Woodford,
where the guide lists "as many as 142 different clubs and associations, and it is not an exhaustive list," Willmott and Young are inclined to write off all this organizational activity as a middle class
trait.[35] Hyperactivity, like neighborliness, seems to be a behavioral
peculiarity which truly distinguishes suburb from city. In Philip H.
Ennis's interviews with New York suburbanites in 1955, one of the
most frequent complaints they expressed "was that their free time
was not their own, that their communities were over-organized and
they were over-worked." [36] Whyte noted the same phenomenon in
his suburbs. The jaundiced eye of the intellectual finds nothing admirable, of course, in this group activity. People may be desperately
busy, but they have forgotten how to perform such elemental human
tasks as rearing children. Exterior busyness conceals an inner vacuum.[37]

Nowhere is this busyness more apparent than in the matter of
gardening. The fellow who could not tell a tulip from a rose in the

city will suddenly become a dedicated son of the soil on removal to his small suburban plot of ground. His land, however limited in size, will not only demand careful lawn care, but painstaking nursing of the flower bed as well. Charlton Ogburn, Jr., for example, has recounted his problems as a suburban husband and father. Ogburn spends a great deal of time tending to and reading about his garden, yet cannot get rid of a nagging feeling that he is neglecting his duties, somehow. The feeling is intensified when one of his friends speaks slightingly of those who are "content to have a mere casual affair with nature." [38] Such ventures are not to be undertaken lightly.

Suburbanites, we have noted, are expected to take care of their lawns, keep them mowed, and relatively free of crab grass: this is one of the few imperatives of suburban life. But taking care of the lawn is one thing; the kind of over-commitment to the task that has been observed by Rolf Meyersohn and Robin Jackson is another thing entirely. These two sociologists, investigating gardening habits in Chicago suburbs, discovered some gardeners who obviously had no aptitude or liking for the task, but who stuck to it when they would rather be off playing golf. "One feels about the overcommitted," they conclude, "that if it were up to them, they wouldn't garden, that gardening was not a leisure activity at all but a necessary chore." [39] Why is it not "up to them"? What is driving them off the golf course and into the yard? Meyersohn and Jackson suggest that gardening may serve as a rather genteel outlet for competitive feelings, a replacement for exhibition of material purchases in an age when everyone knows what "conspicuous consumption" means and how they are supposed to feel about it. The explanation is plausible, but incomplete. For the suburbanite knows as well, sometimes in the front of his mind and perhaps oftener in the back of it, how he is supposed to feel about the land. He knows that nature's noblemen carve a living out of the soil, and he knows that America is the home of the greatest of nature's noblemen. If he cannot find success in the suburbs as a self-sufficient farmer, he can at least try his hand at a bed of flowers. "The joy and profit of suburban life focuses in the garden," John McMahon had written to the pioneer suburbanites of

1917, and though you cannot turn much of a profit on the crop from a 60 by 100 foot lot, you have a duty to seek the joy of watching blades of grass come up.[40]

For many, of course, the gardening hobby comes naturally. Tristram Coffin, for example, writes of the fictional Jeff Jones of Flaming Oaks, who raises petunias as an "antidote for concrete and steel, canned speeches and frozen dinners, computers and traffic jams." Senator Margaret Chase Smith finds it "easier to think" in her suburban Maryland home where she grows roses and feeds birds than in Georgetown, for example. Houston businessmen motor fifty miles every weekend to their gentlemen farms, "with a few cattle grazing and a horse or two galloping over the meadow." Lyndon Johnson goes back to his ranch, and every spring millions of suburbanites go back to their patch of land, with renewed dedication and enthusiasm.[41]

Their gardening efforts may bear fruit, or they may not. But in making the effort at all, the modern suburbanite becomes at least a pale imitation of the yeoman farmer. It is only a token gesture, but it is not wise to underestimate the importance of gestures and what they betoken. The suburbanite tending his garden is performing an act born of a sense of community (everybody shares in the appearance of any given street or neighborhood) evolving out of the fertile myth of the virtuous yeoman farmer. The product, as Douglass points out in this chapter's epigraph, might be the "adolescent, not yet disillusioned part of the city," where the moderately good life can be lived. It is not the perfect life, but where is that to be found?

VIII. COUCH, SCHOOL, AND CHURCH

Biologists discern congestions of germs to match congestions of people and animals. From all the incredible roominess of the world in which they exist, these organisms marshal themselves into unseen, parasitic cities unimaginably more populous than ours. Disease colonizes and settles down with the urban race of men. Sunshine which might destroy or neutralize it cannot penetrate into dark rooms or scant air-shafts.

—*Harlan Paul Douglass, 1925*

PARENTS AND THE PSYCHIATRIC COUCH

The search for a healthful environment has always exerted a strong centrifugal pull on city-dwellers, and it still does. In the quest for sunshine to "destroy or neutralize" disease, for a life free from those "parasitic cities" of germs Douglass warns against,[1] the urbanite packs his bags and his family and moves to the suburbs. When he gets there, however, he may find a less healthy climate than he anticipated. Such, at least, is the judgment of those social critics who cast a jaundiced eye on suburbia. There may be sunshine in the suburbs, the critics concede, and the residents may *appear* to be in good health. But cut through this bland surface, they advise, and you will see the rottenness beneath, the psychological disorganization which infects nearly every suburbanite and every suburban institution. These institutions, the family, the school, the church, are sick at the core, and the flight from the city in pursuit of a healthy living environment has been made in vain.

A number of critics have concentrated their fire on family life in the suburbs, an especially inviting target since many suburbanites avowedly move out from the city in the hope of knitting closer family ties. They should have stayed put, the detractors argue. "Each suburban family is somehow a broken home, consisting of a father who appears as an overnight guest, a put-upon housewife with too much to do, and children necessarily brought up in a kind of communism." [2] Of the children and their communistic existence, more later. For now, let us examine father and mother, especially mother. For if father is divided by his journey from home in the suburbs to work in the city, mother is confronted with even more critical threats to her psychic well-being. Like many another observer, Catherine Marshall writes that "it is the housewife who has to be especially on guard against certain hidden hazards in the otherwise pleasant life of the suburbs." Evidence of such hazards are cited: the Long Island call girl ring of thirteen suburban housewives, reports of excessive use of barbiturates and tranquilizers by women in Connecticut, the high incidence of "stress" diseases such as ulcers, heart trouble, and high blood pressure among suburban women, and "two mounting problems for women in all suburban communities—alcoholism and marital difficulties." [3]

Women are traditionally regarded as the guardians of morals, and suburban moral standards have been falling like temperatures in a Minnesota cold snap, the critics maintain. The evidence for this charge is, to say the least, conflicting. Alcohol consumption per capita in Fairfield County, Connecticut, has been estimated as higher than anywhere in the nation, except Nevada, and there is an "Alcoholism Information Center" opposite a Westport junior high school. [4] On the other hand, twenty-nine residents in the working-class community of Milpitas, California, reported a decrease in drinking after their move to the suburb, while only four acknowledged an increase. [5] In regard to adultery, such extreme cases as that of the Long Island housewife-call girl ring are balanced by the Park Forest court which Whyte says serves as a virtual chastity belt for young marrieds. Similarly, reports from San Francisco suburbs of hundreds of couples openly participating in "wife-swapping" [6] must be measured against the suggestion that there are fewer "extra-marital relationships than the average" in Levittown.[7] Both class and regional differences seem to be operating here; the weeds of immorality thrive in some suburban soils, wither and die in others.

In any case, most of those who point a finger at suburbia's weakening moral and psychological fiber do so without recourse to scientific investigation. The report of David Wallace that there are nineteen psychiatrists to forty-one M.D.'s in Westport, gleaned from the local telephone book, represents more sophistication in the methodology of social science than is usually demonstrated by the enemies of suburbanization.[8] There is, however, one conspicuous exception to this rule, and it is called *The Split-Level Trap.*

A publisher's blurb for this book, which became a national bestseller, calls attention to the credentials of the authors: "Dr. Richard E. Gordon, a psychiatrist who practices in Englewood, New Jersey, and his wife Katherine, a graduate student in social psychology," and to the soundness of their findings, based on five years of "intensive scientific study of emotional problems in a typical section of American Suburbia." The result, according to the blurb, is a "precise, clear picture of the tremendous emotional stresses that are peculiar to the suburbs." [9] One might expect page after page of chart, statistical summary, and the like, but finds instead a series of horror stories, told first in summary (as below) and then in detail:

One of the young husbands who went to work in the morning is feeling ill. . . . Early in the afternoon he suddenly starts to vomit blood. He is rushed to the hospital with a bleeding ulcer.

In one of the split-level houses, a young mother is crying. She is crouching in a dark closet. Voices in the walls are telling her she is worthless. . . .

As night falls, three teen-age boys visit the home of a girl in one of the town's more expensive sections. . . . The boys take turns with her on the living-room couch. . . .[10]

The snake pit has moved to the suburbs. People are in bad shape, *very bad* shape out there, and in case anyone has missed this point, the authors reinforce it by coining a word for the locus of their psychological tales of terror, which lack only the art of Edgar Allan Poe. The word is Disturbia.

To support such a word as Disturbia, the Gordons (with co-author Max Gunther) *do* provide statistical comparisons. They compare figures from their own Englewood hospital, in suburban Bergen County, with those of Olean General Hospital in Cattaraugus County, "a rural county in upstate New York." Figures are taken from a two-year period on the incidence of psychosomatic illnesses, such as peptic ulcers, high blood pressure, heart attack, "physical disorder[s] with emotional roots." The results look bad for suburbanites. "Of all patients admitted to rural Olean General during the period, 2.4 per cent were hospitalized for heart attack. At suburban Englewood, the figure was 11.7 per cent." Again, at "Olean General, 6.7 per cent of the patients were under treatment for high blood pressure. Englewood: 14.3 percent." And at "Olean General, 2.8 per cent were in for duodenal ulcers. Englewood: 9.6 per cent." The inference, they conclude, is plain: "something is troubling people in Bergen—something whose effects are not nearly so intense or so widespread in rural Cattaraugus." [11] At least one other inference, equally plain, is not discussed: some unnamed diseases are much commoner among patients at rural Olean General than at suburban Englewood. Nearly 90 per cent of the rural hospital's patients are suffering from "*non*-psychosomatic" diseases, compared with only 65 per cent of the suburban hospital's patients. By and large, however, there is little point in quibbling with these figures. Life on the farm is undoubtedly far less likely to lead to psychosomatic illness than life in the suburbs, a discovery which will hardly surprise the latter-day preservers of the agrarian myth. (It is worth noting that the scientists who devised this comparison did not see fit to include a *city* hospital's figures within their survey; the suburb is supposed to be a halfway point between city and country.)

The Split-Level Trap offers statistical "support" for its generalization that young married women are especially liable to the psychiatric troubles induced by Disturbia. Who comes in for psychiatric care at Englewood? "A stark picture," the book reports. "Of all the people in the sample, thirty-six per cent—more than a third—are young married women. The number of disturbed suburban young wives is more than half again as big as the number of young husbands [who are, presumably, working in the city while their wives visit the free psychiatric clinic], and more than three times as big as any other group." [12] "Group" is the sort of word that needs to be defined, but is not. It is, however, made clear that by "young married women" are meant those 44 years of age or under. The census figures, *not* provided by the book, reveal that the picture is more predictable than "stark." Bergen County, like most suburban areas, is made up largely of young married people. More than half of the total adult population falls in the 20 to 44 age range, the men in this range making up 23.7 per cent of the adult population and the women 26.7 per cent. The 26.7 per cent who are women (the vast majority are married, of course) occupy 36 per cent of the psychiatrists' time, not a particularly startling figure, especially when the well-established reluctance of older people to seek psychiatric care is taken into consideration. And the 23.7 per cent who are male make up 24 per cent of the psychiatric visits, almost exactly as chance would have predicted. [13]

A similar generalization about the incidence of psychosomatic illnesses among women in two counties of comparison, suburban Bergen and rural Ulster County in New York, can also be partly discounted. The percentage of young women among Englewood hospital's high blood pressure patients was 8 per cent, compared with 1.5 per cent at Ulster's Kingston hospital. Young women made up 12.5 per cent of duodenal ulcer patients at Englewood, compared to 7 per cent for Kingston. [14] The first thing to notice about these figures is the enormous difference between the high blood pressure and duodenal ulcer ratios: Bergen County women are more than five times as likely to contract high blood pressure as their Ulster County counterparts, but less than twice as liable to ulcers. Surely, this is a significant variation. Another thing to notice is that the figures are low in both cases, relative to population. Young women (20 to 44 years old) make up 17.6 per cent of the total population in Bergen, and 15.6 per cent in Ulster County.[15] The logical conclusion is that life for young women is somewhat healthier, at least in terms of these two diseases, in the suburbs than the population figures would suggest, and *far* healthier in rural areas. This generalization does not involve the fact that men generally are more susceptible to these diseases than women, whether they live in a suburb, on a farm, or in a city. Again, the authors provide no figures from city hospitals to use as a standard of comparison.

Still, certain critics continue to view with alarm the physical and psychological pressures which weigh upon the suburban family. Common sense suggests reason enough for this troubled atmosphere, they claim. Anyone can see (and no one more clearly than themselves) what is wrong with the suburbs: they have become the breeding ground of an insidious matriarchy. Women wear the pants not only literally, around the house and in the super market, but figuratively as well. Suburban men have abdicated their traditional role as head of the household. As a consequence, everyone—mother, father, and child—suffers.

The observation about matriarchy in the suburbs has been made so often that it threatens to become axiomatic. It is an axiom which gains authority from repetition in high places. A briefing paper for the 1960 White House Conference on Children and Youth, for example, asserted that in the suburb "the parental roles undergo considerable alteration. The mother has become the authority figure of the family, since the father is away for such extended periods of the day." Dad may carry the luggage, but Mom is the boss.[16] The same phenomenon has been duly noted and recorded by churchmen of all faiths. "Among Protestants residing in suburbia one discovers that the wife inherits the responsibilities which her husband abandons. . . . There appears to be little doubt about the dominant influence of Protestant mothers in suburbia," a Methodist minister has written.[17] A Catholic priest observes signs that roles "in marriage . . . are being reversed. Wives are becoming more masculine, more domineering; husbands are becoming less male and more passive. . . ." [18] Finally, a rabbi comments that his "observation of three decades, and particularly this intensive study of Jewish family life, leads to the conclusion that the wife, by virtue of her increased duties within the family, has become the modern matriarch of Jewish suburbia. Her ideas, opinions, and values clearly dominate." [19]

In this reversal of roles, the father becomes less dominant as the mother becomes more so. This development is inevitable, the critics maintain, inasmuch as the suburban male is so busy commuting that he becomes a "part-time father." [20] Tired out from his work and the long commute, he comes home and falls into a martini. Such at least is the stereotype, as it was expressed by Douglass four decades ago: "Every seasoned suburbanite knows that very definite experience of 'let down' between business and home. . . . When the suburbanite has once slumped down at home it is almost impossible to stir him. It is not good for a boy to know his father habitually in such moods." [21]

Such testimony is not to be lightly dismissed, but neither is it to be accepted without seeking responses to two very important questions. First, is the stereotype true, does it present an accurate picture of suburban life? Second, even if accurate, does this picture represent anything new, or anything peculiar to the suburbs?

There remain serious reservations about the stereotype's accuracy, especially as it pertains to the commuting father. Many suburbanites travel no further from home to work, in respect to time, than do city dwellers. When they get home, these fathers are expected to pitch in and help with the household chores, not to collapse into an unstirrable slump. The days of *Life with Father* may be gone, but Clarence Day's father was something of a tyrant around the house. He used to come home exhausted from his hard day's work, and play the absolute lord and master on arrival. His departure can best be regarded with mixed emotions. Today, instead of the tired businessman limping into the house after a hard day at the office, the standard picture (as Margaret Mead has observed) is of the tired young father limping off to work after a strenuous night of entertaining the children and helping around the house.

Peter Willmott and Michael Young, writing about a London

suburb, conclude that most men "are emphatically not absentee husbands [or fathers]. They hurry back from their offices and factories . . . to spend the evening at home, and they are there for two full days at week-ends. It is their work, especially if rather tedious, which takes second place in their thoughts. . . ." [22] These husbands carry out the rubbish, help with the garden, and play with the children. As in England, so in America. Ernest R. Mowrer's study of the family in suburbia isolated "flexibility of role" as characteristic. Dad feeds and sometimes diapers the baby, while Mom shovels the walk and cuts the grass.[23] The pattern, then, is not so much one of female dominance as of male-female teamwork, not so much a matriarchy as a partnership. There is, probably, nothing new about this shift from the patriarchal family. At the turn of the century, social observers were already lamenting the passing of the good old days when father was the (tyrannical) boss. What *has* changed is the environmental location. In the agricultural society which has gone forever, father was a patriarch. The agricultural society represented the *summum bonum;* therefore, patriarchy is the proper form of family organization. The intellectual, like the Gordons, compares today's suburb to the rural world of the past rather than the city of the present.

Those critics who do not single out matriarchy as the source of the supposed suburban neurosis often point to excessive mobility as the culprit. Even as the Gordons are diagnosing the diseases of Disturbia, it is apparent that mobility—geographic, economic, and social mobility—is at the bottom of most of their horror stories, and not simply the suburban location. Americans, of course, have always been highly mobile: "The red men were nomads; the *voyageurs* and *coureurs de bois* were nomads; the loggers were nomads; the wheatgrowers were nomads, and there is nothing to say that the Wisconsin cheesemen will some day not move on or out." [24] The pioneers had to move, to open up the land. Today, their descendants, constantly seeking a better life in pleasanter, more affluent surroundings, move still more frequently. One out of five American families changes homes each year.[25] And the percentage of suburban families that move is higher than that of city or farm families, so it can be said without exaggeration that the "itinerant family is modal for modern suburban life." [26]

What does all this moving mean to family life? For one thing, it means the breakdown of the three-generation family. The grandparents are rarely around to help young parents over the rough spots, and neither are aunts and uncles. The "wider family," then, "does not flourish in the suburb. . . ." [27] Instead, people are thrown together with equally uprooted strangers. Separation from the "extended family" may, of course, speed up the process of maturation, but it may also disorganize many individuals. Loneliness may be the result, but if so, it is usually a loneliness which is self-imposed, not one imposed by the usually friendly neighbors who are, after all, in the same boat.[28]

Whatever the psychological effects of moving about, no one is likely to suggest seriously that Americans stay put. For the most significant thing about all this moving from place to place and job to job is that it is typically an *upward* movement. The young family moves from Chicago Heights to Wilmette as the breadwinner advances in business, and another young family from south Chicago takes its place in Chicago Heights. This continual movement toward bigger houses and better neighborhoods is the mark of success, and the United States is not ready to reject economic gain as its dominant measure of success. In addition, a high level of mobility stands as proof of the democratic experiment: given equality of opportunity, people *can* rise. The people at the bottom have everything to gain and nothing to lose, and that is just as Americans have always felt it should be. "Without ignoring the dangers it can bring or the problems it creates," as Harvey Cox comments, "it must be insisted that mobility offers positive possibilities for individuals." [29] The dangers themselves may well have been overstated by such observers as the Gordons. There is an admitted psychological hazard involved, but the hazard "is not nearly so destructive as some commentators have imagined," no more destructive, for example, than moving from high school to college or from one job to another.[30] The modern urbanite or suburbanite *expects* to move from time to time; the prospect does not usually appall him or disorganize his life.

Indeed, there is a significant body of evidence, painstakingly gathered by social scientists, to suggest that the move from city to suburb is a healthy one. Herbert J. Gans, who has studied suburbia exhaustively, has concluded that "there is no reason to believe that the move from the city to suburb, or suburban life itself, has any effect on mental health, other than a positive one. Most interview respondents report improvements in health and disposition." [31] Wendell Bell came to the same conclusion after his interviews in Park Ridge and Des Plaines, Illinois. The responses revealed "the definite notion that the move from [city] apartment to [suburban] house was mutually beneficial for parent and child. In fact, several of the wives, according to their own testimony, had been on the verge of nervous collapse living with small children in an apartment. Since moving to a house in the suburbs, they reported that they were no longer 'nervous.' " [32]

Geographical mobility, like the socio-economic mobility it often represents, does not disorganize most Americans. The principal exception is the man who carries with him a Platonic ideal of a secure, non-mobile, peaceful world. But does he really want to return to a time when everyone knew his place and stayed in it? Surely not. "The majority of people in premobile societies lived and worked in ways we would not want to return to. . . . The fact is that most people's grandparents were dirt-poor and lived in hovels." [33] We cannot go back to a stable, pre-industrial, pre-mobile world, and few of us would if we could.

SCHOOLS AND THE SPARED ROD

Mother and father may be able to sidestep the psychological pitfalls of the suburbs, but if the critics are to be believed, the children will not. The irony is obvious; it is most often on account of the children's health and well-being that families move to suburbia in the first place. Four out of five families, in a survey of Chicago suburbs, mentioned better conditions for their children—more space, less traffic, cleaner areas—when asked why they had moved from the city.[34] The suburbs may be superficially clean, roomy, and quiet, the critics concede, but they still breed troubled children. The troubles take two forms. The children are spoiled rotten, one critical school holds, so pampered that they grow up absurdly unprepared for life's defeats and disappointments. The children are scandalously neglected, another school maintains, and turn to stealing hub caps, sports cars, and Cadillacs as they progress through their delinquent teens. There is a certain contradiction here. The children "are simultaneously fattening on a diet of spoon-fed attention, and—wait a minute—rootless and starved for love. It all depends on which expert we've tuned in." [35]

The "pampered" experts outnumber the "neglected" ones, and are examined first. Mowrer's study of the suburban family concluded that children there "tend to be pampered as never before," with the wife serving as chauffeur and the husband as handyman to the youngsters' whims.[36] *The Split-Level Trap,* harping on its theme of mobility, argues that many "mobile people have adopted the notion that you must eternally give to children; otherwise you are not a loving parent." You must give until it hurts, and it "is seen as old-fashioned and unenlightened to discipline kids firmly." These mobile parents, the Gordons argue, have "dropped the ball; the kids have picked it up and are running away with it." [37] Over-permissiveness, Catherine Marshall writes, is "now boomeranging on all fronts." What is needed is a little old-fashioned strictness, for children need the kind of discipline our grandparents provided and are unhappy without it. Carrying the ball all the time gets dull.[38] As you follow the dots and paint in the numbers, the emerging picture is one of children ruling the roost in the suburbs. It is no longer a matriarchy that we must guard against, but a filiarchy, the youngsters holding absolute sway.

Well, one wonders. Even Peter Wyden, who wrote a book about *Suburbia's Coddled Kids,* suspects "that a certain amount of the tut-tutting about suburban youth is little more than a resentful farewell to another age, now gone for good." [39] Should today's children walk five miles to school, simply because father or grandfather once did? Are they spoiled because they ride the bus? A strong orientation toward a more virtuous past almost always crops up, either overtly or covertly, in the indictment against pampering suburban youngsters. The Gordons, for example, are surprised to find that five out of six suburban children do not know how to play mumbly-peg; it used to be that every child in the village or rural town knew how.[40] This habit of looking back on a golden past when children got the right kind of discipline and mumbly-peg training lacks currency—and validity. In the middle of the nineteenth century, keen foreign observers were already remarking on the permissiveness of American child-rearing. These observers included Harriet Martineau, whose interviewees in the United States recommended making friends with children from the very beginning, and Anthony Trollope, who protested in 1860 "that American babies are an unhappy race. They eat and drink as they please; they are never punished; they are never banished, snubbed, and kept in the background as children are kept with us." [41] Americans, it is suggested, have always tended to pamper their children, to worship their young.

There are those, however, who disagree: the experts who maintain that the suburban youngster is in reality neglected, and that he is an excellent prospect for juvenile delinquency. Whatever attention the suburban child does get, these critics argue, is motivated by guilt feelings on the part of the parents and is, therefore, the wrong kind of attention. A false sense of togetherness is generated. For example, Dr. Edward D. Greenwood, a specialist in child psychiatry at the Menninger Foundation in Topeka, Kansas, believes that ". . . suburbia treats youngsters gently until perhaps age 12. Then, as the child's desire for independence grows and his interests begin to diverge from those his parents have so conscientiously shared, the "togetherness" pattern of the child-centered home no longer meets his needs." [42] What the child needs at this stage is the approval and applause of his peers, and one way to earn it is to ignore the adult code, break the adult laws.

That way lies delinquency, of course, and the suburbs *do* grow some delinquent children. "Novelists and writers of serious documents report many instances in lurid detail," Frederick A. Shippey remarks, and these instances are "fact, not fiction." [43] But the "lurid detail" of the reports probably overstates the extent of juvenile delinquency in the suburbs. In one recent case, police unearthed a ring of narcotics users among youths in fashionably suburban Fairfield County, and the story, in rather complete if not in lurid form, made *Time* magazine. In the city, the same story—and the same story repeated many times over in the city—does not constitute news, for in the city two of the users were not "sons of former mayors of Norwalk and Stamford." [44]

David Loth's *Crime in the Suburbs,* published in 1967, undercuts the widely believed theory that suburban crime rates are going up faster than those of cities. "Looking behind the figures at the facts," he writes, "it seems that while crime is increasing there is no proof that the rate really grows faster in the suburbs." He also alludes to an FBI survey of juvenile offenses, covering a little more than half the nation's population. The survey revealed that there were 833,507 youngsters taken into custody in 1965, of which the suburban share was 220,283. "The suburban areas reporting had a little more than 27 per cent of the population and a little more than 26 per cent of the juveniles taken into custody." [45] These figures clearly demonstrate that you cannot escape from crime simply by moving out of the central city. But, when the relative youthfulness of the suburban population mix (compared with that of cities and rural areas) is taken into account, the figures also make it clear that there is substantially less criminal behavior among juveniles there than elsewhere.

Similarly, Gans's thorough but geographically limited study of one suburban community in the East revealed "comparatively few" crimes, suicide attempts, serious delinquent acts, and cases of mental illness. The percentage of such aberrations, "if translated into rates, [ranked] far below those reported for city inhabitants." [46] Such sober reports, however, stand little chance against the colorful subjective judgments of a city-lover like Jane Jacobs, who awakes one night to feed her baby and hears a young man in the street "bellowing terrible language at two girls whom he had apparently picked up and who were disappointing him." Her fellow city-dwellers put their heads out the window to offer the opinion that the troublemaker must be "a wild kid from the suburbs." She transforms the incident into irony in a footnote: "He turned out to be a wild kid from the suburbs. Sometimes, on Hudson Street, we are tempted to believe the suburbs must be a difficult place to bring up children." [47]

The irony depends on the supposition that suburbs are the best places around to bring up children. The idealistic wonder why there should be any suburban delinquency trouble at all. Unlike Mrs. Jacobs, who knows better, they ask: "Isn't this one of the urban blights the suburban adults fled from? Wasn't Suburbia supposed to be the strife-free place purged of dirt, poverty, slum crowding, minorities, low-grade education, and all the other social problems known to be delinquency's breeding grounds?" [48] The suburbs, of course, are not free of all these "social problems," for the suburb is becoming rapidly urbanized. As *Time* editorialized about the Fairfield narcotics case, "in a school of 1,018 pupils so near New York there is bound to be a fast set of hardshell hippies . . . who seem utterly glamorous to more sheltered types. As one Darien mother sighed . . . : 'It's hopeless. We're just nothing but a part of New York—that's all it is.' " [49]

The image of the "wild kid from the suburbs," starved for love but given enough money to indulge himself in drag racing and drunkenness, "is largely mythical," Father Andrew Greeley writes. He wishes, in fact, that suburban children were somewhat wilder, or at least more imaginative. Father Greeley finds the suburban youngster domestic, quiet, docile, unimaginative, sophisticated, worldly-wise, and "just a trifle cynical." In his middle teens he may have had big dreams and noble ideas, but this period does not last long. He adjusts too well and too easily to the world his parents have created, and Greeley finds this adjustment disturbing. "It is the function of the young to dream dreams," he states, "to infuse a little restlessnessness into society." [50] For him as for many critics, suburban children are socialized too early and too completely. The schools, especially, stifle any imagination the child may demonstrate, train out any individuality. The children are not only not wild; they are too darned mild.

A remarkable expression of this point of view came recently from Douglas P. Sarff, a suburban school teacher who bought a full-page advertisement in the local newspaper to unburden himself of his complaints against the youngsters and the community that had produced them.[51] His high school students in Wayzata, Minnesota, a suburb near the shores of Lake Minnetonka, were "frozen solid with sophistication," he wrote. The Class of 1965 was made up of "a mass of bored, indifferent, dulled mediocrities or tittering good-timers." The typical graduate was due to become "either a silly unproductive boob or a sneering sophisticated opportunist with no more conviction than a whore." Whatever sparks of idealism and ambition the students may have felt as freshmen were dampened by the time they were seniors. "They are dead in every sense of the word except viscerally."

This mass dying could be traced, Sarff's ad maintained, to the great dismal swamp of middle class conformity which he apparently equates with suburbia. Sarff was annoyed most of all that his attempts to produce cultural development had not borne fruit. He organized a creative writing contest, but only seven out of 1,000 students entered. He tried to organize a summer writer's colony, but too few students signed up. He started a literary magazine, which came out once and then disappeared. His efforts would have met with success, he argued, but for the ignorance of the Yahoos who occupy the "reechy backwater" of Wayzata. Sarff speaks with the voice of H. L. Mencken, lecturing the boobs on their boobery. You don't care about the important things, he tells the mothers, but only about such popular activities as "pom-pom-waving." You are spiritually poverty-stricken, he tells the fathers, and unable to take any real interest in your children's "cultural development." You do not let the children think for themselves, he tells anyone who may be waiting in the wings to supply the students with advice different from his. Sarff's obvious talent for invective, coupled with the fact that he paid for the full-page "Open Letter to the Community of Wayzata" out of his own pocket, earned him national radio, television, and magazine coverage, and gave him a running start toward the new career as a writer he intends to follow, now that he has resigned as a teacher. For Sarff has given up, convinced that his suburban high school students cannot be defrosted from their frozen sophistication, convinced that the suburban apathy is proof against even such inventive teaching as his own.

But if suburban students are apathetic to cultural opportunities, they are anything but disinterested when it comes to classroom grades. This, at least, is the considered judgment of such a highly trained observer as James Bryant Conant, in *Slums and Suburbs*. In the course of his nationwide survey for this book, Conant found some suburban school districts where upwards of 80 per cent of the graduates went on to four-year colleges or universities. Such figures, he concluded, indicated a relatively homogeneous community: "the vast majority of the inhabitants belong to the managerial or professional class; the average level of income is high; real estate values are correspondingly inflated." In such communities, he also found effective school boards, high parental interest in the schools, and high expenditure per pupil. He called these suburban schools "lighthouse" schools, "beacons lighting the way toward educational progress. . . ." [52]

There is substantial agreement among educators that suburban schooling constitutes the best the nation has to offer in the way of public instruction. Writing in the *National Education Association Journal* in 1957, Thomas E. Robinson counseled young teachers to seek jobs in the greener pastures of fast-growing suburban districts, where they would find more innovations and more equipment, more challenges and more interest, more pay and more jobs. [53] Lured by these inducements, good teachers have flocked to the suburbs. Such high schools as Newton near Boston and New Trier north of Chicago are famous for the excellence of their curriculum and staff. Despite the rave notices, however, the critics point to two key problems which trouble such "lighthouse" school districts. First of all, there is not enough done for the child of little academic talent. Writing about Westport, David Wallace reports that 80 per cent of the 304 June graduates in 1961 went on to college at 135 institutions. Obviously, such students must be carefully groomed to meet college entrance requirements. But what about the workingman's children, Wallace asks? What about the student whose formal education will end with high school? Generally, his needs are neglected, and "efforts to introduce more vocational courses are repeatedly resisted." [54] Conant observed the same neglect, and called for realistic programs for below-average youngsters.

The second problem is psychological, and involves the enormous pressures which come to bear on the more or less typical *average* (not necessarily below-average) student who must achieve grades good enough to get him into college, and into a "good" college if at all possible. Parents, Conant feels, are liable to take the attitude that they do not care where Junior goes to college, so long as it is Harvard. The youth who cannot or does not measure up bears a heavy and unjust burden of guilt. "To counteract the mental anguish of the child who lacks the academic ability to match his parents' ambitions," he writes, "there must be a strong guidance department in the suburban schools." [55] Under pressure some students may be driven to cheat; others tend to develop health-destroying habits of cramming for exams, with the aid of drugs, as early as ninth or tenth grades. The competition is fierce. And it is especially fierce because of a cultural prohibition against trying *too* hard.

Obviously, achievement is critically important to the suburban high schooler, and (perhaps even more) to his parents. At the same time, however, the star achiever in academics as well as sports "must constantly practice 'modesty,' and pass the honor of victory on to the coach, his team-mates, or even his mother who has fed him [or read to him] so well." Success depends on an ability to achieve great things while never seeming to. As Seeley and his colleagues observed in Crestwood Heights: "To succeed in modern, urban society, the child must learn to maintain both competition and cooperation in a delicate balance of forces, and he must develop this balance through the learning situation itself . . . he must learn a kind of covert competition . . . he must compete but he must not seem competitive." [56] This is a tall order for the suburban child, and it is an order he is expected to start filling at an early age. While pretending to be everyone's pal, the youngster must indulge in the bloodiest kind of cut-throat competition for the favor of the Harvard admissions committee.

Such competitive pressure is clearly excessive, and it clearly exists in the suburbs, but "this kind of goings-on characterizes not only the suburbs but the urbs and exurbs as well. In the suburbs it is, if not really more marked, much more apparent." [57] This is true partly because suburban school districts tend to be more homogeneous than city school districts; it is also true because the suburbs are highly *visible* to the naked eye of the observer. It is not suburban location which places a high value on achievement; this is a cultural norm shared by Americans of whatever residential background.

But the fact is that this norm is one the suburban child is far more likely to fulfill than his city or farm counterpart, because the schools and the teaching are excellent, because he or she is being trained specifically for college. A great deal of critical attention focuses on the students who are pushed beyond their capacity. What of those, possibly far more numerous, who need some kind of push to realize their capacity? Similarly, the attack stresses the neglect of the under-achiever, while ignoring the enrichment of curriculum being pro-vided for the high achiever. Obviously, most suburban school dis-tricts need to improve their offerings of practical and vocational courses, as Conant insists. But the schools' failings in this respect would not be so obvious were they not so successful in almost all other respects.

The schools are excellent, of course, because the parents care so deeply about the education of their children. As Douglass observed in 1925, in many suburbs "education is the outstanding community activity," since there is often a minimum of business or industrial activity.[58] Customarily, more than half the local tax bill is paid to support the schools, and suburban school districts grow at an alarming rate. Given these quantitative inducements (they have to pay the taxes), parents express their qualitative concern about education. There is a tremendous amount of citizen participation in matters of school policy. "The program and expenditures of suburban schools are quite likely to engender a brand of active, if not frenzied, political behavior that stands in stark contrast to the more controlled decision-making in other parts of suburban government," Robert C. Wood observes.[59] Political conflict usually takes the familiar form of conservative oldtimers versus progressive newcomers. These newcomers, who want the best for their children at whatever cost, often have "the experience to judge what is good and what is not." Incoming principals and teachers from other communities speak with awe of the knowledge they find among local parents in Westport, for example.[60]

Parents know about education, and they care about education. After all, it is their children who matter: "It is for them we moved here in the first place. It is for them we battle at the village hall in terms of more schoolhouses and playgrounds. They're the reason about a third of our shops are in business and the milkman stays employed. They're responsible for a good part of our reading in books, magazines, and newspaper columns. They explain our having a television set we vowed we'd never buy." [61] Suburban culture *is* child-centered, and children, if they are allowed a vote, like things that way. They should not, of course. Children are not supposed to like being pampered (or being neglected), they are not supposed to like the mild suburban life (or the wild one). But, as critic Peter Wyden admits, "it is one of Suburbia's whopping dividends that almost every youngster loves it there."

Some critics want children to dream bigger dreams, while others complain that the dream is already too big, and that it pushes suburban school children past their ability into a painful and avoidable sense of failure. Who is right? Are suburban youngsters ambitious, or apathetic? Are they wild, or mild? Are they spoiled, or ignored? At the extremes, of course, they are all these things, but there is no reason to suppose that the extremes are an accurate reflection of the vast majority which lies in the middle.

There are, of course, good teen-agers, average teen-agers, and rotten ones in the suburbs. The problem, Tristram Coffin concludes, is to keep them busy and away from booze and sex. And it is a problem, he concludes, which is being solved. Sensibly, though, Coffin cautions that this "does not mean that Adam is going to rediscover the Garden of Eden in Flaming Oaks." [62] Less sensibly, many critics of the suburbs seem to have expected a modern Garden of Eden. The bitterness and contradictory nature of most criticism of suburbia's children and schools reveal a deep disillusionment. Paul Goodman would return us to the one-room country school, and intellectuals generally would return us to the farm. Reinhold Niebuhr, listening to the criticism, has a "negative reaction to the negative interpretation of youthful irresponsibility and delinquency." He sees that there is delinquency in suburbs as well as in slums, and he sees the reason. "I was never a farmer or a farmer's son, but the truth is that our increasingly urban society doesn't have the nice discipline of farm life—and that marks a difference from the past." [63] The rural life of the past was different, and it cannot be transplanted in time or space. A nostalgic yearning after it will solve none of today's problems.

CHURCHES AND COMFORTABLE RELIGION

A religious revival seems to be taking place in the post-war suburbs of the United States. Statistically, there can be no disputing the existence of this revival. The Unitarians now have nine churches in an area outside Washington, D.C., where they had only two a decade ago. More than forty churches serve the booming suburb of Bloomington, Minnesota, where less than a dozen were in existence in the late fifties. Attendance at church schools and Sunday schools follows rapid increases in adult attendance at regular services. As new suburbs spring up, so do churches. Churches are often "the first major organizations to be set up" in new suburban communities; they function as active centers for "social activity, group identification, family counseling, and spiritual security." [64]

Consult the list of functions again, and you find the germ of the critical insistence that the revival is a spurious one, whatever the figures may seem to prove. The new churches abuilding in suburbia may provide a place to square dance or play bingo, a place to obtain amateur psychiatric aid or a comforting sense of security. But they do not, repeat not, renew and revive the dormant faith of the community in general or even their members in particular. According to the indictment, the suburban church has become a spiritual "comfort station." Blinded by its concentration on a host of secular activities, the suburban church has lost sight of its real reason for existence. People join it as they join the country club, for social status. On the golf course, they keep in fair physical trim; at church, they try to maintain a passable spiritual condition. Both places are useful in providing a psychological adjustment and a sense of belonging. As Lionel Trilling observes: "This ease and comfortableness seem to mark contemporary religious conversions. Religion nowadays has the appearance of what the ideal modern house has been called, 'a machine for living,' and seemingly one makes up one's mind to acquire and use it not with spiritual struggle but only with a growing sense of its practicality and convenience." The difference between "religion nowadays" and a more meaningful religion can be assessed by contrasting the platitudes of *The Seven Storey Mountain* with *The Confessions of St. Augustine,* Trilling suggests.[65]

One might think that suburban clergymen would "crow with delight" over rapidly growing church attendance and activity. Not so, Stanley Rowland comments. Many "are shaking their heads gloomily. The suburban church worries the living daylights out of them." Joining a church and participating in church activities has become, for these clergymen and the critics who help them reach this conclusion, merely another indication of stifling suburban conformity. The new suburbanites wish to "be undisturbed in enjoying their grey flannel houses" *and* their grey flannel churches. "Dedicated to a haven scrubbed in detergent, adjusted by psychologists, serviced by your friendly Esso dealer and brimming with baby food and pre-digested opinion, the suburbanite turns to the church and demands more of the same." No breath of the real world penetrates to disturb the vacuum of suburban religious life. Problems "such as slum poverty or race relations rarely obtrude." [66] The emphasis is on the material, not the spiritual, the critics maintain. As one suburban pastor observes: "In the middle of the suburban Paradise Regained, in the middle of the amiably nihilistic, low-keyed, non-believing situation of casual this-worldliness, *it is a miracle to see one man of faith.*" [67]

Clergymen of all faiths have noted the increasing secularism and the widening scope of the suburban church. In suburbs, Albert I. Gordon writes, the rabbi is more of a pastor, counselor, and guide to moral and ethical living than he is a student of the Torah, his class-ical role. Like its Protestant and Catholic counterparts, the Jewish church "is increasingly emphasizing the neighborhood, the com-munity, the ethical, moral, and social values associated with religion, and the needs of living people. Theological and denominational dif-ferences are seemingly less important." [68] They become less im-portant, as well, to the Catholic priest who has a building program and a school to take care of, in addition to his more strictly religious duties. As a consequence, Andrew Greeley writes,

. . . there is at least some reason to think that the Catholic layman views his pastor primarily as an administrator of a large plant and the superin-tendent of an educational institution. The curate is looked upon as a part-time recreational supervisor and a part-time bargain-basement psychiatric counselor. The church is judged as a social service center. . . .[69]

A great deal of church activity is directed toward children. Father Greeley notes that the suburban parish, like the suburb of which it is a part, is child-centered, and the suburbanites are liable to start thinking of "the parish as a glorified day-nursery and the priests and nuns as highly trained baby sitters." [70] In his study of Park Forest Jews, Gans concluded that the community was child oriented when the mothers held out for, and got, a Sunday school for Jewish young-sters, primarily so they wouldn't feel "different" from their Protestant and Catholic playmates.[71]

The community shapes the church, and not vice versa. In serving the suburban middle class, the church, of whatever faith, adopts such suburban middle class values as child-centeredness, conformity, hyperactivity, irresponsibility, and discrimination, to name a few usually cited in the critical attack.

In his influential book, *The Suburban Captivity of the Churches*, Gibson Winter has set forth the terms of the indictment. A successful church, he writes, is impossible without "a fabric of cohesive com-munity." But in the suburbs this fabric becomes a web. Seeking privacy and escape from the city's problems, suburban congregations turn to activities of an "appalling superficiality." The result has been "a growing insulation of the major denominations from the people of the central cities." As the middle class Protestant-Catholic-Jew has moved to the suburbs, his churches have followed him, leaving con-gregations diminished in manpower and monetary resources in their wake. On the surface, it may seem that the new suburban churches welcome parishioners, but appearances are deceiving:

The mark of the primitive church was social inclusiveness—rich and poor, Jew and gentile, slave and free. The characteristic of the church of the metropolis is exclusiveness. The exclusive congregations of the major de-nominations advertise themselves as 'friendly churches' and put a pre-mium on the friendly handclasp, warm cup of coffee, and something for everyone to do. Despite this warmth of sentiment, the typical congrega-tion is a very homogeneous social and economic grouping.[72]

Theoretically, the church's doors are open to anyone. In practice, only people of like social and economic position need apply. "The Church," Winter maintains, "is now a reflection of the economic ladder." For evidence, he proposes a look at the "chaotic crisscrossing of worshippers on Sunday morning. . . . Protestants pass by churches of their own denomination which are higher or lower in social status than their own in order to worship with their economic peers." [73] This exclusiveness prevents the church from realizing what should be its major goal—the goal of service to others. Instead, the concentration is on children and conformity. The Protestant minister "becomes a supplement to the didie service," as do the Catholic priest and the Jewish rabbi. He also becomes an administrator, meeting with the myriad committees which make up the modern religious establishment. In short, the minister becomes the Organization Man of the church, rather than its spiritual guide. What is needed is a return to the condition of the primitive church, the condition of inclusiveness. Break the bond of homogeneity, become a church for rich and poor, free and slave, and it will be possible, Winter believes, to fulfill that "mission to every area of human activity" he regards as the opportunity and duty of the modern congregation. The church must actively stretch its boundaries to take in the poverty-stricken residents of the central city. The church must actively seek membership from several races. It must, in fact, become a *metropolitan* church, rather than merely a suburban church, achieving that same kind of inclusive bigness which political scientists call for in governmental organization.[74]

To summarize the indictment, then, the suburban church is characterized by a large congregation made up of basically insincere members. These members join the church for socio-economic status, not for more altruistic reasons. They engage in a great deal of activity, but the activity is not spiritually oriented. Leaving behind them in the city the problems of poverty and racial strife, they have abdicated that missionary responsibility which is part of the Judaeo-Christian tradition.

How accurate and how meaningful is this indictment? Perhaps its most obvious mistake is its assumption that the shortcomings it describes are peculiar to the suburbs as a *location* and to the present as a *time*. As long as forty years ago, for example, Douglass wrote that a higher proportion of suburbanites than city-dwellers belonged to churches, and that their churches had an unusually large number of subsidiary organizations. In his study of St. Louis, he found that the level of religious activity rose proportionally with the number of miles travelled from the central city.[75] There is nothing new, then, about hyperactivity in suburban churches. Nor is there anything particularly suburban, for that matter, about joining the church as a measure of achievement and adjustment. As Robert S. and Helen M. Lynd wrote of the small town in their 1937 volume, *Middletown in Transition,*

. . . going to church becomes a kind of moral life insurance policy and one's children go to school and college so that they can get a better job and know the right people. Bit by bit in a culture devoted to movement and progress these permanent things of life become themselves adjuncts to the central business of getting ahead, dependent symbols of the community's life.[76]

If the permanent things in life are becoming means to the end of getting ahead, the postwar suburbs are not to blame; it was already happening in depression Middletown.

It is entirely possible, of course, that the suburbanite may use religion cynically, "as an avenue of social mobility or as a means toward respectability." But religion may serve the same purpose for the urbanite or ruralite. And the increasing secularity of church functions, the increasing emphasis on men's groups and women's groups, youth groups and senior citizen groups, cannot be taken as conclusive evidence of this cynicism.[77] In addition, even if the revival of religion in the suburbs has been motivated by the wrong reasons, at least it furnishes an occasion for piety. Certainly, there may be too many secular activities going on. But all these groups and clubs and circles create what George P. Odiorne calls an "available frontier" for bringing people deeper into the spiritual life. "The church gains have not all been in numbers and money," he contends. There has been a concomitant gain in faith.[78] John Cogley, who has no illusions about the selfish motivations that drive most people to join the suburban church, agrees with Odiorne: "The problem of the 'revival' is one of taking advantage of a mood to enlist people in a cause which, if successful, will then destroy the mood. . . . You can't have even a half-souled revival without some people becoming revived. Prophets will yet appear in the suburbs. Hard sayings will yet ring out over the green fields of Westchester County. . . ."[79] All this may be true, the critics concede, but they insist it is also true that the suburban church represents an escape from responsibility to the modern metropolis. In suburbia, religion has retreated from such real problems of the day as racial discrimination, they argue.

By keeping lot sizes large and real estate agents under their thumbs, village councils prevent the problems from coming up. It is not necessary, and it is no longer desirable, to post signs announcing that Negroes cannot buy homes in the suburbs. No signs are needed; the message is conveyed by subtler but equally effective means. While this tacit discrimination goes on, suburban congregations sit idly by. So goes the accusation, but the evidence is less than conclusive. In one case (Deerfield, Illinois), Negro newcomers were met with physical violence and psychological warfare. In another, less publicized case (Main Line suburb of Philadelphia), residents staved off the "blockbuster" out to reap fast, easy profits from devalued homes by greeting a new Negro family on the block with identical signs reading "This House Is Not For Sale." In a third incident, the Jewish Community Council of Levittown, Pennsylvania, passed a resolution when the first Negro family moved in: "We welcome to Levittown Mr. and Mrs. William Myers, expecting no more, no less than is expected of any member of our community." [80]

There are, of course, a great many Negroes now living in the suburbs; it has been estimated, in fact, that 15 to 20 per cent of all American Negroes now reside in suburban homes. But few of them live in integrated communities. Most live in transplanted ghettos, in all-Negro or almost all-Negro suburbs.

The critics believe that suburban churches must help shorten the time and help supply the education which will make fair housing more than a high-sounding principle in the nation's suburbs. It is not fair, however, to conclude that nothing has been done along these lines, especially in the light of the courageous action by clergymen of all faiths and all locations in support of the civil rights movement. Surely, it is significant that neither Gordon nor Gans found substantial evidence of overt anti-Semitism in their studies of suburbs. In Gordon's survey, 63 per cent of the Jewish suburbanites who responded reported "no anti-Jewish feeling in the suburb in which they reside." Another 4 per cent said they were unaware of any such sentiment. A total of 33 per cent, however, believed there was—or might be—" 'some' anti-Jewish feeling, even though they could not often particularize." [81] In his more intensive study of Park Forest, Gans concluded that "there has probably been very little anti-Semitism in Park Forest. . . . And it seems certainly true that if anti-Semitism played any role in the formation of the community, it was the fear and expectation of anti-Semitism rather than actual experience of anti-Semitism in Park Forest, on the part of either children or parents." Certainly there is no stigma against Jewishness in local politics. Jews made up only 9 per cent of the Park Forest population in 1949, yet "all but one member of the first Board of Education, and half of the original six-man Board of Trustees that runs the village, [were] Jewish." [82]

Suburbanites, and their churches, seem to be growing into a mature attitude toward religious and racial discrimination. Phyllis McGinley tells the story of the Japanese-American "Yamotos," who lived in Spruce Manor during "one of the wars." One sweet spring night, someone broke in and uprooted the victory garden the Yamotos had cultivated. The shock, she comments, merely numbed her, but

. . . neighbors protested less and did more. By evening the garden had been replanted. There were no public statements, no petitions, no paid protests. Simply, people with gardens of their own came hurrying spontaneously to the rescue with plants, with seedlings, with spades for digging and stakes to drive into the ground. By an act of common love we wiped out our uncommon shame.

She does not claim that Spruce Manor is Eden, but she maintains that "kindness has become a way of life most of us attempt." [83] Few religions ask more.

Unlike his colleague Gibson Winter, Protestant clergyman Frederick A. Shippey takes a balanced view of the religious revival in suburbia. The attacks of Winter, Rowland, and others, he maintains, have been woefully weak in evidence. "Negative criticisms respecting suburban Protestantism remain unproved and unsupported." [84] To the charge that congregations have insulated themselves from the serious problems beyond their borders, Shippey replies that "an average of thirteen cents out of each budget dollar is sent from the parish to the outside" in the case of 250 suburban Protestant churches studied. Thirteen cents, he comments, may not be enough, but at least the figure shows an awareness of the church's stewardship responsibilities.[85] To the complaints against the increase in suburban church activities, Shippey admits that some "of this busyness probably falls short of intended religious ends" but points out that "many suburban churches in which abundant activity takes place, manage to retain a lively concern respecting the deeper aspects of Christian life."[86]

A basic conflict exists, he realizes, between those who believe the church should function as a spiritual pacesetter and those who believe it should serve as a comfort station, "the primary issue of Calvary versus Zion." Shippey recommends a compromise on this issue, although he recognizes the dangers of too much comfort. The suburban location, he writes, can best be regarded as both a boon and a cross. "The territory has yielded numerous benefits and blessings for many of its residents," and for their churches. At the same time, suburbia "constitutes a real test of faith" for the genuinely Christian person confronted with "material advantages and attractive secular dimensions." But the boon of the suburbs, the opportunities for faith that exist there, tend to outweigh the burden of the cross. "The church has proved a redemptive force in suburbia over and over again," he concludes.[87] Rabbi Samuel Silver, of Stamford, Connecticut, feels the same way:

People of all faiths—Christian and Jew alike—are struggling today to shake off the crass materialistic approach of recent years that has been blatant in many suburban areas, in every religion.

Today, more than ever before, they are seeking true spiritual values. The suburbs, despite the cry of isolation, do provide intercommunications and friendships that may make this search ultimately triumphant.[88]

Despite these hopeful minority reports, however, the critical court continues to judge suburban religion as hollow and insincere. As Shippey comments, "polemical writers have singled out suburbanites and branded them as a type of social criminal who deserves reproach. What provokes this modern witch-hunt?" The provocation, he suggests, proceeds from the high hopes originally held by the polemical writers themselves, and still held (less idealistically) by "thousands of residents of the slum and of the crowded, nondescript city." To the slum-dwellers, "suburbia betokens a heavenly mirage which knows no headaches, no heartaches, and no evils. . . . It beckons as a shining land of beauty and of promise." The critics are busy telling them that the land is not shining, that the land, in fact, has been betrayed, but the slum-dweller with the chance to move out will not listen. When their caustic comments "fall as wasted caveats upon many unheeding ears," the critics are still more incensed, and they return to their typewriters for another attack.[89]

The critical indictment, at bottom, calls for a return to a Golden Age of religion, to a time when the sacred and not the profane (to use the terms of Mircea Eliade) walked the earth. But is such a return desirable? Do we really want to return to the faith of our primitive predecessors, or even to the faith of our Puritan forefathers? The desire to reject the largely desacralized modern world and to return to a sacred past constitutes a refusal of history and more, Eliade writes. Religious man, he claims,

. . . is above all a man paralyzed by the myth of the eternal return. A modern psychologist would be tempted to interpret such an attitude as anxiety before the danger of the new, refusal to assume responsibility for a genuine historical existence, nostalgia for a situation that is paradisal precisely because it is embryonic, insufficiently detached from nature.[90]

Nature, and the land, have lain at the heart of most religions. The practice of agriculture has been celebrated as "a ritual revealed by the gods or culture heroes," by Ceres or Jefferson.[91] And the pull of the land is a powerful one, even on the most urban of peoples. Writing of the Jewish migration to the suburbs, Harry Gersh observes that the first basic change "has to do with the earth and growing things. . . . Our vision of ourselves is of an urban creature isolated by time and trade from the mysteries of seed and soil. The mystery was not displaced by the move to Suburbia. However, it became a known and common mystery, shared by Jew and non-Jew." Gersh confesses that "it is pleasant to walk on your own earth and feel your green grass and plan your own mysteries of birth and bloom and death." [92] In talking about the mystery of growing things, Gersh is talking about the deepest of religious mysteries.

Modern urban man, no matter how profane his life may seem, cannot escape his religious past. To a greater or lesser degree, depending on the mixture of the sacred and the profane of his individual makeup, he will be paralyzed by the myth of the eternal return. And paralysis is not, Eliade maintains, a healthy state of being. "Man makes himself, and he only makes himself completely in proportion as he desacralizes himself and the world. The sacred is the prime obstacle to his freedom. He will become himself only when he is totally demysticized. He will not be truly free until he has killed the last god." That day will not soon come, for such myths as that of the virtue- and health-giving soil do not die easily. Staggering under "a whole magico-religious paraphernalia which . . . [has] degenerated to the point of caricature," the twentieth century intellectual is not free to judge the world around him dispassionately, without bias.[93] Instead of dealing directly with the ethical problems confronting him, he points the finger of ritualistic blame at suburbia, which has turned out not to be a rural paradise regained. The critics argue that there is not enough emphasis on spiritual matters in suburban churches. It may be wiser to argue that there is still too much. As Harvey Cox writes, men "must be called away from their fascination with other worlds—astrological, metaphysical, or religious—and summoned to confront the concrete issues of this one, 'where alone the true call of God can be found.' " [94]

IX. THE SUBURBAN FRONTIER

At Cranbrook in our time [in the thirties], everybody was talking about what a wonderful thing the suburbs were going to be. . . . It was all quite new, and we were full of hope for the pastures. We were all gliding out of town on the freeways.

—*Charles Eames,* 1964

REPUBLICANISM

Suburban politics, like suburban life styles and suburban homes, are a mess—or so the popular indictment runs. What kind of political behavior can be expected of human beings who live in uniform little boxes, consume canned food and entertainment, play bridge out of one book (Goren's) and raise children out of another (Spock's)? The predicted behavior, of course, is one of standardization, a standardization based on rock-ribbed Republicanism and further supported by a framework of economic and social irresponsibility. To elaborate the indictment briefly, the modern American, on taking up residence in the suburbs, is supposed to:

1. Cast off whatever liberal beliefs he might once have held and drift into conservatism, supporting only Republican candidates. (Republicanism and conservatism, though not precisely similar, are regarded as a single phenomenon in this chapter.)
2. Avoid participation in local (or any other kind of) politics, or if unable to do so, participate only in political decisions of infinitesimal importance.

3. Rob the city and the metropolitan area of political efficiency, economic equality, and racial balance in a cowardly flight from responsibility.

Let us, like Al Smith, look at the record in assessing each of these charges, the charges of increasing conservatism, lack of (meaningful) participation and a corollary abdication of power within the suburb, and a profound lack of responsibility to the central city and the metropolitan area which originally spawned the suburban community.

Everybody knows that the suburbs vote Republican. And so they do. Or at least most of them do, most of the time. But it is not safe to conclude that suburbia *creates* conservatism, although the temptation to so conclude is strong. William H. Whyte reached the conclusion in his examination of Park Forest, remarking that whatever the cause, "it is true that something does seem to happen to Democrats when they get to suburbia." [1] *Newsweek* also fell victim to the temptation in reporting that, "When a city dweller packs up and moves his family to the suburbs, he usually acquires a mortgage, a power lawn mower, and a backyard grill. Often, although a lifelong Democrat, he also starts voting Republican." [2]

A funny thing happens to suburbanites on the way to the polling booth; they remember their taxes, they recall the social pressure of their Republican neighbors, and they cast their lot with conservatism, in the process discarding their Democratic heritage. This is the theory of *conversion* from Democrat to Republican, with the suburban experience the root cause of the conversion. The theory has some slight empirical support, beyond the more or less subjective conclusions of those quoted above. G. Edward Janosik, for example, after examining election returns in fifty-seven suburban counties, cautiously decided that even "in suburban areas traditionally Democratic there has been evidence of a tendency toward Republicanism." [3] Fred I. Greenstein and Raymond E. Wolfinger, working with data collected by the Survey Research Center of the University of Michigan, found that the evidence led "tentatively to Whyte's description of the converting effects of suburban living" [4] on voting patterns. Pollster Louis Harris, using research material of the Elmo Roper organization, summarized more boldly. Before they moved to suburbia after World War II, Harris wrote, "the majority of these people were Democrats." But in the Republican suburbs, the lonely Democrats had no choice but to join the dominant party: "Who ever heard of the Democrats out in the suburban town?" [5]

Both the subjective and scientific expressions of the conversion theory are flawed by one important—and intentional—omission in the above summary: In no part of the summary were dates mentioned. But the dates are highly significant: Whyte's book was published in 1956, Harris's in 1954; the *Newsweek* spread on suburbia was printed in 1957, Janosik's article in 1956, Greenstein and Wolfinger's in the Winter 1958–1959 issue of *Public Opinion Quarterly*. All of the comments were produced, in other words, during the two terms in office of Dwight D. Eisenhower, an immensely popular and unexpectedly charismatic President of the United States. Where data are used in those books and articles, they come from the national elections of 1952 and 1956, when Eisenhower scored impressive victories over Adlai Stevenson. Intellectuals and hard-nosed politicians alike were on the lookout for a scapegoat to explain away the liberal defeat, and suburbia was close at hand and eminently safe: you could attack suburbia without, apparently, attacking the people who lived there, or at least without expecting much opposition. You could do it in the 1950s, and you can do it now. So Jake Arvey in Chicago announced that "the suburbs beat us," and Senator Robert Taft, who should have been as aware as anyone of Eisenhower's unusual popular pull, proclaimed that the Democrats would never win another national election unless they could somehow reverse the suburban trend to Republicanism.

It was not the suburbs that beat the Democrats in 1952 and 1956, it was Eisenhower. The point was apparent even at the time to so sharp-eyed a political commentator as Samuel Lubell, who examined the same election returns as did Harris (those of 1952) and reached the conclusion that, compared with 1948, "Eisenhower gained more heavily in the cities than in the suburbs, indicating that many of the newer suburbanites whom the G.O.P. won in 1952 would have voted Republican even if they had stayed in the cities." What's more, he pointed out, the suburbs were no more Republican in 1952 than they were in the 1920s. Cook County's suburbs outside Chicago, for example, voted 84 per cent Republican in 1920, 66 per cent in 1952. Long Island and Westchester were 74 per cent Republican in 1920, 70 per cent in 1952. Analysis of the political effects of the suburban population explosion must wait for "one or more" Presidential elections, Lubell wisely decided. In fact, "some suburban returns I have analyzed point to a long-run trend to make the suburbs somewhat more Democratic, although not on any scale that would threaten Republican ascendancy in these communities." [6] But no one, least of all the Republican party leadership, placed much stock in Lubell's cautions, and it did not matter to the faithful if the *percentage* of Republicanism stayed the same or even dipped a little, as long as the suburbs kept growing fast enough to produce larger and larger pluralities for G.O.P. candidates.

Actually, however, the Republicans had more reason to cry than to laugh, as that most perceptive student of suburban politics Robert C. Wood has demonstrated. The pattern of 1956 followed that of 1952, with Republican gains more marked in the cities than in the suburbs. The carrying power of Eisenhower obscured the real political problems of the suburbs, and of the Republican party. Blinded by the overwhelming majorities for Eisenhower in the suburbs, and encouraged by the surprising support within large cities for their candidate, party brass anticipated a new world for a party whose fortunes had been rocky, to say the least, since depression days. The leaders decided that suburbanization was a secret weapon which would guarantee the G.O.P. more than its share of the political spoils.

The weapon turned out to be a boomerang, for if the voters were not being *converted* to conservatism by the blessings of homeownership and neighborly pressure, but were merely being *transplanted* from city to suburb, with political attitudes intact, the implications were not pleasant to contemplate. Were the Republicans, in flocking to the suburbs, conceding control of the central cities, with their established political machinery and key prestige offices, to the Democrats? In moving to an already predominantly Republican suburb, the emigrants were only dissipating their potential strength. For the suburbs, even more than the cities, are notoriously under-represented in Congress, and seem likely to remain so. Recent Supreme Court "one man, one vote" rulings have mitigated the effect of this under-representation, but the suburbs are sure to lack full proportional representation as long as they continue to grow at their present rapid pace. There are ten years between each census, and a fast-growing suburb can multiply its population several times in a decade. In Bloomington, Minnesota, for example, the community population sprinted from less than 10,000 in 1950 to more than 50,000 in 1960; assuming that other suburban areas in the third district of the state of Minnesota had grown at the same rate (they did not) and further assuming that the district had possessed fair proportional representation even in 1950 (it was in fact underrepresented), the citizens of Bloomington and the third district would be receiving five times less representation in Congress than they deserved, as of 1960. This three-way squeeze—abandonment of city offices, production of virtual one-party suburbs, and underrepresentation in the federal legislature—tends to produce what Wood calls the "impotent" suburban vote.[7]

The picture of the "impotent" suburban vote is based on the assumption that where one lives has little or nothing to do with the way he votes. There is abundant evidence, carefully collected, to support this point of view. Charles Edson, in his study of the St. Louis suburbs, discovered no rush to Republicanism, and no evidence to back up the Whyte-Harris hypothesis of suburban conversion. Party preference, Edson found, was "most directly related to occupational status, combined with the influences of income and parental party loyalties." When voters did change their party affiliation, the switch apparently had little or nothing to do with place of residence.[8] Another study, by Jerome C. Manis and Leo C. Stine, questioned citizens of Westwood, a small suburb of Kalamazoo, Michigan, and concluded that "suburban residence seems in itself to be politically irrelevant" in determining their voting preferences. Occupational status and religion may have some effect, the joint authors stated, but not suburbia.[9]

In the 1960s, two full-scale works have effectively pulled the rug out from under the conversion hypothesis. The two studies are located at opposite geographic and socio-economic poles: one deals with a new mass-produced suburb in California, inhabited largely by working-class families; the other with an old-line Connecticut exurb whose residents are predominantly upper middle class. One community was overwhelmingly Republican, the other Democrat. One suburb's income, education, and educational levels were low to medium, the other's extraordinarily high. The two communities, in short, were as dissimilar as any two suburbs could be, yet the findings were identical. In neither suburb was there any evidence that suburbanization produces conservative voting habits; in both places, in fact, there was a slight, probably insignificant trend toward the Democratic party.

In *Working Class Suburb*, published in 1960, Bennett M. Berger studied the community of Milpitas, California. A suburb of San Jose, Milpitas was populated largely by a group of Ford Motor Company workers whose families had been moved from the industrial city of Richmond, California, and put down near a new Ford plant two and a half years previously. The blue-collar workers and their families settled into suburban life happily, and without any apparent trend toward conservatism. In his interviews, Berger discovered that 81 per cent of the suburb's residents classified themselves as Democrats, 11 per cent as Republicans, 6 per cent as independents, and 2 per cent did not know. The appeal of Eisenhower siphoned off some of the Democratic votes in 1956, after the move to Milpitas, but Eisenhower had garnered even more of these votes in 1952, when the Ford workers were still members of the urban, not suburban, working class. "In terms of *those who voted,* Eisenhower received 26 per cent of the vote in 1952; in 1956 he had not quite 18 per cent. On the basis of these figures alone, we could conclude that the Democratic vote has *increased* since the move to the suburbs." [10]

David Wallace's book, *First Tuesday,* published in 1964, studied the political behavior of Westport, Connecticut, which has been around since Colonial days and is one of the places A. C. Spectorsky had in mind when he wrote *The Exurbanites.* Wallace scattered his fire in approaching this complex community; instead of concentrating on presidential voting, he dispersed his ammunition in three directions, towards local and state as well as national voting. The initial findings were confusing, to say the least. In the presidential elections of 1952 and 1956, the already high margins of Republican voting strength went from a normal 65 per cent to about 75 per cent, before settling back to 65 per cent in 1960. But on the state level, the town voted increasingly Democratic, with the climax coming in 1958 with the first Democratic plurality for governor in over half a century. And locally, Westport's politics were split wide open by a new third party.[11]

Obviously, no simple explanation would suffice to account for this contradictory voting behavior, but Wallace tortured and twisted the election figures to test various hypotheses, including the suburbs-make-Republicans one. The result was conclusive: ". . . whatever we do with the study data there is no support in Westport, Connecticut, for any conclusion that present suburban voters are becoming more Republican than their parents. In this community at least a better case might be made for movement to the Democrats. . . ."[12] Wallace attributed voting preferences to a set of attitudes learned early in life and clung to throughout life. Even in Westport, with its cosmopolitan life style and high socio-economic-intellectual standards, most people voted the way their parents had, and showed little indication that they would change in the future: "By and large, three out of four persons somehow managed to see greater virtue in the political party that their parents favored . . . and almost six out of ten never, on any occasion in their lifetime, had crossed party lines."[13]

What happened in Westport was what has been happening throughout the country. Most suburbs were Republican before the postwar population boom, and most remained Republican, in about the same proportion, after the boom. The inescapable lesson is that Republican suburbs attract Republican newcomers, or enough of them to maintain a high G.O.P. percentage.

Several recent studies lend weight to Berger's and Wallace's findings. John H. Millet and David Pittman, working with election figures in the suburbs of Rochester, New York, found no evidence to support "the often cited hypothesis that voting behavior changes with a move to the suburbs." Bernard Lazerwitz's study of national elections from 1948 to 1956 revealed that "as the suburban population has grown, there has been a slow but steady growth in suburban Democratic Party strength. The position that residents moving to the suburbs from the central city shift from the Democratic Party to the Republican receives no support." And Frederick M. Wirt points out that John F. Kennedy got 49 per cent of the suburban vote in 1960, while in 1964 the median vote for Barry Goldwater in the suburbs was down to 33.8 per cent, and for Republican Congressional candidates to 47.6 per cent.[14] Suburban living does not change voting behavior: the behavior is determined long before the move to suburbia.

PARTICIPATION

The critics of suburbia tumble into one of the occasional pitfalls of contradiction when they attempt to negotiate the subject of political participation. Some claim that there is little participation in the affairs of local government; others note feverish, compulsive activity, but dismiss it as inconsequential. In a few cases, the two contradictory views are expressed by the same critical observer.

A century and more ago, Alexis de Tocqueville reported with fascination the extremely high level of associational participation in Jacksonian America. People were always bustling about to do one thing or another—as a group:

No sooner do you set foot on American ground than you are stunned by a kind of tumult; a confused clamor is heard on every side. . . . Everything is in motion around you; here the people of one quarter of town are met to decide upon the building of a church; there an election is going on; a little further the delegates of a district are hastening to the town in order to consult upon some local improvement. . . .[15]

No one, according to one version of the indictment, is going to be stunned by such a tumult in mid-twentieth century suburbia. There, the citizens have all but given up their political rights in a retreat to apathy. People spend their time *Kaffeeklatsch-ing* or barbecuing, not mending the holes in their (artificial) governmental fences. Commuters, especially, are too tired to pay any attention to local issues; when they finally get home, they want to be greeted by a martini, not a zoning crisis. Wood adds his considerable weight to the proposition that suburbanization will result in less, and not more political participation. It is at least clear, he remarks, "that one result of more people moving into smaller towns has been to reduce the likelihood of vigorous political activity, party or otherwise." [16]

This view of suburban political activity is at odds with that expressed by Whyte and others, that there is so much activity, at all hours and affecting every conceivable issue, that no one has time to sit down and think in isolation. There is more support for the Whyte hypothesis than for that of Wood. Certainly, suburbanites turn out for national elections in greater percentages than either city dwellers or rural residents. And voting on the local level similarly favors the idea that interest in politics runs higher in suburbia than elsewhere. Wattel reports that only 40 per cent of eligible Levittown voters show up at the polls for school bond elections, but adds that this percentage "is much larger than that of other communities in the county" and even more significant since most residents of Levittown are emigrants from New York City, where administrators, not citizens, make decisions on school policy matters.[17]

The suspicion grows that when the critics of suburbia, whether social commentators or social scientists, talk about the lack of "*vigorous* political activity," they mean a lack of *meaningful* political activity, as seen by their lights. Levittown Hall may be busy every night of the year, but what is being discussed inside may not seem of much importance. What goes on in suburbia is inconsequential:

who cares about zoning and street lights and garbage collection
when the larger problems of the metropolitan area, the state, the
nation, and the world are in balance? Suburbanites *do* care about
such trivialities, and they are roundly chastised for their trouble.

In such a political climate, suburban citizens lose touch with the
big picture and submerge themselves "in a new cult of urban local-
ism" where they concentrate on "the history, folkways, politics,
housing arrangements, zoning laws, and a hundred other things"
pertaining solely to their own community.[18] More important matters
are ignored while the suburbanite devotes himself to his newly-
acquired grass roots. This is the charge that David Riesman elaborates with customary brilliance in his article, "The Suburban
Sadness." His suburban prototype is bland, not political at all but
only "parochially civic-minded, tending to a 'garden' which includes
the local schools and waterworks—he is apt to be an Eisenhower
Republican, seldom informed, rarely angry, and only spasmodically
partisan." Riesman acknowledges that such piddling activity may
seem to represent an attempt to come to grips with political problems, but dismisses it as "enjoyable as recreation but hardly a challenge or a source of significant political experience." [19]

Child's play or not, it is worth asking rhetorically whether the
twentieth century American would have the opportunity to indulge
his political inclinations anywhere other than in the suburb. Any
such level of activity, whether designated as trivial or not, would
gladden the hearts of democratic observers if it took place in the city
or small town.

But that is not likely: there are certain qualities of the suburban
experience that tend to guarantee greater participation. In the first
place, the new suburban resident often becomes a homeowner for
the first time in his life, and is confronted by the problems of fighting city hall that he formerly left to the landlord or consigned to
such institutions as the army or the university. *He* is going to have
to pay the special assessments for the storm sewer and the sanitary
sewer, *he* is going to have to pay the taxes that keep the schools and
the local government running, and if taxes and assessments do not

necessarily make him more Republican, they are certainly going to catch his attention. "There is some evidence," as Berger writes "that homeownership contributes to an increased interest in politics—not to an increased propensity toward Republican politics, but only toward politics in general." [20]

Secondly, the suburbanite frequently is a refugee from the city, where his life was conducted in comparative anonymity. It is, of course, possible for the suburban resident to avoid any sort of participation in local affairs, but there is no gainsaying the point that such an avoidance is more difficult in the suburb than it was in the city. There "the individual is known. His neighbors demand something from him [some civic-mindedness, at least], and he dare not altogether refuse." [21] What's more, the suburbanite has an advantage in pursuing political goals that the small-towner does not: the suburb is far less likely to be run by a clique—the turnover is too high.

A third aspect which contributes to greater political activity is the relative homogeneity of the suburban community. People are, by and large, of similar age, occupational level, and income, and they are more likely to unite in common cause than the more heterogeneous populations of the city or small town. "The lack of common interests and other differences which so frequently limit interaction between urban neighbors is . . . likely to be missing in the suburb." [22]

But if the people within any given suburb tend toward homogeneity, suburbs themselves do not. One way in which suburbs can be classified, however, is by age. There are the relatively new suburbs, often created out of cornfields, which sprang up in the wake of the postwar housing boom. And there are the older suburbs, developed several generations ago but subject to vast alterations in the last twenty years as they have been invaded by emigrants from the cities. In the new communities, government had to start from scratch. In the older suburbs, the newcomers brought a host of problems with them to upset a relatively stable order. In both cases, conditions favored political democracy, as these terms are defined in the perceptive essay by Stanley Elkins and Eric McKitrick on "A

Meaning for Turner's Frontier." [23] Frederick Jackson Turner had announced that democracy came, stark and strong, out of the American forest. But he had done little to justify his announcement; there was no thread to hold the argument together. Elkins and McKitrick, convinced that Turner had been right (although unscientific), supplied the necessary connecting links.

Political democracy, they wrote, is best understood to mean a high level of participation in government by a great many citizens. Such a level was reached in the frontier communities of the Old Northwest, where settlers were confronted by a bewildering variety of problems which could be solved only by their own resources. Democracy is not a matter of forms, they stated. "It is the result of an experience: the experience of setting up institutions . . . in new *surroundings.*" [24] Settlers on the frontier of the Old Northwest had no choice but to establish such institutions; or rather the choice was between community and anarchy, in the face of a host of problems crying out for solution. So they went ahead to establish their communities, and to take political office without the benefit of previous experience. "With the organization of each wilderness county and pioneer township, the roster of offices to be filled in and operated was naturally a perfect blank (how long had it been since this was so in Philadelphia?); somebody, willing or unwilling, must be found to fill each one." [25]

Elkins and McKitrick formulated the ideal conditions for the growth of democracy in this way: "Political democracy evolves most quickly during the initial stages of setting up a new community; it is seen most dramatically while the process of organization and the solving of basic problems are still crucial; it is observed to best advantage when this flow of basic problems is met by a homogeneous population." [26] By homogeneity, they meant both a similar level of social and economic status and aspirations, and lack of a ready-made structure of leadership in the community.

The situation is exactly that facing a brand-new suburban town carved out of a cornfield, and the historians were not insensitive to the analogy. In fact, they used the example of a contemporary federal housing project to illustrate the democratic process operating in current surroundings. This project, called Crafttown, was beset from the start by a plethora of problems. When government (the federal housing authorities had sent along a project manager) moved too slowly, the residents—mostly blue collar workers—banded together in voluntary associations of the kind that had amazed de Tocqueville to solve their problems. "The key," according to Elkins and McKitrick, "was necessity," and persons with no previous experience whatever plunged into political action.[27]

Just as the conditions for democracy were right in Crafttown, so were they present in the hundreds of privately developed suburbs which were thrown up after World War II. Private developers were even less likely, as a matter of fact, than their government counterparts to have done any intelligent thinking or planning about the ingredients of community.[28] They put up the houses, sold them, and moved on to the next project without looking back. Frequently, the streets were not paved; usually, there were no community water or sewer facilities, but only individual wells and cesspools; almost always, there was that roster of offices to be filled, and no built-in leaders to fill them. Schools and churches had to be built; police and fire departments formed. A great many things needed doing in the "initial stages" of these suburban communities, the problems were crucial, and the residents who were forced to solve the problems (the key was necessity) were notoriously homogeneous, in both Elkins-McKitrick senses of the term. Suburbia provided the contemporary frontier, the modern locus for the growth of democracy.

But what happens after the initial flurry of activity? What occurs when the most pressing problems have been solved? Clearly, there is *some* hardening of the political arteries as the suburban community ages, but liberating forces remain in the bloodstream to free the flow of access to political participation. The formative years, however painful, stand the fledgling community in good stead as it grows older. The early "time of troubles" in Crafttown, for example, produced a body of shared traditions which could later function as a reservoir of resourcefulness. "In such a usable fund of tradition,"

Elkins and McKitrick predicted, "resources for meeting a new crisis, should one appear, would remain always available." [29]

Their prediction was borne out in the crisis which confronted Bloomington in 1961. Unlike Crafttown, Bloomington was not quite brand-new when the suburban migration started in 1945; there were a few thousand residents, mostly farmers, even then. But the community's sensational growth during the next dozen years provided much the same kind of crucial problems which ordinarily face wholly-new communities. By the early 1960s, population had grown from less than 4,000 to more than 50,000 persons, but the initial "time of troubles" appeared to be over. The suburb was beginning to settle into relative stability. Then, in 1961, state inspectors discovered that water in many of the suburb's individual wells was polluted, and Bloomington faced a crisis.

The polluted water posed too serious a danger to be ignored. The residents either had to act, or leave. Spurred by economic reality and by a healthy tradition of widespread community participation, they decided on action. Neighborhood groups quickly organized, and petitions circulated calling for a suburb-wide sewer and water system, to be paid for at a stiff special assessment price by the homeowners themselves. A water testing station was set up across from city hall where skeptical residents might find out for themselves just how polluted their water was. The suburb's officials rapidly united across party lines to urge an immediate solution; separate hearings were held in each of the neighborhood areas, starting with those in which pollution was most widespread. It is likely that a majority of Bloomington's adult citizens attended one or more of these hearings, although no one took time to keep an audience total. Supported by the residents' petitions, the city council was able to speed project after project. Bloomington city employees, particularly the administrators and engineers, worked long overtime hours. In less than eighteen months, the community had *completed* more than $20 million worth of improvements, and the crisis was over. Largely as a consequence of this accomplishment, the National Municipal League designated Bloomington an All-American City, and its residents deserved the award. They could have panicked and fled; instead they chose to stay and to act—and to add several thousand dollars apiece to their own private obligations as the lesser of economic evils. It is hard to say how a community which had never experienced an early time of troubles would have reacted to such a crisis; it seems certain that Bloomington's "usable fund of tradition" served the community well in its later crisis.

This suburb's initial time of troubles was marked by a clash of interests which typically accompanies invasion of a more or less established community by a horde of newcomers, and which produces anew those conditions of crucial decision-making that lead to democratic action. The clash takes place, of course, between the old residents and the newcomers, and it follows an almost invariable pattern from suburb to suburb. The older residents support a low-tax, economy-minded governmental structure; the newcomers want improvements. The oldtimers, who have often sold their farm land at inflated prices to developers, typically remain in control of local government for a period of time, and manage to hold taxes, and services, down, while resisting the expansionist demands of the newcomers. The new suburbanites, sooner or later (the length of time depends on the original population of oldtimers and on the size and speed of the in-migration movement), outnumber their rivals and gain control of local government. In go the paved streets, up go the modern schools, out go the community garbage trucks—and up go everyone's taxes.

This ubiquitous conflict between old and new residents creates a climate of political participation. If the newcomers are not actually building institutions from scratch, as they must do in the cornfield suburb, they are willing and eager to work such changes in the existing institutions as to render them unrecognizable. The struggle between the old and new produces that high level of citizen participation in politics that defines American democracy.

In Bloomington, old and new residents conflicted on liquor laws. The suburb was dry, and the oldtimers wanted it left that way. Most of the newcomers, however, were attracted by the probable economic benefits of liquor licensing, property taxes from restaurants, motels, and so forth. The Democrats appropriated the issue to their cause by taking a position in favor of municipal liquor stores, an option not available to the suburb by virtue of state law. The idea of municipal ownership appealed to the Democratic newcomers as a logical, if impossible, solution to the liquor question (Democratic candidates promised to get the state law changed, if elected, but were unable to fulfill such promises); and it appealed to the nominally Republican oldtimers as well, more because of its impossibility than its logic. Through this device the local Republicans became identified, quite accurately, as the proponents of private liquor licensing; and the Democrats, through their coalition of liberal newcomers and status quo-minded oldtimers, held sway in local government for the half decade from 1955 to 1960.[30]

But such coalitions between old and new residents are rare. Usually, the two groups oppose each other in active political warfare. Considering their socio-economic differences, such warfare seems almost inevitable. In Westport, Wallace found that it was far easier to distinguish newcomer from oldtimer than to tell Republican from Democrat. The latter pair looked surprisingly alike. Recently settled Westport Democrats, for example, ranked slightly (but only slightly) higher on the socio-economic scale than their Republican counterparts. Recent arrivals of whatever political persuasion, however, ranked far higher, earned substantially higher salaries, and possessed far better educations than long-time residents of the Connecticut suburb. Especially where school policy matters were concerned, the "big cleavage" was between the newcomers, who wanted the best education for their children at almost any price, and the anti-academic keep-the-taxes-down oldtimers. This basic conflict resulted in the wide-open split in local Westport elections of the 1950s, when a Taxpayer party, composed primarily of old-time residents, challenged and nearly won control of the township government from the numerically predominant Republicans.[31]

Westport and Bloomington are only two examples of a phenomenon which has been observed throughout the country. Louis Harris has called attention to the old versus new resident conflict, and so have Wood and Dobriner.[32] In all accounts, there seems to be agreement that the newcomers eventually emerge victorious from the conflict. Once the battle is won, it is logical to expect a period of greater political stability and less citizen activity to set in, and this expectation is usually confirmed by facts. But there is little danger that any suburb will reach such a state of political stability as to produce an apathetic citizenry. For one thing, the citizenry itself, in most suburbs, is in a process of rapid turnover: most suburbanites are far more geographically mobile than residents of central cities or rural towns. For another, once the battle lines are drawn, as in the old versus new conflict, they are not easily erased. For a third, these suburbs have established a tradition of political participation, either by necessity as in the cornfield community or by choice as in the old-line suburb invaded by newcomers. Suburban political arteries may tend to harden, but that ingredient of participation which is the life-blood of democracy will keep them from congealing.

In the cities, politics seem terribly impersonal, complicated, and remote. The average citizen concludes that there is no real chance for him to participate in a government he can neither understand nor identify. As Louis Wirth wrote: "There is little opportunity for the individual to obtain a conception of the city as a whole or to survey his place in the total scheme. Consequently he finds it difficult to determine what is to his own 'best interests' and to decide between the issues and leaders presented to him by the agencies of mass suggestion." [33] In the small town, there is no such lack of identification, no reason for anomie. Everybody knows everybody else, and everybody knows who runs the town. Usually, it is run by an entrenched oligarchy. It is no longer possible to go West in search of political opportunity: the United States ran out of geographical frontier seventy-five years ago. But there is still an internal political frontier in America, located in the suburbs.

ESCAPE FROM RESPONSIBILITY

When and if the anti-suburban commentators of the fifties are persuaded that suburbs do not, ordinarily, convert Democrats into Republicans; and when and if they are convinced that suburban life encourages political participation, they will still be inclined to view government in the suburbs with a jaundiced eye. Satellite communities purchase their political independence at too high a price, they maintain: the price is governmental inefficiency, economic inequality, and racial or religious discrimination.

In the course of the twentieth century, units of government in America's metropolitan areas have multiplied almost geometrically. Now, there are 600 such units serving the Detroit complex, 1,400 for New York. Chicago had 55 units in 1890; 109 in 1920; 960 in 1954. Most of these new units have been established to govern the widening ring of suburban communities which surround central cities. Political commentators view their proliferation with alarm. Such fragmentation "results in a lack of civic responsibility for the problems and expenses of the city in which the suburbanites work." [34] It deprives the city of its natural leaders, men who move to the suburbs and leave the city's problems behind.

In addition, such fragmentation of government is grossly inefficient. A freeway to hook up Miami's south suburbs to the central city runs into the middle of a Miami Housing Authority project. While police argue about which municipality should be called to put it out, fire burns down a building unlucky enough to be located on the border between Miami and West Miami. Local governments, working separately and often at cross purposes, cannot be expected to solve area-wide problems. Water supply, transportation, and land-use control involve the whole metropolitan complex, not a single suburban town, village, or city. "Once an indivisible problem is divided, nothing effective can be done about it," as Luther Gulick comments.[35]

Inefficiency is bad enough. What is worse is that the suburbs are "milking the city," which is deteriorating and dying without the funds to do much about it. The people who move out to the suburbs from the city are typically (though not always) members of the middle and upper middle class, usually on their way up in the world, in short, those most able to pay taxes. Obviously, one immediate effect of their exodus is to change the economic character of the core city. "With the middle income classes moving out, the Cen-

tral City becomes the home either of the well-to-do or the poor." [36]
Commerce (and later, industry) follow the middle class to suburbia,
further eating into the city's tax base. Shopping centers spring up,
and downtown stores set up branches whose volume soon challenges that of the "main store" itself. Some stores simply pack up
and move their whole operation to greener pastures. "In two years
in the early 1950s San Francisco lost 289 retail stores to the suburbs," [37] and the Bay City's experience is hardly unique. In time, as
city property taxes skyrocket to compensate for loss of residential,
commercial, and industrial tax base, even the well-to-do may be
unable to stand the gaff.

Not only does the city face a diminishing tax base, but it is also
required, according to the critics of suburbia, to subsidize the suburbs. The reasoning is that cities pay a proportionally higher share
of state and county taxes than do the suburbs. Charles Adrian, in
making this point, uses the Minneapolis metropolitan area as an
example. "In Minneapolis in 1949," he maintains, "about 87 per cent
of the Hennepin County taxes were paid by city taxpayers who received no benefits, or only very small benefits, from nine of the
county functions, including some of the most expensive ones." [38]
Adrian supplies no further specifics, but a recent study has demonstrated that if his estimates were accurate in 1949, they are no longer
accurate in the 1960s. After a three-year study of exactly this area,
James Banovetz concluded that Minneapolis does *not* subsidize its
suburbs in Hennepin County, at least not to any appreciable extent.
According to one yardstick, Minneapolis may be subsidizing the
suburbs slightly, about $574,000 worth, or one-half of one per cent
of the total value of public services included in his study. Using
another yardstick, the *suburbs* may be subsidizing Minneapolis
slightly, about $1 million worth, or about one per cent of the value
of services. By either yardstick, the claim of suburb subsidization is
effectively refuted, at least in the case of Minneapolis and Hennepin
County. What seems to be true is that the city pays more for some
things and the suburbs more for others. [39]

If the cities have their financial complaints, so do many of the suburbs. Their local government, like that of the city, is largely financed by the property tax, and when the property tax is "divided among so many jurisdictions, the sum of the parts [does] not equal the whole." The result is municipal poverty, "in good times as well as bad." [40] The plight of the have-not suburb, in fact, deserves as much sympathy, and attention, as that of the core city. The have-not suburb typically occurs when a small community lacks proper sites or services to attract the tax dollars of business and industry, or when the community is so rapidly built the homes gobble up such sites. Such a suburb is made up of little houses on little lots, with the people inside producing large families, and large sewer and school, police and fire protection bills.

Still, there is the charge of inefficiency. The very multiplicity of governmental units is an affront to common sense, to principles of scientific management, and worst of all to our sense of modernity. "The automobile, rapid transit, the organization of modern industry, and many other technological and social changes have rendered the older set of political implements not only obsolete but also grossly inefficient." [41] Thomas H. Reed metaphorically diagnoses the status quo as a case of "suburbanitis." This disease, accompanied by intense suffering and caused by vast and unruly growth, "is endemic to every urban community" in the United States. His proposed cure is drastic: "many of the existing organs—cities, counties, towns, and villages—must be removed and the body sewed together again so that it will function successfully." [42]

One answer to this argument is that the "set of political implements" *is* changing, that at least minor surgery is already being performed upon the urban body politic. The most popular technique results in creation of an entirely new body altogether: the metropolitan authority or district empowered to work out solutions to a particular set of problems—those affecting transportation or water pollution, for example. But it has disadvantages. Often it is established on an undemocratic basis, remote and unavailable to civic criticism or recall. And, of course, such authorities merely add to the already bewildering variety of governmental units: "What happens to political visibility when the suburbanite finds himself bound into a murky structure of overlapping, submerged, and superimposed election districts, school districts, sanitation districts, fire districts, police jurisdictions, postal areas, incorporated and unincorporated villages, towns, and cities?" [43] Fewer jurisdictions are called for, not more, the political scientists agree. With Reed, they call for surgery: cut out the existing organs and reassemble them in one metropolitan government body.

Despite a near-unanimity of opinion among professional planners that metropolitan government—or Metro, as it usually comes to be called—holds the answers to the area's political woes, few communities have initiated this form of government. Where Metro has been tried, the reviews are mixed. Toronto's experiment in city-suburb federation began in 1953, with a twenty-five-man metropolitan council at the reins (twelve representatives from the suburbs, twelve from the city, and a chairman selected by these). The new government took over control of assessments, water and sewer, highways, capital expenditures for schools, housing projects, and most health and welfare projects. But the individual communities retained their identity, and some reason for existence, by keeping control of certain governmental functions—fire and police, local school operations other than building, local streets, licensing, civil defense, health clinics, off-street parking, and so forth.

There is no question that Metro has been getting things done in Toronto, though there *is* a question whether these things might not have been accomplished even without the new governmental framework. All communities have been reassessed to assure equality of taxation rates, schools have been built, a sewer project developed, housing projects put up, expressways completed. Speaking in 1955, recently re-elected chairman Frederick G. Gardiner proclaimed that "Metro is certainly better than anything we've had before." But the *Toronto Globe and Mail* qualified its praise by finding the new government ". . . cumbersome and unwieldy, subject to serious delays and confusion." Similarly, have-not suburbs "are delighted with the system," while those in good shape prior to Metro feel they are putting "everything we have into a church poorbox." [44]

The *Globe and Mail*, like the two evening papers, continues to support Metro for the Toronto area, and agrees substantially with the 1965 judgment of a Royal Commission of inquiry that Metro "was a bold experiment which had been justified by its accomplishments" but that additional consolidation was needed for more equitable government. The commission proposed reducing the area's thirteen municipalities (an unusually small number to begin with, compared with most United States cities) to but four. Early in 1966, the Ontario government passed a compromise, cutting down from thirteen to six the number of municipalities, and granted Metro additional responsibilities, including area-wide school taxation to help "equalize educational opportunity." But the six-borough plan has failed to eliminate "the cities-versus-suburbs type of conflict, which," the newspaper believes, "has obscured the point of many a debate in Metro Council." What has happened in Toronto is that the suburbs, which have grown faster than the central city, have secured a majority on the Council, so that the city proper has been "thrust into a minority position." [45]

In Miami, the third county manager in less than a decade for Dade County's version of Metro took over early in 1965. He was greeted with an unenviable situation. Many felt that Metro was "a government that does a lot of talking and little else." As in Toronto, projects and reforms have been subject to serious delays. Miami's reassessment program is still going on; in 1964 alone, 65,000 property owners protested their new assessment rates. The commission which governs Miami's Metro has rarely reached consensus; it split badly on the selection of its new manager. As a consequence, his "first big task will be solidifying his commission support. He's coming here on the strength of a bare majority vote from a commission that has no real policy leadership and no real controlling bloc." [46]

The reviews, then, have been mixed, but one thing is clear: most people do not want Metro in their own backyard. In Toronto, significantly, attempts to establish the new form of government on a voluntary basis broke down; Metro was imposed from above by the Ontario legislature, a proceeding offensive to the American tradition of home rule. And in the United States, Miami is one of the rare exceptions to the rule laid down in 1962 that almost "no metropolitan area . . . has by the vote of its people indicated a desire to extend the geographic limits of the local government to cover its metropolitan region." [47]

Why is it that citizens generally, and suburbanites particularly (for it is in the suburbs that opposition to Metro is most violent) oppose the initiation of metropolitan government? Often, the motivations of the suburbanite who says no to Metro have been pictured as ignoble. He moved to the suburbs to achieve a "status" address, some critics maintain, and is not willing to give it up. He is trying to escape the city's social, racial, and criminal ills. He is afraid that such a government will strain his pocketbook. He is swayed by local officials whose own motivation is simply to hang on to their jobs. Or he is simply so appalled by the prospect of change that he cannot see the real merits of the proposal.

But there is another and more fundamental reason for the suburban resistance to Metro. The reason stems from Thomas Jefferson, who cordially detested cities, who preferred the moral and political choices of the plowman to the professor, and who identified the New England town governments as "the wisest inventions ever devised by the wit of man for the perfect exercise of self-government." [48] His heritage persists to this day, as Wood has observed: ". . . it is a serious mistake to believe that an ideology simply reflects the social and political organization in a particular period of history, lingering for a while, but ultimately giving way to an expression of a new reality. When they are powerful enough, ideologies may shape —as well as mirror—the world about them." [49] The heritage is so persistent, in fact, that it seems liable to remain anachronistically triumphant, no matter what the cost.

Surely, the problems of our metropolitan areas demand cooperative solutions. Undoubtedly, the nation's suburbs must in the future show more willingness to act in concert, less insistence on solo performances. Perhaps, as Gulick comments, there are but two paths open. One is to drift into worse and worse traffic, housing, and other difficulties; the other "starts with knowledge of the facts and is followed by the decision to work together, making full use of all three 'extensions' [federal, state, and local] of government. . . ." [50]

What the suburbs must do is live up to their obligations to the wider metropolitan area of which they are a part. It is undoubtedly true, as the critics maintain, that some (but by no means all) suburbs represent secluded enclaves where businessmen and their families try to escape from the economic and the political and, especially, the racial problems of the central city. Their departure, of course, only exacerbates the city's difficulties. Furthermore, the problems they hoped to leave behind are pursuing them into the suburbs, which are becoming increasingly urbanized and less and less the rural retreats promised in the real estate advertisements. Partly as a consequence, those who have consistently opposed Metro in the past are now modifying their position. In the Minneapolis metropolitan area, for example, the suburban newspapers campaigned against almost all forms of metropolitan authority until 1967, when they came out for the establishment of an appointed Metro Council, whose job it will be to recommend further steps in consolidation of services. As Don Heinzman, executive editor of the Twin Cities Suburban Newspaper chain, comments, there is now "very little standing in the way of a more powerful metropolitan government." And, as he further acknowledges, one of the principal reasons is the nearly universal concern over minority problems: "it is difficult for any of us to deny an effort which will clean up the cities and rebuild the rotting schools in the ghettos. Frankly, all of us will have to pay the price to rebuild portions of Minneapolis." [51]

Suburbia cannot much longer escape its obligations, nor should it wish to. Certainly, Toronto's plan to provide equal educational opportunities for all residents of its metropolitan area deserves emulation; far-sighted educators, like superintendents Fred Atkinson of the Bloomington school system and Donald G. Emery of the Scarsdale schools, openly support such plans.[52] John Finley Scott and Lois Heyman Scott have proposed a number of steps, short of metro-wide taxation for schools, to improve the quality of ghetto education.[53] Most such steps (premium pay for hazardous teaching duty, high school scholarships for the disadvantaged, bussing of the city's Negro youths to white suburban schools) will require federal support, but there are other ways that well-to-do "lighthouse" school districts can help their less financially fortunate neighbors. What is true of schools should, of course, also be true of other local services in a land which honors the concept of equality of opportunity. Metropolitan cooperation, if not full-scale metropolitan government, must be achieved, even at the expense of the deeply cherished illusions willed to us by the Jeffersonian myth.

X. TWO STUDIES IN DEPTH

It is wretched, dispiriting advice to hold before him the dream that ideally there need be no conflict between him and society. There always is; there always must be. Ideology cannot wish it away; the peace of mind offered by organization remains a surrender, and no less so for being offered in benevolence. That is the problem.

—*William H. Whyte, Jr.,* 1956

In the early 1950s two teams of sociological researchers set out to examine an institution which is peculiar in its galloping growth to mid-twentieth century America—the institution of suburbia.[1] One group of twenty-four persons went to Toronto for a five-year study of the pseudonymous community of Crestwood Heights; another group scattered among the "package suburbs" built after World War II around several large United States cities, the suburbs of Levittown and Drexelbrook, Pennsylvania; Park Merced, California, and especially Park Forest, Illinois, a suburb of Chicago.

The studies culminated in the publication of what remain two of the most professional and thorough investigations of this phenomenon. The first, called *Crestwood Heights*, was written by John R. Seeley, R. Alexander Sim, and E. W. Loosley, and was published in 1956. William H. Whyte, Jr. wrote the other book, which was also published in 1956. Its title, of course, was *The Organization Man.*

Both books represent exhaustive studies of suburbia, yet their findings are markedly dissimilar. This is not to say that Whyte on the one hand, and Seeley et al. on the other, did not discover similar points in the two communities of Park Forest and Crestwood Heights, for the fact is that they did find several such common points. This is what we should expect them to find. But Seeley and Whyte also uncovered many significant differences between the ways of life in these two communities, and this is *not*, perhaps, what we expected.

Neither Seeley nor Whyte claims that his particular sociological poaching ground is typical of the culture—not yet. Crestwood Heights, for example, houses a much higher proportion of Jews than do most American suburbs. "What we have, then, is a community which is typical of but few communities in North America. It is, moreover, a community with a very high degree of self-conscious-ness, both individual and collective, and in this sense also it differs significantly, probably, from all but a handful of similarly situated suburbs." [2] For this reason, Seeley et al. are reluctant to extrapolate from Crestwood Heights to the suburban experience in general. This reluctance, however, they are able to overcome (note the subtitle: *A Study of the Culture of Suburban Life*) by deciding that this community "represents what life is *coming to be* more and more like in North America—at least in the middle classes—rather than what it already is." In this sense, Seeley et al. consider Crestwood Heights normative or "typical." [3] Whyte assumes much the same posture. He stresses that Park Forest and the other suburbs briefly referred to in his study, the new package suburbs, "are a new social institution" and therefore atypical. But, these communities, like Crestwood Heights, are seen as the communities of the future: "The values of Park Forest, one gets the feeling, are harbingers of the way it's going to be." [4]

Essentially, then, both Crestwood Heights and Park Forest emerge as representative middle class communities of the future. Crest-wooders may have climbed a little further up the social and eco-nomic ladders than Park Foresters, but both communities are un-mistakably middle class suburbs. And both, in the view of their observers, are accurate predictions of what the suburb of the future will look like. But predicting what is going to happen on what both

Whyte and Seeley et al. admit are shaky empirical grounds is a risky business. And an additional germ of doubt that is liable to fog the sociological microscope is present in both community studies: Park Forest and Crestwood Heights are "model" communities, made self-conscious not only by their exposure to the researchers who helped to produce these books but also by the periodic visits of experts in many fields, come to study Crestwood's unusually efficient public safety department, Park Forest's highly successful uni-denominational Protestant church, or the highly-regarded school systems in both suburbs.

What most interests the authors (and their audience), of course, is not so much the communities *per se* as their effect on the people who live in them. Here there are a few areas of substantial agreement between Whyte and Seeley et al. accompanied by an abundance of divergent findings. The writers reach common accord that suburban life tends to break down kinship ties, although Whyte puts the matter more strongly than Seeley et al. "Almost by definition, the organization man [who populates Park Forest] is a man who left home, and, as was said of the man who went from the Midwest to Harvard, kept on going." [5] The young parents of Park Forest rarely see or communicate with *their* parents, who probably live somewhere other than Chicago or environs and may well belong to a separate social class. The matter of social standing does not really mean much in these suburbs populated by families on the move, anyway. In leaving home, Whyte points out, they leave any local prestige behind them. Besides, "what is one town's upper-upper would be another's middle class." [6] Income, rather than social class, is apt to determine one's status.

Seeley et al. paint much the same picture. Although Crestwooders are less likely to be transients than Park Foresters, they do not see much of their kin, either. "The newly formed family is frequently isolated geographically and often socially from the parental families." [7] Here, too, class distinctions are greatly reduced and resist rigid classification. As a consequence, "prestige depends more on wealth than on lineage." [8]

Popular fiction and humor to the contrary notwithstanding, Whyte and Seeley both give suburban morality high marks. Both studies find sexual habits in their respective suburbs highly moral and monogamous. The attitude is that, in Crestwood Heights, as one of its citizens puts it, "no man who engages in extra-marital relations is responsible." [9] What occasional deviation there is meets with strong disapproval. In Park Forest, "Young suburbanites talk a great deal about sex, but it's all rather clinical, and outside of the marriage no one seems to do much about it." [10] If adultery is rare, divorce is rarer, and in these respects the two communities are similar. But an examination of the reasons underlying these moral standards shows a significant difference between the communities. They are alike in sharing the *end* of family solidarity; most unlike in the *means* of holding the family together.

The ingredients which prevent philandering and hold marriages together in Park Forest are *social* in origin; in Crestwood Heights, they are basically *economic*. The tyranny of the group [11] is perhaps never so benevolent as in its effect on Park Forest morality. Apartments and homes are arranged facing a central court, and the court, according to Whyte, is "the greatest invention since the chastity belt . . . it's almost impossible to philander without everyone's knowing about it." [12] These courts develop into compact and highly organized social worlds of their own, with friendships dictated by the happenstance of geography. Though these relationships may be formed illogically, they are powerful ones. The court group, in fact, is the principal reason divorces are so rare. Here is the minister of the United Protestant church in Park Forest on the subject of divorce: "Few people, as a rule, get divorces until they break with their groups. I think the fact that it is so hard to break with a group here has had a lot to do with keeping some marriages off the rocks." [13] The sanction is social.

In Crestwood Heights, however, the sanction is economic. It is no longer possible to keep job and family separate, as the Victorians could and did, according to Seeley. Just as "the family may be used primarily to promote the career," [14] a failure in family relationships is frowned on at the office. A man is held accountable for insuring domestic tranquillity, just as he is held accountable for doing his job well. Failure in either realm is an indication that the man is "weak" or spoiled. This is true whether the moral transgressor is husband or wife: if the man slips, he is obviously at fault; if the wife breaks the code, he is still at fault, for he chose her in the first place.

The distinction becomes even clearer in the authors' elaboration of cases in which adultery has been allowed to strain the marriage bond. In Crestwood Heights, ease of occupation is recognized as a contributing cause, if not a justification, of adultery. One Crestwood Heights husband remarked that "brokers were more likely to deviate and, next to them, persons with inherited wealth, those persons who had never had to work." Professional men he placed much lower on the list.[15] In Park Forest, however, what talk there is about moral laxity centers around the custom of wife-trading,[16] not around individual activity. Even when they sin, in Park Forest, they do it in groups of four or more.

Neighborliness is the dominant and accepted value among the courts of the package suburb, while in Crestwood Heights Seeley et al. find a lack of strong neighborhood friendships [17] and conclude that "in their relationships with other human beings, Crestwooders are highly individualistic." [18] The contrast with Park Forest is startling. Here, Whyte is able to predict, through traffic patterns, who will make friends with whom and which families will be invited to the Saturday night party at the Joneses. Park Foresters conform to the cult of neighborliness, but they do not do so unconsciously. "They know full well why they do as they do, and they think about it often. Behind this neighborliness they feel a sort of moral imperative and yet they see the conflicts also." [19]

In brief, the principal distinction between the ways of life in the two communities is that Crestwooders are family oriented, Park Foresters group oriented. The attitude toward child rearing bears out the point. In both suburbs, children stand at the center of the world, with all other concerns rotating around the filial axis. "The major institutional focus," Seeley et al. write, "is upon child rearing," [20] and the institutions of Crestwood Heights "tend to converge upon the family, existing as they do to regulate the life of a purely residential community devoted to child-rearing." [21] Significantly, children also have a cohesive effect in Park Forest, but what they hold together is not the family alone, but the family *as part of the group.*

It begins with the children. There are so many of them and they are so dictatorial in effect that a term like *filiarchy* would not be entirely facetious. It is the children who set the basic design; their friendships are translated into the mother's friendships, and these, in turn to the family's. . . . 'When your kids are playing with the other kids, they force you to keep on good terms with everybody.' [22]

The group is united in its concern with parenthood, and the group itself, as Whyte remarks, becomes a kind of substitute for the big family of former years, a "foster family" to the transients who live in Park Forest for a time before moving on.[23]

To borrow from politics, the style of government in Crestwood Heights is democracy within the family, a purely local democracy, while in Park Forest, the basic tradition is the dictatorship of the group. "The Crestwood family now seems a little like a country which, having operated under an authoritarian form [the Victorian patriarchy] of government, has suddenly switched to a democratic form, without too much preparation for the change." [24] The family is a true democracy, if the state is not; conflicts in Crestwood families are solved by discussion, with parents exerting pressure as subtly— and as powerfully—as possible. The age gap no longer has much importance, and an emphasis on responsibility at all ages, and on outward acts of affection, typify the family. Once again, the contrast with Park Forest is striking. In the package suburb the group decides how the family should behave, and the price of non-conformity is exile.

Take the matter of consumption, for example. Both communities betray traits of the consumer society one expects to find in a present-day suburb, but the attitude toward consumption is vastly different. Crestwooders are more or less free to consume as conspicuously as they please, and the problem of status incongruency, while present, is not dominant. It is possible for man to walk into his house and announce to the family over dinner that "today I have satisfied a life long ambition" by buying a Cadillac.[25] So conspicuous a purchase would result in social ostracism in Park Forest, where the problem is "not to keep up with the Joneses. It's to keep *down* with them . . . what in one block would be an item eminently acceptable [as a purchase] might in another be regarded as flagrant showing off." Thus it is the group which determines *"when a luxury becomes a necessity* . . . and just as the group punishes its members for buying prematurely, so it punishes them for not buying." [26]

The dictatorial group also has a devastating effect on privacy. In Crestwood Heights, privacy is no problem, since there is no over-powering emphasis on neighborliness. But in Park Forest, "there isn't much privacy . . . people don't bother to knock and they come and go furiously." In Drexelbrook, Whyte notes, a harassed mother may draw the venetian blind across the picture window as a signal that she's had it up to here with continual socialization, but the blind is drawn with a sense of guilt. "Privacy has become clandestine. Not in solitary and selfish contemplation but in doing things with others does one fulfill oneself." [27] Those who seek privacy too often are stigmatized; the comparable stigma in Crestwood Heights would result from failure to associate on an equal-to-equal basis with one's wife and children, but only the members of the family, not the whole neighborhood, would observe the stigma.

The battle of the sexes, Seeley et al. tell us, is fought daily in Crestwood Heights. "The differences in values, attitudes, and out-look between men and women . . . are . . . in some families the cause of considerable conflict." The problem of authority within the family constitutes "another frequent source of strain." [28] To counter-act these pressures, the family tends to wed itself to a strict routine, with life so ordered in time as to minimize opportunities for conflict. Whyte, on the other hand, observes no war between men and women, and implies, by reason of this state of truce, that David Riesman's concept of "the homogenization of the sexes" holds true for Park Forest.

Like the Crestwood Heights family which keeps busy to avoid intra-family conflicts, most Park Foresters are active in civic and community affairs, more active, in fact, than most Crestwooders. And their activity is of a different kind. Crestwood Heights parents seem to devote their principal energies to the Home and School Association; Park Foresters get involved not only in school matters but also in local politics and government and church and hobbies. This suburbia "is a hotbed of Participation . . . the active are so active that they generally feel compelled to laugh [hysterically?] at themselves for their folly." [29] They are so busy, as the gag goes, that mom and dad must make an appointment to see each other.

Sociologists and novelists, and following in their wake, the public, are perhaps equally guilty of generalizing about the suburbs. For there are suburbs and suburbs, and most generalizations about them are bound to miss the mark when they purport to apply equally to Bloomington (annual mean spendable income in 1960: $7,201 per family) and to Edina (annual mean spendable income in 1960: $12,082 per family).

Crestwood Heights and Park Forest are clearly very different kinds of suburbs. Crestwood Heights can be regarded as a *traditional* suburb, Park Forest as a *transient* suburb. The designation of transiency is one Whyte stresses. People live in Park Forest only a few years on their upward path; then they move into the more traditional suburbs like Winnetka or Glen Cove or Greenwich or White-fish Bay or Clayton. If only because of its many apartments, Park Forest must be regarded as different from any of the other places mentioned. But the really distinctive thing about Park Forest, whether compared with Crestwood Heights or Coral Gables, is its *newness*. It has sprung up, literally from nothing, since World War II. It is this newness that accounts for the unusual concentration of local activity in Park Forest. Changed from cornfield to going political community in only a few short years, Park Forest has had to deal with governing itself; and the incoming families, provided with a greater chance to participate in governing this embryo community, responded with a vengeance.

Seeley et al. do not deal at any length with political activity in

Crestwood Heights, and one may logically infer that there was not much to write about. Crestwood was older, more traditional, its political patterns fixed by the time the decade of the 1950s rolled around. Thus in this suburb of Toronto, there was "no clear-cut action either for or against . . . [metropolitan] annexation." [30] Faced with the same kind of issue, Park Foresters would have been fighting against annexation, one feels sure, with all the considerable vigor they could command. What's more, the Park Forest newspaper could have and probably would have given the fight a unity of focus Crestwood Heights could not muster. (It is significant that Seeley et al. never refer to a suburban newspaper serving Crestwood Heights; if there is such a paper, it apparently does not play a very important part in the community.)

What happens when the politically active Park Forester moves to a more traditional community in his way up the organization ladder? Typically, he tries either to join or to start an action group Moved to a traditional town where civic interest is low, Whyte's new suburbanites see a challenge; they have learned to take the initiative at Park Forest.[31]

Another index of the traditionality of Crestwood Heights is its path of upward mobility. While Park Foresters can go up the organization ladder only by moving to other places and other groups, Crestwooders can and do achieve upward mobility while staying in one spot. The case of an insurance man named Robert is an example. Robert struggled along for some time, carefully being one of the boys and knowing everybody, and as time went on, he finally achieved business success. But, unlike Whyte's organization man, he cannot transfer his fund of good will and clients from one suburb to another.[32] It may be argued with justice that what is true of Robert is true of insurance men generally, but the point is that Robert can begin and end his career with Crestwood Heights as his home base. By way of contrast, no really ambitious insurance man would settle in so transient a community as Park Forest in the first place. Were he to do so, his home would be only a way-station on the road to Winnetka if he hoped to prosper in Chicago insurance circles.

Crestwooders are older than Park Foresters, too. In both communities the families are small, including one or two, or at the most three children, but the children are in high school in Crestwood, while they are still toddlers in Park Forest. "What might be called the modal [Park Forest] man . . . is a twenty-five-to-thirty-five-year-old-white-collar organization man with a wife, a salary between $6,000 and $7,000, one child, and another on the way." [33] Seeley offers no comparable picture of the modal Crestwooder, but it is clear that he is older and somewhat better off financially, with his youngsters in junior high or high school. In terms of age, then, the traditional versus transient dichotomy holds true, for only the younger families can endure the transient life. A man of forty-five, put down in Park Forest, would clearly be a failure-in-the-making; in Crestwood Heights, he is probably only the average citizen.

Another important distinction between the two communities is that Crestwood Heights is Canadian (or North American, as Seeley et al. usually refer to it) while Park Forest is very much a part of the United States (or American, as we pre-empt the term). Riesman, in his introduction to *Crestwood Heights*, makes much of this difference in nationality, suggesting that it may account for the battle of the sexes among Crestwooders. Such a sharp division of the sexes, Riesman comments, cannot easily be transplanted to the United States; it is in fact reminiscent of an older America of tired businessmen and *The Male Animal* and Carol Kennicott on *Main Street*. "Even in my own lifetime," Riesman writes, "this has drastically changed: the avant garde exurbanites are men . . . and in many suburbs men as well as women read *The New Yorker* and learn to laugh ironically at suburban life and values." [34]

The fact that Crestwood Heights is a traditional, Canadian suburb and Park Forest a transient, American one may help to account for the differences in the ways of life of the two communities, but there is one other reason why Whyte and Seeley et al. found different things while looking at what are supposed to be two examples of the same phenomenon. The reason has to do with the technique and style of the authors.

Whyte looks at his package suburbs through a set of glasses fitted for observation of the organization man at home. He is interested in these communities as the habitat of his new species, the organization man, and he will logically limit his findings to those which bear on the life and times of this species. There is nothing particularly wrong with this technique, especially since he is completely honest in telling us what he is up to. (His book does *not* carry a subtitle claiming it to be a study of suburban culture.) His purpose is didactic, and he freely admits it. "While the burden of this book is reportorial, I take a position," the position of urging the individual to do battle with the corporation.[35] And, again, he tells us that awareness of the problem faced by organization man is more than half of this battle, and he is supplying the awareness.

If Whyte's method is thorough, that of Seeley must be called exhaustive. A team of two dozen researchers spent five years studying Crestwood Heights, and they started, according to the authors, with no preconceived ideas as to what they were looking for. Seeley and his fellow researchers brought with them the basic tools of sociological study—directed interviews, informal "classes" with junior high students, careful analysis of all aspects of community life. The method is taken from anthropology. And in the very intensity of their study, according to Riesman, lies one of the reasons the book never quite comes off.

So intertwined . . . is the research with the community that this book gives the impression that its authors are still stuck in the tar-baby; their moral intensity about their task and their responsibilities both as research- ers and as reporters, is, in all its humorlessness and intensity, rare and admirable.[36]

As Seeley et al. are aware, the social scientist "is involved [with his data] in a way that differs radically from the manner in which the physical scientist is involved with his data." Under these cir- cumstances, "perhaps the most that can be asked for," as *Crestwood Heights* states in conclusion, "is that another and more extended effort than is represented by this book make a fresh attempt to take a new look from a new perspective at what we have been doing and pool afresh such wisdom as we have or as we might, in the sharing, find." [37]

In contrast, Whyte's ringing conclusion measures up as nothing short of dogmatism. The individual, he concludes, must fight the organization, the seemingly benevolent villain who is robbing him of his autonomy as an individual. There is always going to be conflict between the individual and the society he lives in, Whyte realizes, and the fight becomes progressively harder to win as the seeming, or actual, benevolence of the suburbanized, organized society becomes more and more apparent.[38] The individual must swim for all his might, or he will be carried along by the powerful current of conformity which, Whyte maintains, pulls him away from the port of self-realization. Almost everything about the suburbs annoys the author, who continues to fish in the stream of American individualism. *The Organization Man* was a very influential book; Whyte's negative attitudes toward suburban architecture, life style, and politics were adopted wholesale as official intellectual dogma of the 1950s.

XI. CONFLICT IN THE
SUBURBAN NOVEL

THE SOCIAL ETHIC

Between 2000 and 1000 B.C., greater Ur in Mesopotamia reached a population of 360,000, but the inner-walled city of Ur held a mere 34,000 persons. The barrier not only served for military purposes, but to restrict the working class and pariahs, who lived outside the wall.

It is a long way from Mesopotamia to the modern United States, and the pre-industrial city of Ur, Mesopotamia seems light years removed from Upper Montclair, New Jersey. In Mesopotamia, presumably, the social goal of the pariah was to be admitted inside the walls of the city; now society's outcasts *must* live inside the city, whose walls are now less visible, but no less real. They are not allowed to live in the suburbs surrounding the city. There the American middle class has staked its claim to comfort and conformity. In their mid-century flight to the suburbs, Americans seek a compromise between the jangling tempo of city life, which they want to leave behind, and the economic and cultural opportunities of the metropolis, which they are loath to give up.

In these suburbs populated by a middle class that is determined to have its cake and eat it, too, there supposedly flourishes an attitude toward life that William H. Whyte, Jr. calls the Social Ethic. It is an attitude that exalts conformity and ducks controversy, and the best place to see it in action, according to Whyte, is in the American suburb.

He set forth his theory in *The Organization Man.* Basically, the Social Ethic involves "a redefinition of [the organization man's] place on earth ... something that will do for him what the Protestant Ethic did once." [1] According to the Social Ethic, the ideal life is one in which man, as a unit of society, submerges himself in society; for by so doing "he helps produce a whole that is greater than the sum of its parts. There should be then no conflict between man and society," [2] and what appear to be conflicts are merely misunderstandings or breakdowns in communication. Gone is the Protestant Ethic's emphasis on achievement, replaced by the Social Ethic's emphasis on adjustment. Controversy is only misunderstanding, conflict unnecessary.

This philosophical faith, as Whyte points out, is utopian. More than that, it is positively evil as it is applied by the organization and by the group, the dominant, tyrannizing force in suburbia. And the evil is the more insidious because it is so carefully concealed. It is not something one can attack mounted on a charger, for both the group and the organization are beneficent. Modern man, or at least modern middle class American man, "is imprisoned in brotherhood." [3]

Whyte, who was to have such significance for modern novelists, used a novel himself to buttress his case for the dominance of the Social Ethic in American life. The novel is Herman Wouk's *The Caine Mutiny,* like *The Organization Man* a striking popular success. The central dilemma in the novel involves the character Captain Queeg, an incompetent, a coward, a paranoiac. In the midst of a typhoon at sea, Queeg is relieved of command by his junior officers, and eventually, in a court martial, these officers are absolved of guilt. But Wouk does not let them off so easily; instead, he makes it clear that Queeg is the real hero of the book, because he has stuck with the system (the Navy) through good times and lean. In fact, it would have been better, Wouk says through his spokesman, for the ship to go down, as it surely would have under Queeg's panicky command, than for these junior officers to challenge their superior, incompetent though he may have been. In short, there would have been no conflict at all, if only everyone had followed the rules. As well he might, Whyte finds this kind of thinking intolerable, and it is a mode of thought that he says is coming to dominate popular fiction:

In older fiction there was some element of conflict between the individual and his environment; no matter how much assisted by coincidence, the hero had to *do* something—or at least seem to do something—before he got his reward. Rarely now. Society is so benevolent that there is no conflict left in it for anyone to be rebellious about. The hero only *thinks* there is.[4]

In short, the vision of life in popular fiction is one in which conflict is giving way to adjustment. What's more, it is not only true that heroes are no longer masters of their own destiny, but it is made clear that they cannot and *should* not be. Society itself tends to become the hero. This is Whyte's argument, but one suspects that he was over-selective in his choice of literary sources. Certainly it is no longer true (as it was for Wouk, in 1951) that society is regarded as the hero; the modern hero may be the non-hero, the poor sap, Yossarian, but the sympathy of the novelist lies with him and not with society. Society is the villain and there is plenty of conflict in the four novels about suburbia discussed here.

FOUR NOVELS OF CONFLICT

Some time ago in the magazine *Commentary* there was an article on the types of short stories appearing in American magazines. The author, after reading a dozen or so collections of short stories published in the last few years, decided that there are two current types: first, the sophisticated or 'Connecticut' story and second, the southern or 'Yoknapatawpha' story.[5]

William Van O'Connor, who wrote the lines above, warned in the same article that "one ought to be wary of finding sociologically valid descriptions of a society in highly imaginative fiction." [6] The warning is a sound one, and is powerfully illustrated in the anecdote O'Connor uses about Sherwood Anderson, who was at a loss as to how to behave when he was complimented on the realism of *Winesburg, Ohio*. Anderson, as it happens, found sources for the characters in his famous novel among fellow residents of a Chicago boarding house, most of whom had never gone near a small Ohio village.

But four novels are safer than one, and especially since they are self-consciously suburban novels in the same way that the "Connecticut" story is self-consciously suburban. Both in content analysis, the sociologist's way of studying fiction for insights, and in the use of metaphor, the literary scholar's way of discovering hidden elements of culture,[7] the novels are useful for illumining the canvas of suburban life today.

The four novels are *Revolutionary Road*, by Richard Yates, published in 1961; *Peaceable Lane*, by Keith Wheeler, published in 1960; *Leave Me Alone*, by David Karp, published in 1957, and *The Blind Ballots*, by Georg Mann, published in 1962. From the dates, there can be no doubt of contemporaneity or of the possible influence of Whyte. Two of the novels, *Leave Me Alone* and *The Blind Ballots*, are essentially concerned with the suburban experience; in the other two, suburbia serves more as a setting than as the source of the drama itself.

Revolutionary Road is a psychological rather than social novel. It tells the story of Frank and April Wheeler, who live in Connecticut mostly because it is the thing to do. Once there, they get in the habit of belittling their neighbors as unfeeling automatons, as veritable paragons of comfort and conformity. Intellectually, they reject the other suburbanites as a "type" they refuse to be molded into.

"It's all the idiots I ride with on the train every day. It's a disease. Nobody thinks or feels or cares any more; nobody gets excited or believes in anything except their own comfortable little God damn mediocrity," Frank Wheeler, who is quite a talker, remarks.[8] Frank may talk that way, and belittle his job in New York, but the fact is that he wants to conform and be "accepted" as much as anyone on Revolutionary Road. The desire for acceptance, Yates makes clear, stems from his own particular brand of unhappy childhood and not totally from the environment. April also had an unhappy childhood, but she is strong enough to want to make the break with suburban conformity, and strong enough to commit suicide when she realizes Frank is a phony in all his talk about the "others."

As for the author, Yates conceives of suburbia as an unreal world, a way of hiding from reality, a world of light without shadow. After April's suicide, Frank runs wildly and woefully through the suburb. But

the Revolutionary Hill Estates had not been designed to accommodate a tragedy. Even at night, as if on purpose, the development held no looming shadows and no gaunt silhouettes. It was invincibly cheerful, a toyland of white and pastel houses whose bright, uncurtained windows winked blandly through a dappling of green and yellow leaves. Proud floodlights were trained on some of the lawns, on some of the neat front doors and on the hips of some of the berthed, ice-cream colored automobiles.[9]

This toyland is anything but harmless, though; it stifles those who live there. April at one point has Frank persuaded that they should go off to Europe, two children and all, where Frank could "find himself" while she worked. For a while, he is enthusiastic: "You know what this is like, April?" he asks. "It's like coming out of a Cellophane bag. It's like having been encased in some kind of Cellophane for years without knowing it, and suddenly breaking out." [10] The Cellophane bag is a marvelous image, with its suggestion of both consumption and the inhibiting conformity of suburban life.

Peaceable Lane deals with a particular and timely problem, the problem of segregation in the suburbs. Once again, Connecticut is the setting, and the eleven homes on Peaceable Lane house daily commuters to high middle management jobs in New York City. There is an ethnic mixture here. Like the typical Hollywood war movie, there is a representative of every religious and racial strain in the platoon of families who live on Peaceable Lane—everything, that is, except the Negro. When a Negro decides to try to move in, the Lane unites against him—at first, anyway—by buying the house out from under him.

Author Wheeler is a sensitive observer of his suburbanites, and they are not, except for one family, painted in the single dimension of racial hate. The principal motive the residents hold for wishing to exclude a Negro family is economic, and this is not necessarily a completely bad motive, as the author depicts it. In fact, the real villain of the book turns out not to be any of the residents of Peaceable Lane, although a couple of them behave very badly indeed *after* the Negroes move in, but a colored block-buster named Francis Barton who uses violence as part of his two-edged plan to integrate the neighborhood and turn a fancy profit into the bargain.

Wheeler offers no solution to the problem of suburban segregation. He does adequately make the point that when the residents determine not to panic, integration can proceed smoothly enough. There is often no resistance when Negro families move into mostly white suburbs. Trouble may develop, however, in lower middle class communities where many white families have come to the suburb from city neighborhoods which have already been blockbusted. Whyte observed the phenomenon in Park Forest, where "an acrid controversy over the admission of Negroes" developed. For a small group, admitting Negroes would have meant a fulfillment of personal social ideals; for another, slightly larger group, "many of whom had just left Chicago wards which had been 'taken over,' it was the return of a threat left behind." [11]

There was nothing noble about the way Peaceable Lane reacted. Conflict disorganized these suburbanites; controversy unsettled them, and those responsible for creating the controversy faced ostracism. The same theme turns up more explicitly in David Karp's thoughtful novel, *Leave Me Alone*. The hero is Arthur Douglas, editor of a New York publishing house. At the insistence of the wife and children (like every other hero in these four novels, his family consists of a wife and two children, two offspring apparently being par for the suburban course), he moves to the Long Island suburb of Oakstown. Oakstown is not Westport; it is not nearly as "sophisticated" as the Connecticut of the modern short story. But Eleanor and the children thrive in the suburbs, if Arthur does not. [12]

Somewhat against his better judgment, Arthur is persuaded to take on the task of bringing a public library to Oakstown, a measure opposed by the community's old guard and its conservative Catholic element. The project goes badly, and blows up when the other members of the committee, most of whom apparently equate a Democrat with a card-carrying Communist, veto on red herring grounds Arthur's selection of a speaker to arouse public opinion for the library. At this point, Arthur tells off his fellow Oakstowners:

You are possibly the most dreary collection of slack-jawed yahoos it has ever been my bad luck to meet. I don't know what sins against the human spirit and the intellect can be excused on the grounds of neighborliness and civic pride, but however many there are, I've gone over my quota tonight. Those of you who aren't cowards are bigots, and those of you who aren't bigots are sheep, and some of you are all three.[13]

Whew. Ignoring the point that no one really talks that way, Arthur's speech is quite an indictment of the suburban attitude. A good-guy real estate man named Steel tries to calm Arthur down: people, he explains, do not come to the suburbs to start fights; they come looking for friends and a chance to belong. They may not like what they see, sometimes, but they keep their reservations to themselves.

Steel, as a Jew, shares the ostracized feeling Arthur as an intellectual gets. But, he asks, what are we supposed to do? "Destroy ourselves? Or do we keep to ourselves what we are and share with the rest of the world what there is to share?" Steel's answer is that we must compromise by sharing. "No intelligent person thinks less of another intelligent person for the compromises he must make in life." [14]

This concept launches Arthur into an interior monologue that is straight from Whyte. "There it was . . . pressure. Pressure of the most benign sort—but pressure nonetheless, and it was hard to resist. . . . There is a tyranny of good intentions, he decided, and it is the very benevolence which makes rebellion impossible. Compromise, indeed, but how far, how much, for how long?" [15] His answer is that you adjust so far, but no further. "Living here in Oakstown is part of the adjustment you have to make," he tells his wife. "But do you want to know something? There are things you don't adjust. You just damn well leave them alone." [16] His solution, then, is to live *in* the community, but not as a member *of* the community.

Arthur sees the suburb as a nice warm round foetal ball that shuts out conflict. In his summary speech, he makes a ball with his hands and comments:

I have the feeling that we're being locked up, wrapped up, snuggled down, tucked in, and what kills me is that everyone's so damned anxious to get inside, to get tucked in and wrapped up. No one wants to be left out in the cold and . . . it's cold out there—so cold that people run off to find some other warmth—the comfort of belonging to any society, even one composed of fairies. But the people outside the circle aren't all crackpots, nuts, cranks, loonies. These are the ones I worry about.[17]

The most optimistic view of life in suburbia occurs in Georg Mann's novel, *The Blind Ballots*. Harry Beauclerk and friends live in the midwestern suburb of Ryswick (the only non-New York suburb of the four) where the old guard still runs the show. Like Arthur Douglas, Harry, a lawyer, is an intellectual. He and his small band of non-conformists do not sell out. Through their not-so-great books club, they hit on the idea of tackling the adjustment oriented school system in Ryswick through political action. In a proposed new junior high school "no room will have more than one jukebox or snack bar, in addition to minimal provision for ping-pong, bridge, and shuffleboard." [18] This is burlesque, of course (the book is labeled a comic novel), but the heart of the matter is there and the Ryswick intellectuals are moved to attack.

To their surprise, they succeed in electing their candidate, while the old guard licks its wounds. But it turns up a hollow victory when their candidate is indoctrinated by the adjustment minded majority on the school board. Next, another battle ground is seen—the proposed industrialization of the area's one natural asset, some lovely sand beaches. Harry pursues this battle alone, and finds he is taking on just about every high level politician and businessman in the state, all of whom stand to make a tidy profit on the project. He can wage his war, he finds, only through the somnolent Democratic organization, an organization that has not produced a majority in the county "since Buchanan was elected in 1856." [19] Of course, he fails in his bid for office, but at the end he is only down, not yet defeated.

The fight Harry fights is not an easy one, for the reasons Whyte isolated. "The old, big issues we grew up with have been flushed down the drain. . . . When a head, ornamented by office, showed itself, you automatically threw a rock. All the ammunition you needed was a conviction that people in themselves were basically good, and a belief that social institutions oppressed man for the profit of men." [20] Now there is no one left to fight except the benevolent organization. Nonetheless, Mann provides an element of hope for the individual in his struggle with the established order. There are, he writes, three tangential rings in modern society, but they do not interlock, like those in the Ballantine beer advertisements. One circle is the government, another the working situation, and "the third stockade is one's neighbors. Add them up together, they spell Sing Sing. [Albeit a comfortable cell, still a cell.] Fortunately, all three circles, touching, miss a tiny triangle where a man can operate as himself." [21]

The nook between the encircling rings of government, job, and neighborhood is still there, Harry Beauclerk finds. At the beginning, he is very much the cynical intellectual taking his comfort and conformity as he finds it. "In this historical lull, as we wait for the man in the classified job to drop the other bomb, time passes painlessly. In an age that's zoned out heroes, I've become a locally recognized authority on comfort." [22] Which having said, he sets out to become a hero, even in the manicured frontier of the suburbs. The individual *can* reject the Social Ethic, he *can* fight the system, and because of the climate of conflict that is peculiarily suburban, it is easier for him to do it there than anywhere else. Most of the neighbors will wonder what in Heaven's name he's doing (after all, politics isn't polite) but at least there is a chance to assert himself, and Harry takes it.

At the end, having lost his bid at the polls to defeat the insidious industrial project, Harry reflects on the difficulty of the battle, but optimistically decides that "perhaps we can tilt, nudge our way to freedom and some small social usefulness." [23] Between the three enclosing rings, he has found the triangle where there is room to assert his individuality. Joyfully, he concludes that if he can't whip the Riverport project at the ballot box, he can and will at least "sue the sons of bitches." [24] He has escaped from the warm foetal ball which encompassed Arthur Douglas in *Leave Me Alone*, the cellophane bag which restricted the Wheelers in *Revolutionary Road*. Individually, *The Blind Ballots* ends on a strong note of affirmation. But this note is one that is rarely heard among the modern literary musicians whose compositions deal with suburbia; usually, they strike a bitterly satirical chord. "The suburb," as Harlan Paul Douglass observed as long ago as the thirties, "is consistently portrayed in fiction as petty, frivolous, and lacking in virility." [25]

XII. THE FICTIONAL TREATMENT

An artist's use of language is the most sensitive index to cultural history, since a man can articulate only what he is, and what he has been made by the society of which he is a willing or an unwilling part.

—*F. O. Matthiessen,* 1941

The stars were people like Aline Luville and W. B. Parker. Joe Sarno directed and wrote it, and Bradley Burton was executive producer. The movie was called *Sin in the Suburbs,* and as the house lights went down, the screen lit up with its explicit tales of illicit sex. "The whole scandalous story . . . shock by shock" unfolded: the faithless wives, abandoned too long by husbands who had to catch "that damned 7:21," the workmen who dropped in on hot-eyed suburban wives for an hour of pleasure, the younger set made up of boy rapists and girl lesbians, the sex club members who played musical beds on Tuesday and Thursday evenings.[1]

It seemed that suburbia was under attack in this "adults only" film, and so it was, but only as part of a larger milieu. A preview of coming attractions clarified the point. The upcoming feature was *Hot Nights on the Campus,* where, apparently, life and love in the groves of academe were to be scandalously exposed. What do the campus and the suburbs have in common? They are both, largely, middle class or upper middle class locales, and the films were sighting their weapons on the ways of the middle classes.

Assuming that this conclusion is valid, that this kind of film *is* attacking the middle class as part of its appeal to lower and lower middle class audiences, is it of any importance to cultural history? The answer is that trash nearly always reflects the culture, and expresses some of its most obvious antagonisms. Nathaniel Hawthorne, with justice, complained about the "mob of scribbling women" whose books badly outsold his novels during his lifetime. But such novels, as Matthiessen remarks, offer "a fertile field for the sociologist and for the historian of our taste," [2] and for the historian of ideas as well. The attitudes and prejudices toward suburbia revealed in second- to fourth-rate books or films are additionally important when they turn out to be nearly, if not entirely, identical with most of those attitudes and prejudices found in more serious works of art.

The difference between the truly trashy book or film on the suburbs and the merely commercial version can be measured on a descending scale of salaciousness. The theme of the "nightstand novel" set in suburbia is always and predictably the same. "Problems in Bed . . . were no problems at all," one back cover blurb reads, "to the members of Eastport's highly secret suburban switch club. Who could have problems with eight beautiful, different women to choose from? For that was the lot of each man in this fantastic sex-prowling group." [3] In these books, as in the sex films, a sublimated class hatred is operating. Everybody is too social, everybody is too eager to get ahead, everybody is too concerned with appearances. "Unless you're smothered in diapers and are a card-carrying PTA member," one rebellious female complains, "they hate your guts." [4]

Where the near-pornographic concentrates explicitly on sex, the commercial film which seeks a wider audience focuses on symbols of suburban life: "Picture windows, patios and barbecues, power lawn mowers, the problems of commuting, and the armies of children manning their mechanized vehicles down the sidewalks, are only secondarily facts; primarily they are symbols whose function is to evoke an image of a way of life for the non-suburban public." [5] The movie supplies the symbols, and the public supplies the required negative reaction. Despite its celebrated neighborliness, the suburban world remains an impersonal one, according to an unpublished playscript which led to the screenplay for *Wives and Lovers*. The script sets the scene in the living room of a new suburban home in Pompton, Connecticut: "It is bright and gay and loaded with brand-new antiques, but there is nothing in the room that would indicate its belonging to Joe and Bertie. It is the work of a decorator who to all intents and purposes never made their acquaintance." [6] A piece of dialogue in *Bachelor in Paradise* questions whether the suburban paradise may not be a prison of sorts:

Real estate promoter: 'You'll find this truly *is* a paradise. Schools, churches, country club, playground, pool, shopping center. . . . (chuckles) As we say, a family can live a full and happy life and never leave Paradise Village!'
Hero: 'But they're allowed to, aren't they?' [7]

When sex is introduced, in commercial movies like *Boys' Night Out*, it is presented as something everyone talks about, but nobody does much about.[8]

There is an impassioned and articulate echo of the agrarian ideal in *Please Don't Eat the Daisies*. The heroine, who is married to a New York theatre critic, moves the family up to the country so her critic-husband "can get some perspective . . . make friends with *people* . . . be himself again." In suburban Hooton, she is determined to be "putting down roots for us in the community—making a niche for us. From now on we're going to *belong* somewhere." [9] *The Tunnel of Love* takes another tack, and ends with the message that the suburbs are no place to belong to. In the midst of an argument, the heroine tells her husband (another writer): "I'm sick of you and Westport and everybody in it. . . . I never want to see a tree, or a blade of grass, or a piece of chintz again as long as I live!" After they make up their quarrel, the couple heads back to the city, because "the country's no place to bring up kids. Our baby's going to be born in Manhattan—in a normal, *healthy* atmosphere!" [10]

All of these movies (*Bachelor in Paradise* excepted) commit the "Connecticut fallacy." That is, they center on the life of rather well-to-do suburbanites who commute to New York City. The film *No*

Down Payment presents the "other" kind of suburb, the transient community for young couples on their way up the economic and social ladder. *No Down Payment* has everything the most profit-conscious producer could demand: there is sexual immorality, there is too much drinking, there is thievery and rape and accidental death. Better yet, there are multiple "messages." Don't get caught in the dollar rat-race. Don't let the organization run your life. Don't discriminate against your fellow man. In Sunrise Hills, the walls are paper thin and there are two-foot side-yard setbacks; there is an outdoor barbecue and drinking-dancing party nightly. Everyone says how wonderful it all is for the children, but they're inside, watching westerns on TV, anyway. All the wives are good-looking, and all the men have flat stomachs. When the rapist dies an accidental death, and the local atheist decides to go to church, and the Japanese family is finally admitted to the community, the movie ends with an ironic shot of the development sign: Sunrise Hills Estates, The Happy Ending Homes.[11]

Most novels cut no deeper than motion pictures beneath the facade of visible symbols which have come to represent suburbia. As Joseph Bensman and Bernard Rosenberg wrote in 1962:

A serious account of the suburbs does not yet exist inside or outside of fiction. Instead, there are pot-boilers. We have the man-in-the-gray-flannel-suit, crack-in-the-picture-window-exposé—which is merely a first attempt to capitalize on the shock value of dealing with a new phenomenon.[12]

Few novelists have been able to resist the temptation to paint a stereotyped picture of the suburbs. Two very popular novels of the postwar period, for example, share a propensity to let the symbols stand for the real thing. One is Sloan Wilson's *The Man in the Gray Flannel Suit,* the other is John P. Marquand's *Point of No Return,* and both are, basically, novels "against" the organization rather than novels "against" the suburbs which happen to be the home of the organization man. Phyllis McGinley has written that if she had been acquainted with John Marquand, she would surely have gone up to him at a cocktail party and asked him to explain why he kept denigrating her suburb, however wittily and skillfully. Her suburb, she felt, was "a lively, interesting, and desirable dwelling-place," while for Marquand it was at best a subject for satire.[13] McGinley asked for a reason, and a reason can be found in the comparison of Sycamore Park, the suburb in which Charlie Grey lives, and Clyde, Massachusetts, the small town in which Charlie Grey grew up (*Point of No Return*). Clyde and its highly involved class structure had been sketched in a "Yankee City" kind of book. This class structure was not a bad thing but a good one, Charlie thinks. "Everyone had a place in that plan and everyone instinctively seemed to know where he belonged." It all "fitted together and it fitted beautifully and there was no reason to disturb it." Watching his own son grow up, Charlie reflects that he will not have a secure base to build on, such as he himself brought from Clyde. "The impermanance of a New York suburb with its shifting population of unrooted communities, with order that existed only on the surface, was as hard for a boy to grasp as it was for him to explain." [14]

In this comparison, Marquand betrays the attitude typically expressed by oldtimers when their suburb is invaded by newcomers. Such an invasion forms a central incident in *The Man in the Gray Flannel Suit:* an attempt to slice the ten-acre zoning law down to more workable size meets with determined opposition. "If we replace the big estates with housing projects," one old resident argues, all of South Bay will be a slum in ten years. Ten-acre zoning had been instituted "to preserve the rural beauties" of the community, which also had its own nice system of social class neatly worked out and stratified—until the newcomers moved in. Tom Rath, the hero of the novel, fights the good fight against the oldtimers, and eventually leaves the organization; on his own, he plans to subdivide the land he has inherited and make money in that safely countrified way, not in the caverns of the city.[15] He is driven, it turns out, by the same motivations, the same rural hankerings, which led the oldtimers to oppose him and John P. Marquand to compare Sycamore Park unfavorably with Clyde, Massachusetts. Here, then, is a reply to Miss McGinley's question: the suburb is denigrated in fiction because the author finds it infuriatingly inferior to the rural small town of the past he has either once known or, more likely, idealized from a distance.

The same disillusionment may well account for what might be called the "hysterical" novel about the suburbs. The best workman in this genre is Peter De Vries, who writes acidly witty portrayals of suburban immorality and dullness, novels which seem always on the verge of turning from a laugh to a scream. Perhaps the best known novel of this type, however, is *Rally Round the Flag, Boys,* by Max Shulman, like De Vries a very funny man indeed.[16] Russell W. Nash has interpreted this novel as a reaction to "the Spectorsky sort of book" (*The Exurbanites*) about the suburbs. But most of the characters in the book seem to lack the dignity or intelligence that would lend credence to this interpretation. Instead, Shulman has, perhaps subconsciously, isolated the importance of the dominant agrarian myth in his plot line. For the hero of Putnam's Landing turns out to be Corporal Opie Dalrymple of Altus, Oklahoma, a "farm boy" and "country music" star. Opie marries Comfort Goodpasture, whose name is perfect for the daughter of the oldtimer who wants no changes—none—in his home town of Putnam's Landing.[17]

S. J. Perelman, a wise and wonderful writer, effectively demolishes the agrarian ideal and its charms for the suburbanite in his *Acres and Pains,* written in 1947. For about a month after he first moved to Bucks county, Perelman wrote, "I was a spare, sinewy frontiersman in fringed buckskin, with crinkly little lines about the eyes and a slow laconic drawl. One look told you that my ringing ax and long Kentucky rifle would tame the forest in jigtime." But he almost blew off a toe cleaning an air rifle, and he changed his image from Natty Bumppo on the frontier to "the honest rural type" of the middle landscape. In this role, "I started wearing patched blue jeans . . . and crumbled bits of earth between my fingers to see whether it was friable enough. Friable enough for what I wasn't quite sure. . . ." As for the benefits to the youngsters, another Bucks county friend with "a pair of rose-colored bifocals askew on his nose" volunteered the information that "Junior grew fourteen inches the first week. He's only nine, and he can split a cord of wood, milk twenty-one cows and cultivate a field of corn by sunup. Sister's not even three but you ought to taste her preserves." [18] The tone is obvious, and so is the good-natured message that the yeoman image is better smiled at than swallowed whole. But few of our serious writers, unfortunately, have been as sensible as the humorist Perelman.

In his stage directions for *The Bald Soprano*, Eugene Ionesco suggests a "middle-class English interior, with English armchairs. An English evening. Mr. Smith, an Englishman, is smoking his English pipe and reading an English newspaper, near an English fire." His wife sits in another armchair, darning "some English socks." The clock strikes seventeen, and she speaks. "There, it's nine o'clock. We've drunk the soup, and eaten the fish and chips, and the English salad. The children have drunk English water. We's eaten well this evening. That's because we live in the suburbs of London and because our name is Smith." [19] Life in the suburbs of London, to Ionesco, is dull, dull, dull. So it is, also, in an extraordinary short story by no less a personage than Bertrand Russell. His story, "Satan in the Suburbs," recounts the substantial trade drummed up by a horror-manufacturer to relieve the "humdrum uniformity of life in the suburbs of our great metropolis." [20] Ionesco and Russell both find the suburbs of London dull, just as serious writers everywhere find suburbs everywhere dull.

Most of those who turn their attention to suburbia expose sins worse than dullness. Here, for instance, is Josephine Miles's poem, "Housewife:"

Occasional mornings when an early fog
Not yet dispersed stands in every yard
And drips and undiscloses, she is severely
Put to the task of herself.

Usually here we have view window dawns,
The whole East Bay at least some spaces into the room,
Puffing the curtains, and then she is out
In the submetropolitan stir.

But when the fog at the glass pauses and closes
She is put to ponder
A life-line, how it chooses to run obscurely
In her hand, before her.[21]

The theme here is not dullness, but waste of life. The suburban housewife is severely

Put to the task of herself

when an early fog obscures the weather the real estate man had promised: a soft east wind puffing the curtains and everyone outside talking to her neighbors. Left to herself in the fog, she examines her life-line, which "chooses to run obscurely" before her eyes. The life-line runs of its own volition; she has nothing to say about it. Her life is being spent emptily in the "submetropolitan stir," but the housewife does not think about it. At least she does not think about it until

She is put to ponder

by the fog at the glass. This two-beat line, like the final line of the poem, is so much shorter than the other lines that it takes on tremendous importance. It is being "put to ponder," "put to the task of herself" which reminds the housewife of the shallowness of her life in the San Francisco suburbs.

Richard Wilbur, in "To An American Poet Just Dead," explicitly identifies the suburbs as the source of the "sleep of death:"

In the *Boston Sunday Herald* just three lines
Of no-point type for you who used to sing
The praises of imaginary wines,
And died, or so I'm told, of the real thing.

Also gone, but a lot less forgotten,
Are an eminent cut-rate druggist, a lover of Giving,
A lender, and various brokers; gone from this rotten
Taxable world to a higher standard of living.

It is out in the comfy suburbs I read you are dead,
And the soupy summer is settling, full of the yawns

Of Sunday fathers loitering late in bed,
And the ssshh of sprays on all the little lawns.

Will the sprays weep wide for you their chaplet tears?
For you will the deep-freeze units melt and mourn?
For you will Studebakers shred their gears
And sound from each garage a muted horn?

They won't. In summer sunk and stupefied
The suburbs deepen in their sleep of death.
And though they sleep the sounder since you died
It's just as well that now you save your breath.[22]

The tone of ironic bitterness is established in the first stanza where
Wilbur scans the obituary in "no-point type" for a poet dead of drink.
The obituary is sandwiched among somewhat longer accounts of
the lives of American materialists—cut-rate merchants, money lend-
ers, stockbrokers—who have at least escaped high taxes in their
departure from greater Boston. Next Wilbur shifts from an inspection of the *Boston Sunday Herald* to the site of the poet's death—
"out in the comfy suburbs." The suburban location is tarred with the
same brush as that which smeared the druggist and the lover of
Giving; suburbia *is* the temple of the money-changers. The association of the suburbs with crass materialism is reinforced in the fourth
stanza which asks if the sprinklers will weep for the dead poet, if
the deep-freeze will melt in mourning for him, if the Studebakers
will sound "a muted horn." The question is rhetorical, as the first
brief powerful sentence of the last stanza makes impressively clear:
"They won't." The suburbs may appear to be alive, but they are
dead, and cannot mourn. What's more, they cannot be resurrected;
their sleep of death is "sounder since you died," Wilbur tells the dead
poet, and there is no hope:

It's just as well that now you save your breath.

Wilbur clearly links the deadly dominant materialism of American
life with the suburbs. Even nature is commercially neutralized by
the sprinkler systems and deep-freeze units.

Phyllis McGinley presents a different view of nature in her poem,
"June in the Suburbs:"

Not with a whimper but a roar
Of birth and bloom this month commences.
The wren's a gossip at her door.
Roses explode along the fences.

By day the chattering mowers cope
With grass decreed a final winner.
Darkness delays. The skipping rope
Twirls in the driveway after dinner.

Through lupine-lighted borders now
For winter bones Dalmatians forage.
Costly, the spray on apple bough.
The canvas chair comes out of storage;

And rose-red golfers dream of par,
And class bound children loathe their labors,
While pilgrims, touring gardens, are
Cold to petunias of their neighbors.

Now from damp loafers nightly spills
The sand. Brides lodge their lists with Plummer.
And cooks devise on charcoal grills
The first burnt offerings of summer.[23]

In this poem, nature in the suburbs is delightful, not oppressive, like a Marin County fog, nor merely mechanical, like the little lawns of the comfy Boston suburbs. In McGinley's suburbia, roses explode, loafers collect sand in walks along the shore, and even "darkness delays" to allow children to skip rope after dinner. Her sure touch with language and her sense of humor (note the "pilgrims" who are not impressed with the neighbor's petunias, the "first burnt offerings of summer," the echoed rejection of T. S. Eliot's "The Hollow Men" in the first line) rescue this celebration of nature from the realm of sentimental *kitsch*, from kinship with the works of Edgar Guest and Norman Rockwell.

In her awareness of the joy of life, wherever lived, Phyllis McGinley is cousin not to the purveyors of *kitsch*, but to the short story writer and novelist, John Cheever. More than almost any modern writer of stature, Cheever writes "out of an abundant love of created things" wherever he may encounter them. This love he communicates to the senses of the reader, who can find in *The Wapshot Chronicle,* for example, "what things a New England evening wind smells of, which ingredients to add to carp before boiling, [and] how to traverse, naked and at night, the multiple roofs of a millionaire's castle in search of your lover's terrace. . . ." [24] The two writers are akin, also, in their refusal to join the parade of literary detractors of suburbia. This is not to say that Cheever, like McGinley, has embarked on a crusade to defend the besmirched name of suburbia, for he certainly has not. Instead, he has written about suburbia with precision and acuteness, at the same time always realizing that it is *people,* and not *places,* that make the difference. As he said in an interview: "There's been too much criticism of the middle-class way of life. Life can be as good and rich there as anyplace else. I am not out to be a social critic, however, nor a defender of suburbia. It goes without saying that people in my stories and the things that happen to them could take place anywhere." [25]

His fiction bears out the statement. St. Botolphs, of the Wapshot novels, is a weird place, inhabited by a gallery of characters who are every bit as eccentric as the citizens of Winesburg, Ohio but somehow lovable despite it. Cousin Honora, the rich Wapshot, eventually dies of starvation rather than face the consequences of never having paid federal income taxes. Uncle Peepee Marshmallow regularly exhibits himself on warm spring days. The minister drinks to excess. Still it is a romantic picture, as its creator acknowledges; it is not, however, a place where it is possible to live in the twentieth century: "The air smelled of brine—the east wind was rising—and would presently give to the place a purpose and a luster and a sadness too, for while the ladies admired the houses and the elms they knew that their sons would go away. Why did the young want to go away? Why did the young want to go away?" [26] The young, and especially the young men, must leave St. Botolphs, a woman-dominated town, to seek their fortunes, and so Moses and Coverly Wapshot, like all the other young men, run off to the city to get rich and to the suburbs to live. In the city and suburbs, they find much the same world they thought to have forever left behind. As Coverly muses: "You have come to feel—you may have been told—that the beauties of heaven centered above your home, and now you are surprised to find, stretched from edge to edge of the dissolute metropolis, a banner or field of the finest blue.[27]

Cheever writes about people who live in the suburbs because he knows a great deal about people who live in the suburbs as he does. Once, he lived in Quincy, Massachusetts, the model for St. Botolphs, and later he lived in the city, during his young manhood, but now he lives in the suburbs, like most other middle class people. If he seems to look back on Quincy (St. Botolphs) with nostalgia, it is no more a consuming nostalgia for him than it was for Henry Adams, another boy who summered at Quincy and wrote that "Town was restraint, law, unity. Country, only seven miles away, was liberty, diversity, outlawry, the endless delight of mere sense impressions given by nature for nothing, and breathed by boys without knowing it." [28] For all his nostalgia, the adult Henry Adams never went back to Quincy to live, and neither will John Cheever. As a professional writer, Cheever writes about what he has come to know, or imagine, best. When he was younger, and lived in the city, he wrote stories about young couples who happened to live in the city. Now he writes about what happens to people who happen to live in the suburbs.

No matter where in space and time he places his fiction, Cheever has a special ability to communicate the crazy or the bizarre which is at once the moving or the pitiful. Back in St. Botolphs, this curiously touching craziness took the form of Leander Wapshot trying to sell his body to medical science, or of Honora sending the streetcar company a Christmas check in lieu of purchasing tokens during the year. In the suburbs of Proxmire Manor and Shady Hill, the same quality is suggested by the incredible grocery story contest that gives Melissa Wapshot a trip to Rome, and by Cash Bentley's insistence, when he is a little drunk, on hurdling whatever furniture is readily available. The bizarre exists everywhere in Cheever's imaginative world, but so does petty cruelty and scandalous neglect. Two especially powerful stories, for example, deal with the problem of children all but abandoned by their well-to-do parents. The setting of one, "The Sutton Place Story," is given in its title; the other, "An Educated American Woman," takes place in exurban "Gordenville."

Cheever is no Pollyanna in his attitude toward the suburbs. In fact, he explicitly tells his readers what is wrong with them. Coverly and Betsey Wapshot live for a time in a brand-new suburb inhabited by those who (like Coverly) work at a nearby missile installation. After a quarrel with Betsey, Coverly takes a walk:

But Remsen Park was not much of a place to walk in. Most of its evening sounds were mechanized and the only woods was a little trip on the far side of the army camp and Coverly went there. . . . Making a circle around the woods and coming back through the army camp and seeing the houses of Remsen Park he felt a great homesickness for St. Botolphs— for a place whose streets were as excursive and crooked as the human mind. . . .[29]

The world of Remsen Park is mechanical, even hostile, while that of Proxmire Manor, where Moses and Melissa live, is eminently respectable on the surface (it is known on the railroad line as the "place where the lady got arrested" for a minor parking infraction) but rotting away underneath. Cheever never loses sight of the differences between suburbs. Shady Hill is upper middle class, a "destination" suburb, while Maple Dell is merely a stopover:

It was the kind of place where the houses stand cheek to jowl, all of them built twenty years ago, and parked beside each was a car that seemed more substantial than the house itself, as if this were a fragment of some nomadic culture. And it was a kind of spawning ground, a place for bearing and raising the young and for nothing else—for who would ever come back to Maple Dell? [30]

While Cheever is aware of the shortcomings of suburbia, or of some segments of suburbia, he is also aware of the advantages it may offer. Shady Hill, for example, makes an inviting target for the abuse of "city planners, adventurers, and lyric poets, but if you work in the city and have children to raise, I can't think of a better place." [31] The "I" speaking here, it should be clarified at once, is not the author but a 36-year-old businessman named Johnny Hake who is made to feel "the pain and sweetness of life" as he watches his lovely wife salt the lovely steaks for a lovely cookout on a lovely summer night. Hake's endorsement of the suburban life loses much of its force when it is revealed, as the story proceeds, that he must steal from his neighbors in order to keep himself and his lovely wife installed in their nice suburban house "with a garden and a place outside for cooking meat." Money, indeed, is the serpent in the garden for Cheever's suburbanites. "The Swimmer," for example, tells the terrifying tale of Neddy Merrill, who gives "the impression . . . of youth, sport, and clement weather" but who has taken to drink to forget the loss of most of his money and all of his house and the beautiful suburban life in Bullet Park.[32]

But if the bitch goddess success has ruined life in the suburbs, she has equally contaminated life everywhere. The age of missiles and other symbols of mechanization extends far beyond the borders of Remsen Park. As Cheever insists, he is no social critic and he is not interested in attacking the middle class way of life. To the extent that he does criticize the world around him, it is a broader world than that of the suburbs, it is American, even international (as in some of his exquisite stories about Americans in Italy) where people are dollar fiends and nations concentrate on the tools of annihilation.

The reaction of literary critics to Cheever's work is interesting. Generally, their critical assessment has become less favorable as he has increasingly concentrated his stories in a suburban locale. The reception of *The Wapshot Chronicle*, his first novel which won the National Book Award for 1957, was almost unanimously favorable. A typical review demurs on the episodic nature of the book, but praises the writer's "blend of gusto, nostalgia, and profoundly innocent ribaldry."[33] In 1958, following the appearance of *The Housebreaker of Shady Hill*, Granville Hicks commented wonderingly on Cheever's ability to make "rich and exciting" stories out of suburban subject matter that is dull and "not inviting."[34] The tone remained one of admiration, but the seeds of critical disapproval had been planted. They sprang into full bloom with the publication of *The Wapshot Scandal* and *Time's* cover story identifying John Cheever as a latter-day "Ovid in Ossining." Once *Time* magazine approved the author, he became fair game for almost all other magazines. Thus Cynthia Osick in *Commentary*, ignoring the author's explicit warning and misreading his fiction, maintains that Cheever has failed as a social critic (something he never intended to be) by idealizing

St. Botolphs (something he carefully avoids doing).[35] Finally, James Scully, reviewing *The Brigadier and the Golf Widow* for *The Nation*, concludes that "Cheever, alas, has been sucked in, not by the market, but by his subject." [36] The critic, presumably, is annoyed by the use of the suburbs as the locale for serious fiction. He does not see, as Cheever does, that suburbia is but another place where people retain a readiness for delight, as well as a sense of the tragic.

What the suburbs provide, to those like McGinley and Cheever and Margaret Halsey (to whom the following quotation belongs), is this kind of scene:

I stood in the front yard in the spring twilight, and all down the hill people were out of doors, watering lawns, edging turf and setting out plants. On the slanting sidewalk, Cora and her friends played hopscotch and some younger children toiled up the slope with their small-size bicycles like a collection of diminutive Sisyphuses. Next door a catbird in a birdbath scattered crystal into the dusk.[37]

This is a highly domesticated version of the middle landscape, far closer to the city than the agrarian ideal Americans and their artists persist in celebrating. And as Matthiessen remarked in the epigraph, an artist can only communicate what he is, what the culture has made him.[38] It is a rare novelist or poet who can escape "the most prevalent vision of them all," the vision of peaceful times on the farm with the children growing tall and healthy like the corn. The vision *seems* innocent enough, as Conrad Knickerbocker observes:

It is an innocent vision, hallowed by three centuries of belief in the ultimate goodness of living near the *land*. Innocent but destructive. The pastoral dream may have made some sense in 1920, when nearly half of the nation still lived on farms or in small towns. But it has helped destroy the cities of today and it casts a nightmarish shadow over the city of tomorrow.[39]

In search of this vision, Americans have deserted their cities for suburbs. But the search has not been successful, for the suburbs are not replicas of ideal farming villages, after all. Disillusioned by the failure of their search, the embittered seekers have turned on their suburbs in apoplectic rage.

XIII. THE SUBURB, NOT THE FARM

The soil and the pavement grow different crops, even though the soil is cut up into minute suburban plots.

—*Harlan Paul Douglass,* 1925

In his reminiscent book, *The Suburban Child,* Britisher James Kenward looks back on the "great days" of suburbia, the days of buttercups and carriages, badminton and roses. For the reader's enlightenment, Kenward gives an ostensive definition of what he means by suburbia: it is the place between the shops and the fields. "If you walk for so many minutes in one direction you come to the shops, and if you walk for so many minutes in the other direction you come to the fields." [1] The direction he preferred is obvious. His most powerful memory is of being taken

when I was about four years old . . . past the last houses of all, and I remember being lifted over a fence between oak trees into a field of buttercups. . . . For a few moments the world stood still with us. The miracle that stupidly wise people fail to understand happened. The sun waited in the sky. Then, moved by a common instinct, together we spread out our arms and ran in among the buttercups, hugging, snatching, wading, gathering, shouting, and shouted at, trampling disastrous lanes far out into the centre of the field. It was sheer greed of gold. [2]

The great days of suburbia are over for Kenward because the fields have receded before the population migration and are now more than "so many minutes away." The middle landscape loses its appeal when it moves closer to the shops, further from the fields.

This desire for pastoral felicity, powerfully evoked by Kenward, still retains its vigor for Americans, as for Englishmen, despite the ubiquitous urban environment of both countries. The avowedly emotional (note the anti-intellectual slur on "stupidly wise people") commitment to a mildly domesticated nature is nowhere more evident than in the rural "survivals," or practices and beliefs of the past which are "retained under changed conditions to which [they are] no longer well adapted." [3]

Such survivals often take the form of imagery, and can be seen in the real estate advertisements of American Sunday newspapers. The "country" symbols fairly leap from the full-page advertisements for suburban developments. The reader is invited to wander along rural "lanes" and "roads," not citified "streets" and "avenues." The development itself will have a rustic-sounding name, something like the Sunrise Hills of *No Down Payment*. Some suburbs can afford more symbols than others. David Wallace, for example, acutely describes the impression of a motorist who sees Westport, Connecticut for the first time, ". . . trees, moss-covered stone walls, prevailing rusticity. He would see few lawns of the standard suburban type; more often he would glimpse only the opening of a drive, banked perhaps by free-growing ivy, myrtle, or pachysandra." What will catch his attention most of all, however, "are the omnipresent standard RFD mail boxes, each on its own post and bearing its owner's name in homemade lettering on the side. . . ." [4] A dozen years ago, a group of Westport residents acquired flocks of sheep to keep their lush lawns trimmed. A sheep-shearer takes their wool, making a modest kickback to the commuters in the form of an annual blanket.[5] Such suburbanites can afford to be fleeced, like their sheep; most must content themselves with less expensive symbols.

The most obvious of these symbols is, of course, the well-cared-for lawn. The brilliant green of the lawns in suburban developments bespeaks the considerable effort, and expense, that go into the care of this particular rural survival. For the lawn is, at bottom, such a survival. Thorstein Veblen, writing in 1899, made an unmistakable connection between lawns and cow pastures. "The close-cropped lawn is beautiful in the eyes of a people whose inherited bent it is to readily find pleasure in contemplating a well-preserved pasture or grazing land." [6] The frequently-noted compulsion to garden is further evidence that not only conformity drives the suburbanite out of his air-conditioned house to work on the lawn and garden. We love our gardens, Phyllis McGinley writes, "as alcoholics love the martini." [7]

In their most remote origins, all these symbols—the lawn, the lane, the rural place name, the sheep—trace back to the beginnings of mankind's consciousness. Primitive man was born into a world of nature. Is it then surprising, Erich Fromm asks, "to find a deep craving in man not to sever the natural ties, to fight against being torn away from nature, from mother, blood, and soil?" [8] In America, this instinctive drive gained vigor from the vastness, richness, and beauty of the country, and from the conviction of those religious Englishmen who first settled the land that this was indeed *the* place. Such fervor, in a new and shining land, led to the development of a highly charged and stubbornly persistent myth, the myth of the yeoman farmer living in perfect harmony with nature.

The good life was to be lived on the land; but when men stopped living on the land, they did not stop believing in its efficacy. It has been said that the "proper time to influence the character of a child is about a hundred years before he is born." [9] Certainly the rural ideal seems to have lasted, intact, over the past century, and even to have gained power as it was losing pertinence. There is no need to learn this pastoral ideal; it is communicated with the culture, in many subtle ways and in other more obvious ones, like *Petticoat Junction* and *The Beverly Hillbillies*. The country mouse is always the better mouse.

Ernst Cassirer has commented on the importance of *place* to the mythological imagination. "For mythical thinking the relation between what a thing is and the place where it is situated is never purely external and accidental. . . ." [10] Mircea Eliade, in his study of primitive religions, took note of the phenomenon in the concept of the center of the earth, or *axis mundi,* as the holy place. Primitive men defined the *axis mundi* as the place where they themselves lived. Americans have simply done the same thing: the holy place is here, on American land, in harmonious unity with nature. The holy place, or to secularize the myth, the ideal place, is located not in the howling wilderness but in a more peaceful version of nature: "Americans have consciously or unconsciously sought to establish a midpoint between savagery and civilization, to establish a national identity which was neither primitive in the frontier sense nor excessively civilized in the European sense." [11] The perfect "midpoint between savagery and civilization" was defined by Jefferson (and is still defined by Secretaries of Agriculture) as the "family farm." But as the farmers' families deserted the farms for the cities, the ideal midpoint became located on the frontier of suburbia. Thus in the suburbs Robert C. Wood finds a curious and highly significant reluctance to part with "long-established American traditions." Far from epitomizing modern culture, Wood sees suburbs as looking to the past for their values. In particular, he calls attention to their reluctance to part with the ideal of the country village.[12] This reluctance goes back to the notion that virtue and health inhere in the land, that the soil and the pavement do indeed grow different crops, as Douglass put it four decades ago.[13]

But the close-cropped suburban lawn is *not* a cow pasture, and the tiny suburban lots are *not* homestead farms. Maurice R. Stein writes, "we are far too deeply committed to urban-industrial civilization even to think of abandoning it now." [14] Today the farms are becoming citified, as mass media advertising spreads the gospel of cosmopolitan life styles into large city and remote hamlet alike. Labor-saving devices give the farmer and his wife the leisure to imitate their city cousins. Just as the city man tries to pretend he is a farmer on his removal to Westport, so the countryman begins to act like a city man.[15]

The suburb, in other words, may want to preserve the image of a simple rural village, but the image cannot be successfully retained. Not without plenty of money, anyway; enough money to hire a private flock of sheep, for example, or enough money to restore a colonial village. Retreat from the twentieth century is only possible for the wealthy; it is an expensive retreat. The agrarian ideal has become intermingled with the powerful drive for economic success; the garden has been invaded by the serpent of materialism. "More so than ever before," one social critic comments, "energies have been thrust into creating a worldly paradise based on material acquisition. This version of the American Dream is embodied with greatest clarity in the prosperous suburb. . . ." [16] In this process of intermingling, the agrarian dream has been corrupted into an ugly replica of its former self. The suburb does not represent a return to the best of all possible worlds, but merely the most comfortable of all present worlds.

The suburb is not a natural paradise, and it was unreasonable to expect that it would be. Reason is not a long suit for those who persist in sentimentalizing the pastoral ideal. What's more, as Jane Jacobs points out, those Americans who are "probably the world's champion sentimentalizers about nature, are at one and the same time probably the world's most voracious and disrespectful destroyers of wild and rural countryside." [17] Suburbanites kill the thing they love, and then wax poetic about it, like Dobriner in this passage about a small village which has suffered from the encroachments of urban anonymity and transiency:

You sense the shift in internal balance in the village by the domination of the [new] suburbanites at school board meetings. You know it on an autumn's evening, in the crisp sea air, and in the deepening twilight around the mill pond. The great shuddering bulk of the mill squats in the hollow, intimidated by the headlights of the commuters as they race down and through the valley, dreary from the city and hungry for home. Pencils of light search into the gaping slats and crudely intrude upon the embarrassment of the mill's decay—the rusting gears, the splintered shaft, the rotting timbers, and marsh slop heaped up by the last high tide.[18]

The mood is mellow and nostalgic, and the author resents the automobiles and shopping centers. But the world of the mill has departed, and however powerful the nostalgic wish, that world will not return.

If the natural landscape has been polluted in a betrayal of one-half of the Jeffersonian dream, the other half, which involves the individualistic, self-sufficient yeoman, has fared little better. More than any other single American idea, the doctrine of individualism seems proof against change. In *The Organization Man,* Whyte articulates its current expression: "Thousands of studies and case histories have dwelled on fitting the individual to the group, but what about fitting the group to the person? What about *individual* dynamics? The tyranny of the happy work team? The adverse effects of high morale?" [19] Both in its thought and paradoxical style, the passage is reminiscent of the great Transcendental individualist, Emerson. Imitation is suicide, Emerson wrote. Each man should be his own man, independent of the group:

But now we are a mob. Man does not stand in awe of man, nor in his genius admonished to stay at home, to put itself in communication with the internal ocean, but it goes abroad to beg a cup of water of the urns of other men. We must go alone. I like the silent church before the preaching begins, better than any preaching. How far off, how cool, how chaste the persons look begirt each one with a precinct or sanctuary! So let us always sit.[20]

Like Whyte in 1956, Emerson in 1840 saw society steadily encroaching on the individual and threatening his fulfillment. Two centuries earlier, Anne Hutchinson rebelled against the same sort of group control, expressing her Antinomianism in a flight from the Puritan society she found too restrictive.

The American creed has remained faithful through the centuries to the merging concepts of individualism, a beneficent nature, and the virtuous small village. As social democracy flourished, the individualist was alarmed. As highway and building programs ate away the countryside, the naturalist became exasperated. As the quest for roots proved unsuccessful in an increasingly mobile society, the modern Jeffersonian was frustrated. Unwilling to give up his creed, the practicing intellectual cast about for a scapegoat and settled on the accessible target of suburbia. Here were new communities which might have done something different, communities which might have helped to make the impossible dreams come true. When the postwar suburbs failed to "restore" utopia, the social critic turned the full fury of his alarm and exasperation and frustration on them. Like jilted lovers, the critics belabored the suburban landscape with bitter invective.

The reach of the expectations and the consequent depth of the disillusionment account in large part for the contradictory nature of the attack on suburbia, for its confusion of cause and effect, for its illogical blaming of all the ills of society on a given modern location. But the roots of the propensity to criticize society lie still deeper than the hallowed ideals of our nation. They lie, in fact, in the nature of man's psychic mechanism. Certainly, in the United States, the critic finds it easy to articulate his disenchantment. Speaking in another connection, Carl Rowan noted that one "glaring characteristic of our society, I suppose of any free society, is its penchant for self-criticism. We Americans have carried it further than perhaps any society in history—so far, indeed, that we can be sometimes accused of self-flagellation." Self-criticism is a healthy thing, good for the soul, he adds, but it "can be carried to the point of defeatism." [21] Daniel Lerner comments that "our intelligentsia" accept anti-American slogans, such as those produced in France, without examination. The French talk of our bathtub culture, and we do not pause to ask what is wrong with being clean. They talk of Coca Cola culture, and we do not reflect that addiction to Coke may be preferable to alcoholism.[22] Now, accused of "suburban" culture, the American intellectual nods his head guiltily and returns to the typewriter to indicate his agreement.

We criticize our societies, Freud tells us, out of a sense of guilt.[23] The individual, naturally aggressive, finds himself held in check by the needs of society. His aggressive instincts, finding no overt outlet, turn inward to form a hyperactive superego, or conscience, which intensifies the individual's restrictions. Two trends in every man's make-up, "one towards personal happiness and the other towards unity with the rest of humanity, must contend with each other." And every time he lets the trend toward personal happiness become dominant, every time he becomes more rich or comfortable or secure than others, he is attacked by his superego. In this sense, then, the critics serve as a cultural superego to chastise Americans for daring to be prosperous, for the nerve to be content in their secure suburban communities. You are *not* living in paradise, they tell the suburbanite, to whose less-well-developed conscience it had never occurred that he ought to be living in paradise. But civilizations, as well as individuals, can become neurotic when the superego stifles the ego, and the continued harping of the superconscientious critics may end by convincing the fellow out in the suburbs that he ought to be unhappy with his lot.

There is some evidence that this process is indeed taking place, that the disillusionment of the critics is being experienced by new suburban residents who make the trip from city to suburb with a moving van full of utopian expectations. "They thought moving out of the city would solve all their problems," a Chicago psychiatric social worker remarked about new suburbanites in 1964. "Living in the suburbs didn't come up to expectations because those expectations were too high to begin with." [24] Such disillusionment may lead to withdrawal from involvement with the problems of the community, local or metropolitan. Those who remain hopeful, on the other hand, often adopt boosterism, chauvinistically asserting the virtues of *their* suburb and refusing to contaminate themselves by cooperating with the other communities that make up the metropolitan area. To avoid development of a neurotic civilization (if in fact we do not already have one), Americans would do well to reflect that there is an inevitable conflict between the individual and society, and that perfect societies of totally independent individuals, self-sufficient yeoman farmers, are impossible. "The liberty of the individual is not a benefit of culture," as Freud bluntly put it.[25] Writing in 1955, Richard Hofstadter observed:

Much of America still longs for—indeed, expects again to see—a return of the older individualism and the older isolation, and grows frantic when it finds that even our conservative leaders are unable to restore such conditions. . . . But actually to live in that world, actually to enjoy its cherished promise and its imagined innocence, is no longer within our power.[26]

We cannot go home again to our pastoral dream-house, but the real house in the suburbs may be better, anyway. At least it exists.

NOTES

CHAPTER I: ONSLAUGHT AGAINST THE SUBURBS

1. Maurice R. Stein, *The Eclipse of Community* (New York, 1964), p. 295.

2. Louis Gottschalk, *Understanding History* (New York, 1950), p. 160.

3. William H. Whyte, Jr., *The Organization Man* (New York, 1956). Whyte's section on suburbia was earlier printed in *Fortune*.

4. Harlan Paul Douglass, "Suburbs," *Encyclopedia of the Social Sciences*, eds. Edwin R. A. Seligman and Alvin Johnson, Vol. XIV (New York, 1934), p. 434.

5. Max Lerner, *America as a Civilization* (New York, 1957), p. 173.

6. Lawrence Lader, "Chaos in the Suburbs," *Better Homes and Gardens*, Vol. XXXVI, No. 10 (October 1958), p. 12.

7. Hal Burton, "Trouble in the Suburbs," *Saturday Evening Post*, Vol. CCXXVIII, No. 12 (September 17, 1955), p. 20.

8. "Suburbia: The New America," *Newsweek*, Vol. XLIX, No. 13 (April 1, 1957), p. 36.

9. Dr. Marvin A. Rapp, "Challenge to Leadership," *Vital Speeches*, Vol. XXX, No. 21 (August 15, 1964), p. 655.

10. C. W. Griffin, Jr., "The Ugly America," *Reporter*, Vol. XXX, No. 3 (January 30, 1964), p. 53.

11. A. W. Zelomek, *A Changing America: at Work and Play* (New York, 1959), p. 157.

12. Bennett H. Berger, *Working Class Suburb* (Berkeley, 1960), p. 3.

13. William M. Dobriner, *Class in Suburbia* (Englewood Cliffs, New Jersey, 1963), p. 6.

14. Phyllis McGinley, "Suburbia: Of Thee I Sing," *30th Anniversary Reader's Digest Reader* (Pleasantville, New York, 1952), p. 228.

15. Stanley Rowland, Jr., "Suburbia Buys Religion," *Nation*, Vol. CXXCIII, No. 4 (July 28, 1956), p. 78.

16. Zelomek, *Changing America*, p. 136.

17. McGinley, "Suburbia," p. 228.

18. No apology need be made for including Keats's diatribe, *The Crack in the Picture Window* (Boston, 1956) in a review of periodical literature on the suburbs. Although his comments are presented in book form, they are ephemeral in style, research, and thought.

19. *Ibid.*, p. 24.

20. Bruce Bliven, Jr., "Life and Love in the Split-Level Slums," *Reporter*, Vol. XVI, No. 3 (February 7, 1957), p. 46. Keats's book generally received unfavorable reviews, but people read the book, not the reviews.

21. Burton, "Trouble," p. 152.

22. Anthony Winthrop, Jr., "The Crab-Grass Roots of Suburbia," *New Republic*, Vol. CXXXVI, No. 6 (February 11, 1957), p. 20.

23. Keats, *Crack*, p. xi.

24. Harold L. Wattel, "Levittown: A Suburban Community," *The Suburban Community*, ed. William M. Dobriner (New York, 1958), p. 297.

25. R. W. Emerson, "Self-Reliance," *Selections from Ralph Waldo Emerson*, ed. Stephen E. Whicher (Boston, 1957), pp. 148, 149.

26. Keats, *Crack*, p. 61. The author consistently uses loaded words like communism and gangrene to beg his question.

27. Daniel Bell, *The End of Ideology* (New York, 1961), p. 35.

28. Lerner, *America*, p. 178.

29. Dobriner, *Class*, p. 86.

30. Lerner, *America*, p. 175.

31. "Suburbia," p. 37.

32. Thorstein Veblen regarded the primitive state of man, that of savagery, as preferable to the intermediate state of barbarism. The apparent contradiction in terms has rarely troubled utopian social and political thinkers in America.

33. "Quit Picking on 'Suburbia,'" *Changing Times*, Vol. XVII, No. 10 (October 1963), p. 35.

34. J. D. J. Sadler, "Utopia Reconsidered," *House and Garden*, Vol. CXIII, No. 3 (March 1958), p. 158.

35. "Quit," p. 36. See also Berger, *Working Class Suburbs*.

36. "Suburbia," p. 37.

37. Sadler, "Utopia Reconsidered," pp. 158, 160.

38. Thorstein Veblen, *The Theory of the Leisure Class* (New York, 1931), p. 87. In this passage the word *best* is obviously used ironically.

39. Keats, *Crack*, p. 144.

40. "Quit," p. 35.

41. Peter De Vries, "Humorists Depict the Suburban Wife," *Life*, Vol. XLI, No. 26 (December 24, 1956), p. 150.

42. Robert J. Blakely, "The Lonely Youth of Suburbia," *PTA Magazine*, Vol. LV, No. 8 (April 1961), p. 16.

43. Helen Puner, "Is It True What They Say About the Suburbs?" *Parents' Magazine*, Vol. XXIII, No. 7 (July 1958), pp. 42, 97.

44. "Suburbia: Lost Paradise?" *America*, Vol. CVII, No. 5 (May 5, 1962), p. 199.

45. Griffin, "The Ugly America," p. 53.

46. Lader, "Chaos in the Suburbs," pp. 10, 12.

47. Michael Harrington, *The Other America* (New York, 1962), pp. 10, 156.

48. Rowland, "Suburbia Buys Religion," pp. 79–80.

49. Edgar C. Hanford, "Surprises in the Suburbs," *American Mercury*, Vol. XXCI (September 1955), p. 69. Also "Suburbia," p. 41.

50. James B. Conant, *Slums and Suburbs* (New York, 1961), p. 109.

51. Kenneth Rexroth, "Book Week," *New York Sunday Herald Tribune* (March 8, 1964), p. 2.

52. "On the 5:19 to Ulcerville," *Newsweek*, Vol. LIV, No. 7 (August 17, 1959), p. 32.

53. "Quit," p. 34.

54. Lader, "Chaos in the Suburbs," p. 166.

55. Winthrop, "Crab-Grass Roots," pp. 19–20.

56. S. I. Hayakawa, "Popular Songs vs. the Facts of Life," *Mass Culture*, eds. Bernard Rosenberg and David Manning White (Glencoe, Illinois, 1957), pp. 393–403.

CHAPTER II: CITY AND COUNTRY: MARRIAGE PROPOSALS

1. David Riesman, "The Suburban Sadness," in Dobriner, *Community*, p. 375.

2. Ebenezer Howard, *Garden Cities of Tomorrow* (London, 1965), p. 48. Italics his.

3. The term "middle landscape" is borrowed from Leo Marx, *The Machine in the Garden* (New York, 1964). Marx applied the concept of the middle landscape primarily to literature, not to intellectual history, but it has relevance to both disciplines. Note, for example, its application to Crevecoeur's "middle settlements" in J. Hector St. John de Crevecoeur, *Letters from an American Farmer* (London, 1926), pp. 44–45.

4. Alexander Jackson Downing, in John Burchard and Albert Bush-Brown, *The Architecture of America* (Boston, 1961), p. 101.

5. *Harper's Weekly*, Vol. XX, No. 1006 (April 8, 1876), p. 294.

6. *Harper's Weekly*, Vol. XX, No. 1027 (September 5, 1876), p. 709.

7. Henry George, *Progress and Poverty* (New York, 1884), p. 405.

8. Carl N. Degler, *Out of Our Past* (New York and Evanston, 1959), p. 327.

9. In A. Whitney Griswold, *Farming and Democracy* (New Haven, 1952), pp. 179–80.

10. Adna F. Weber, *The Growth of Cities in the Nineteenth Century* (Ithaca, New York, 1963), p. 475.

11. Frederic C. Howe, *The City: The Hope of Democracy* (New York, 1905), p. 204.

12. Josiah Royce, *Race Questions, Provincialism and Other American Problems* (New York, 1908), pp. 97–98, and George Santayana, *The Background of My Life* (New York, 1944), p. 298.

13. Louis Sullivan, *The Autobiography of an Idea* (New York, 1922), pp. 98–99.

14. Robert Ezra Park, *Human Communities: The City and Human Ecology* (Glencoe, 1952), pp. 34, 140.

15. John Dewey, *The Public and Its Problems* (New York, 1927), pp. 211, 214. See also Morton and Lucia White, *The Intellectual versus the City* (New York, 1964), pp. 177–79. The Whites maintain that the attitude of the intellectual toward the American city underwent a change in the late nineteenth century, from an attitude of basic hostility to one of belief in the potentiality of the city, once it was reformed. But the reformers seemed almost invariably to want to change the city back into the rural village.

16. John R. McMahon, *Success in the Suburbs* (New York and London, 1917), pp. x–xi.

17. McMahon, *Success,* pp. 16, 24, 193–94.

18. *Ibid.,* vii, 173, 201.

19. Paul K. Conkin, *Tomorrow a New World* (Ithaca, New York, 1959), pp. 51–53.

20. Ralph Borsodi, *Flight from the City: The Story of a New Way to Family Security* (New York, 1933), pp. 1–19.

21. Newspaper advertisement, undated, in files of Bloomington Historical Society, Bloomington, Minnesota.

22. Twelve Southerners, "I'll Take My Stand" (New York, 1930), *City and Country in America,* ed. David R. Weimer (New York, 1962), pp. 121–22.

23. Harlan Paul Douglass, *The Suburban Trend* (New York, 1925), p. 327.

24. Conkin, *New World*, pp. 6–7. In reviewing the community building programs of the New Deal, this essay relies heavily on Conkin's excellent book.

25. Conkin, *New World*, pp. 87–130.

26. Conkin, *New World*, pp. 153–325.

27. Jane Jacobs, *The Death and Life of Great American Cities* (New York, 1961), pp. 444–47.

28. Frederick A. Shippey, *Protestantism in Suburban Life* (New York and Nashville, 1964), p. 117.

29. Quoted in Anselm Strauss, "The Changing Imagery of American City and Suburb," *Sociological Quarterly*, Vol. I, No. 1 (January 1960), p. 21.

30. Burchard and Bush-Brown, *The Architecture of America*, p. 121.

31. Thomas Ktsanes and Leonard Reissman, "Suburbia—New Homes for Old Values," *Social Problems*, Vol. VII, No. 3 (Winter, 1959–60), p. 195.

32. *Life*, Vol. LIX, No. 26 (December 24, 1965), pp. 37, 139.

33. Wolf von Eckardt, "New Towns in America," *New Republic*, Vol. CXLIX, No. 17 (October 26, 1963), p. 17.

34. Albert Mayer in consultation with Clarence Stein, "New Towns: and Fresh In-City Communities," *Architectural Record*, Vol. CXXXVI, No. 2 (August 1964), pp. 131–32.

35. "Reston," *Architectural Record*, Vol. CXXXVI, No. 1 (July 1964), p. 120.

36. Mayer and Stein, "New Towns," pp. 134–36.

37. Ada Louise Huxtable, " 'Clusters' Instead of 'Slurbs,' " *New York Times Magazine* (February 9, 1964), p. 44.

38. Morton and Lucia White, *The Intellectual versus the City* (New York, 1964), p. 238.

CHAPTER III: SUBURBS AND SUBURBS

1. Berger, *Working Class Suburb*, pp. 11–12.

2. Oscar Handlin, Arthur M. Schlesinger, Samuel Eliot Morison, Frederick Mork, Arthur M. Schlesinger, Jr., Paul Herman Buck, *Harvard Guide to American History* (Cambridge, 1954), p. 32.

3. Stein, *Eclipse*, p. 199.

4. Dobriner, *Community*, p. xvii.

5. Douglass, *The Suburban Trend*, p. 154.

6. Herbert J. Gans, "Urbanism and Suburbanism as Ways of Life: A Re-evaluation of Definitions," *Human Behavior and Social Processes*, ed. Arnold M. Rose (Boston, 1962), p. 636.

7. Melvin M. Webber, "Transportation Planning Models," *Traffic Quarterly*, Vol. XV, No. 2 (July 1961), p. 378.

8. A. C. Spectorsky, *The Exurbanites* (New York, 1955), pp. 6–7.

9. *Ibid.*, p. 53.

10. *Ibid.*, pp. 69–70.

11. Otis Dudley Duncan and Albert J. Reiss, Jr., "Suburbs and Urban Fringe," *Social Characteristics of Urban and Rural Communities, 1950* (New York, 1956), in *Community*, pp. 48–85.

12. Almost anyone who has ever lived in the Twin Cities area could successfully draw distinctions between these three adjoining communities. To lend demographic weight, census figures were used. Final Report PHC(1)-93, *U.S. Censuses of Population and Housing: 1960* (Washington, 1962), especially pp. 14, 42, 96, 126, 154.

13. Douglass, *The Suburban Trend*, pp. 74–121. As early as 1943, Chauncy Harris proposed a systematic division of suburbs into six separate classifications: industrial fringe, industrial, complex with industrial more important, complex with residential more important, dormitory, and mining and industrial. See "Suburbs," *American Journal of Sociology*, Vol. XLIX, No. 1 (July 1943), pp. 1–13.

14. Berger, *Working Class Suburb*, p. 10.

15. Dobriner, *Class*, pp. 27, 48, 106. Dobriner also distinguishes suburb from suburb on the basis of age.

16. *Ibid.*, pp. 111 ff.

17. *Ibid.*, p. 127.

18. Scott Donaldson, *The Making of a Suburb: An Intellectual History of Bloomington, Minnesota* (Bloomington Historical Society, 1964), pp. 45–49.

19. Peter Willmott and Michael Young, *Family and Class in a London Suburb* (London, 1960), pp. 6–8.

20. Dobriner, *Class*, p. 27.

21. Bernard De Voto, "The Easy Chair: Beating the Bali Ha'i Racket," *Harper's Magazine*, Vol. CCXII, No. 1268 (January 1956), p. 10. Italics mine.

22. Douglass, quoted in Dobriner, *Community*, p. 87.

23. De Voto, *Racket*, p. 10.

24. Robert C. Wood, "The American Suburb: Boy's Town in a Man's World," *Man and the Modern City*, eds. Elizabeth Geen, Jeanne R. Lowe, and Kenneth Walker (Pittsburgh, 1963), p. 114.

25. Bryon E. Munson, "Attitudes Toward Urban and Suburban Residence in Indianapolis," *Social Forces*, Vol. XXXV, No. 1 (October 1956), p. 77.

26. Quoted in Dobriner, *Class*, pp. 8–9, 62.

27. Lewis Mumford, *The City in History* (New York, 1961), p. 483.

28. H. G. Wells, *Anticipations* (New York, 1901), p. 55.

29. Douglass, *The Suburban Trend*, p. 164.

CHAPTER IV: LITTLE BOXES

1. Malvina Reynolds, words and music, "Little Boxes," 1963. Additional quotations from the lyric head the sections of this chapter.

2. Lewis Mumford, *From the Ground Up* (New York, 1956), p. 236. Actually, 1960 census figures revealed that Manhattan, Brooklyn, the Bronx, Jersey City, and Newark all lost population during the decade 1950–1960. Mumford understates the point.

3. "The Contemporary Suburban Residence," *Architectural Record*, Vol. XI, No. 3 (January 1902), p. 69.

4. The Editors of Fortune, *The Exploding Metropolis* (New York, 1958), p. ix.

5. "The Changing Suburbs," *Architectural Forum*, Vol. CXIV, No. 1 (January 1961), p. 47.

6. *Ibid.*, p. 67.

7. H. E. Bates, "Landscape Lost," *Spectator*, Vol. CXCIX (November 22, 1957), p. 668.

8. Mumford, *The City*, p. 496.

9. Huxtable, " 'Clusters,' " pp. 40, 37.

10. Mencken's correspondence, as might be expected, was particularly lively. To answer letter writers who took violent exception to the journalist's ideas, Mencken developed a formula note that read simply: "You may be right. Signed, H. L. Mencken."

11. Mumford, *The City*, p. 483.

12. *Ibid.*, p. 482.

13. *Ibid.*, p. 485.

14. *Ibid.*, p. 485.

15. Burchard and Bush-Brown, *The Architecture of America*, p. 169.

16. Mumford, *The City*, p. 495.

17. Burchard and Bush-Brown, *The Architecture of America*, p. 169.

18. *Ibid.*, pp. 272, 365.

19. Mumford, *The City*, p. 492.

20. "The Contemporary Suburban Residence," p. 74.

21. Burchard and Bush-Brown, *The Architecture of America*, p. 303.

22. Burchard and Bush-Brown, *The Architecture of America*, p. 272.

23. Mumford, *The City*, p. 506.

24. *Ibid.*, p. 487.

25. John R. Seeley, R. Alexander Sim, E. W. Loosley, *Crestwood Heights* (New York, 1956), p. 55.

26. Edgar Kaufmann and Ben Raeburn (eds.), *Frank Lloyd Wright: Writings and Buildings* (New York, 1960), p. 284.

27. *Ibid.*, p. 51.

28. *Ibid.*, p. 50.

29. Frank Lloyd Wright, *The Future of Architecture* (New York, 1953), p. 129.

30. Mumford, *The City*, p. 486.

31. "The Changing Suburbs," p. 76.

32. Bernard Rudofsky, *Behind the Picture Window* (New York, 1955), p. 26.

33. *Ibid.*, p. 164.

34. *Ibid.*, p. 167.

35. *Ibid.*, p. 8.

36. Wright, *The Future*, p. 21.

37. Rudofsky, *Behind the Picture Window*, pp. 172, 175.

38. Seeley et al., *Crestwood Heights*, pp. 42–43.

39. Robert Erwin, "Up, Up and Away with the Arts," *American Scholar*, Vol. XXXI (Autumn 1962), p. 578.

40. Rudofsky, *Behind the Picture Window*, p. 10.

41. *Ibid.*, p. 106.

42. *Ibid.*, p. 94. The non-erotic suburban bedroom has been enormously productive of children, however. Ask any school administrator.

43. *Ibid.*, p. 193.

44. *Ibid.*, p. 194.

45. Seeley, et al., *Crestwood Heights*, p. 50.

46. Mumford, *Ground Up*, p. 184.

47. "The Contemporary Suburban Residence," p. 76.

48. Seeley et al., *Crestwood Heights*, p. 45.

49. Lewis Mumford, "The Future of the City," *Architectural Record*, Vol. CXXXII (December 1962), p. 105.

CHAPTER V: FUTURE UTOPIAS

1. Burchard and Bush-Brown, *The Architecture of America*, p. 441.

2. Mumford, *Ground Up*, p. 88.

3. *Ibid.*, p. 11.

4. Peter Blake, *Architecture and Space: Frank Lloyd Wright* (Baltimore, Maryland, 1960), pp. 111–13.

5. Mumford, *The City*, p. 511.

6. Mumford, "The Future of the City," *Architectural Record*, Vol. CXXXIII (February 1963), p. 125.

7. Eliel Saarinen, *The City: Its Growth, Its Decay, Its Future* (New York, 1943), p. 251.

8. The Editors of *Fortune, The Exploding Metropolis*, p. xii.

9. *Background Booklets Nos. 1 and 2*, Goals for the Region Project, New York Regional Plan Association (New York, 1963).

10. Robert Woods Kennedy, *The House* (New York, 1953), p. 4.

11. Clarence S. Stein, "New Towns for New Purposes," *Roots of Contemporary American Architecture*, ed. Lewis Mumford (New York, 1952), pp. 336, 346.

12. Eugene Henry Klaber, "Comment re 'Visual Communities,'" *Journal of the American Institute of Planners*, Vol. XXIV, No. 1 (1958), p. 41.

13. Herbert J. Gans, *The Levittowners* (New York, 1967), p. 411.

14. "The Changing Suburbs," pp. 81, 82.

15. *Ibid.*, p. 58.

16. *Ibid.*, p. 96.

17. *Ibid.*, p. 97.

18. *Ibid.*, p. 97.

19. Peter Blake, "The Suburbs are a Mess," *Saturday Evening Post*, Vol. CCXXXVI, No. 34 (October 5, 1963), p. 14. Clusters may also attract a wider variety of settlers in suburbia, preventing development of a WASP (White Anglo-Saxon Protestant) ghetto.

20. Huxtable, "'Clusters,'" p. 42. Huxtable admires clusters, but reserves most of her praise for the revived New Town movement in the United States.

21. Montgomery Schuyler, "The Chicago Renascence," in Mumford, *Roots*, p. 210.

22. Whyte, *Organization Man*, p. 304.

23. Rudofsky, *Behind the Picture Window*, pp. 198–99.

24. "The Changing Suburbs," p. 101.

25. *Ibid.*, p. 102.

26. Suzanne Gleaves, "Levittown Revisited," *New York Sunday Herald Tribune Magazine* (August 16, 1964), p. 12.

27. "The Changing Suburbs," p. 103.

28. Wright, *The Future*, p. 255.

29. J. M. Richards, *Modern Architecture* (Baltimore, 1962), p. 124.

CHAPTER VI: THE TERRITORY BEHIND

1. R. W. B. Lewis, *The American Adam* (Chicago, 1955), p. 3.

2. William H. Whyte, Jr., *The Organization Man* (New York, 1956), pp. 276–77.

3. Marx, *Machine*, p. 100: "The ideal lies between the howling wilderness where dark scorpions abound in the poisonous fields, and the snake seeks human prey, and the European city where ten thousand baneful arts combine to pamper luxury and thin mankind. . . ."

4. Wright Morris, *The Territory Ahead* (New York, 1963), foreword.

5. Marx, *Machine*, p. 6.

6. *Ibid.*, p. 141.

7. Arthur K. Moore, *The Frontier Mind* (New York, 1963), pp. 216–17, 237.

8. William E. Taylor, *Cavalier and Yankee* (New York, 1963), pp. 105, 165.

9. Henry Steele Commager, *The American Mind* (New Haven and London, 1950), p. 34.

10. Norman Mailer, address to joint meeting of American Studies Association and Modern Language Association, Chicago, December 28, 1965.

11. Quoted in Morris, *Territory*, p. 2.

12. *Ibid.*, pp. 44–45.

13. Charles L. Sanford, *The Quest for Paradise* (Urbana, Illinois, 1961), pp. 181–82.

14. Huxtable, " 'Clusters,' " p. 37.

15. Quoted in Whites, *The Intellectual*, p. 59.

16. Nathaniel Hawthorne, *The House of the Seven Gables* (New York, 1961), p. 155.

17. Harriet Beecher Stowe, *Oldtown Fireside Stories* (Boston, 1872), pp. 53, 103.

18. William Dean Howells, *Suburban Sketches* (New York, 1871), p. 12.

19. *Ibid.*, p. 86.

20. *Ibid.*, p. 221.

21. William Dean Howells, *A Modern Instance* (Boston, 1957), p. 142.

22. Henry B. Fuller, *The Cliff-Dwellers* (New York, 1893), pp. 102–04.

23. Sanford, *Quest*, pp. 255–56.

24. Maxwell Geismar, Introduction, *The Ring Lardner Reader* (New York, 1963), p. xxiv.

25. *The Ring Lardner Reader*, p. 274.

26. *Ibid.*, pp. 370, 405.

27. Marx, *Machine*, p. 357.

28. F. Scott Fitzgerald, *The Great Gatsby* (New York, 1953), p. 182.

29. Morris, *Territory*, p. 159.

CHAPTER VII: LIFE STYLES: CONFORMITY, NEIGHBORING, AND HYPERACTIVITY

1. Hal Burton, "Trouble in the Suburbs," p. 114. In the motion picture, Miss Lang retains the beauty of youth, although she is very old in terms of actual years, as long as she remains in Shangri-La. When she attempts to leave, the years take their toll of her beauty.

2. Douglass, *The Suburban Trend*, in Dobriner, *Community*, p. 91. See epigraph.

3. Robert C. Wood, *Suburbia: Its People and Their Problems* (Boston, 1958, pp. 4–5.

4. Ktsanes and Reissman, "Suburbia," p. 189.

5. "Quit," p. 35.

6. John Keats, *Crack*, p. 61.

7. Reynolds Farley, "Suburban Persistence," *American Sociological Review*, Vol. XXIX, No. 1 (February 1964), pp. 38–47.

8. Quoted in Albert I. Gordon, *Jews in Suburbia* (Boston, 1959), pp. 195–99. For the accuracy of historian Schlesinger's comment on Republicanism in the suburbs, see the chapter on politics.

9. Ktsanes and Reissman, "Suburbia," pp. 189–90.

10. Henry David Thoreau, "Civil Disobedience," *Walden and Other Writings* (New York, 1950), p. 649.

11. Douglass, in Dobriner, *Community*, p. 95.

12. Quoted in Gordon, *Jews*, p. 199.

13. Quoted in Ralph Henry Gabriel, *The Course of American Democratic Thought* (New York, 1956), pp. 310–11.

14. Charles Duff, *Anthropological Report on a London Suburb* (London, 1935), pp. 20–25, 43–44.

15. Bell, *Ideology*, pp. 34–36. This lack of opposition can lead to real frustration, of the kind that developed on the Berkeley campus of the University of California in 1964–1965 when the rebelling students could find no opposition, until they finally came up with the filthy speech movement.

16. William N. Leonard, "Economic Aspects of Suburbanization," in Dobriner, *Community*, p. 191.

17. McGinley, "Suburbia, of Thee I Sing," pp. 228–29.

18. Robert Gutman, "Population Mobility in the American Middle Class," *The Urban Condition*, ed. Leonard J. Duhl (New York and London, 1963), pp. 176–79.

19. Herbert J. Gans, "Effect of the Move from City to Suburb," in Duhl, *Urban Condition*, p. 191.

20. Dennis H. Wrong, "Suburbs and Myths of Suburbia," *Readings in Introductory Sociology*, eds. Dennis H. Wrong and Harry L. Gracey (New York, 1967), pp. 358–64.

21. Douglass, *The Suburban Trend* (New York, 1925), p. 224. Italics mine.

22. Rolf Meyersohn and Robin Jackson, "Gardening in Suburbia," in Dobriner, *Community*, p. 271. The imagination of intellectuals generally, not just sociologists, seems to have been over-stimulated by the always visible suburbs.

23. Wood, *Suburbia*, p. 131.

24. Irving D. Tressler, "So You Live in a Suburb," *Best of Modern Humor*, ed. P. G. Wodehouse and Scott Meredith (New York, 1951), pp. 208–13.

25. Wattel, "Levittown," in Dobriner, *Community*, p. 297.

26. Sylvia Fleis Fava, "Contrasts in Neighboring: New York City and a Suburban County," in Dobriner, *Community*, pp. 126–27; see also Berger, *Working Class Suburb*, pp. 57–59, and Gans, in Duhl, *Urban Condition*, p. 187.

27. Willmott and Young, *London Suburb*, p. 129.

28. Herbert J. Gans, "Planning and Social Life: Friendship and Neighbor Relations in Suburban Communities," *Journal of the American Institute of Planners*, Vol. XXVII, No. 2 (May 1961), pp. 134–40.

29. Harry Henderson, "The Mass-Produced Suburbs," *Harper's Magazine*, Vol. CCVII, No. 1242 (November 1953), pp. 31–32.

30. Gans, in Duhl, *Urban Condition*, p. 187.

31. The close relationship of the two myths is discussed in Alan Gowans, *Images of American Living* (Philadelphia, 1964).

32. Douglass, *The Suburban Trend*, p. 188.

33. Andrew M. Greeley, *The Church and the Suburbs* (New York, 1959), p. 12.

34. Bell, *Ideology*, p. 36.

35. Willmott and Young, *London Suburb*, pp. 87–90.

36. Philip H. Ennis, "Leisure in the Suburbs: Research Prolegomenon," in Dobriner, *Community*, p. 264.

37. Stein, *Eclipse*, p. 283.

38. Charlton Ogburn, Jr., "Help! Help!" *Harper's Magazine*, Vol. CCXXIX, No. 1374 (November 1964), p. 69.

39. Meyersohn and Jackson, in Dobriner, *Community,* pp. 281–84.

40. McMahon, *Success,* p. 193.

41. Tristram Coffin, "Maryland's Montgomery County: The Changing Suburban Dream," *Holiday,* Vol. XXXVIII, No. 1 (July 1965), pp. 54–55.

CHAPTER VIII: COUCH, SCHOOL, AND CHURCH

1. Douglass, *The Suburban Trend,* p. 307.

2. John Keats, "Compulsive Suburbia," *The Atlantic,* Vol. CCV, No. 4 (April 1960), p. 47.

3. Catherine Marshall, "What's Happening to Our Homemakers?" *Suburbia Today* (July 1964), p. 6.

4. "Exurbia: The New America," *Newsweek,* Vol. XLIX, No. 22 (June 3, 1957), pp. 84–85.

5. Berger, *Working Class Suburb,* p. 79.

6. J. Robert Moskin, "Morality U.S.A.," *Look,* Vol. XXVII, No. 19 (September 24, 1963), p. 81.

7. Wattel, "Levittown," in Dobriner, *Community,* p. 298.

8. David Wallace, *First Tuesday* (Garden City, New York, 1964), p. 37.

9. Richard E. Gordon, M.D., Katherine K. Gordon, and Max Gunther, *The Split-Level Trap* (New York, 1964), p. 8. Perhaps it is unfair to visit the sins of the blurb-writers on the heads of the authors of books.

10. *Ibid.,* pp. 12–13.

11. *Ibid.,* p. 23.

12. *Ibid.,* p. 26.

13. *U.S. Censuses of Population: 1960,* Vol. I, Part 32—New Jersey (Washington, 1963), pp. 32, 129.

14. Gordon et al., *Trap,* p. 27.

15. See New Jersey census report cited above. Also U.S. Bureau of the Census, *U.S. Censuses of Popualtion: 1960,* Vol. 1, Part 34—New York (Washington, 1963), pp. 34, 172.

16. Peter Wyden, *Suburbia's Coddled Kids* (New York, 1962), pp. 27–30.

17. Frederick A. Shippey, *Protestantism in Suburban Life* (New York and Nashville, 1964), pp. 128–29.

18. Greeley, *Church,* p. 93.

19. Gordon, *Jews,* pp. 59–60.

20. "Some Drawbacks of Suburban Life," *Science Digest,* Vol. XXXVII, No. 1 (January 1955), p. 33.

21. Douglass, *The Suburban Trend,* p. 221.

22. Willmott and Young, *London Suburb,* pp. 21–22.

23. Ernest R. Mowrer, "The Family in Suburbia," in Dobriner, *Community,* p. 156.

24. Burchard and Bush-Brown, *The Architecture of America,* p. 49.

25. Gordon et al., *Trap,* p. 17.

26. Shippey, *Protestantism,* pp. 123, 124–26. Also see "The Church in 'Outer Space,'" *America,* Vol. XCVIII, No. 20 (February 22, 1958), p. 585, where it is reported of a suburban church congregation of 1,300 families, that 300 moved away and 400 more moved in during one year in the late fifties.

27. Willmott and Young, *London Suburb,* p. 35.

28. Sidonie Matsner Gruenberg, "The Challenge of the New Suburbs," *Marriage and Family Living,"* Vol. XVII, No. 2 (May 1955), p. 133.

29. Harvey Cox, *The Secular City* (New York, 1965), pp. 53–54.

30. Gutman, "Population Mobility," in Duhl, *Urban Condition,* p. 180.

31. Gans, "Effects of the Move," in Duhl, *Urban Condition,* p. 191.

32. Wendell Bell, "Social Choice, Life Styles, and Suburban Residence," in Dobriner, *Community,* p. 239.

33. Cox, *Secular City,* p. 52.

34. Bell, in Dobriner, *Community,* p. 233.

35. Anne Kelley, "Suburbia—Is It a Child's Utopia?" *The New York Times Magaine* (February 2, 1958), p. 22.

36. "A Look at Suburbanites," *Science Digest,* Vol. XL, No. 6 (December 1956), p. 20. See also "Spur to Conformity," in *Commonweal,* Vol. LXIV, No. 24 (September 21, 1956), p. 602.

37. Gordon et al., *Trap,* p. 92.

38. Marshall, *Homemakers,* p. 6.

39. Wyden, *Coddled Kids,* pp. 128–29.

40. Gordon et al., *Trap,* p. 125.

41. Seymour Martin Lipset, "A Changing American Character," *Culture and Social Character* (Glencoe, Illinois, 1961), p. 153.

42. Quoted in Dorothy Barclay, "Adolescents in Suburbia," *National Education Association Journal,* Vol. XLVIII, No. 1 (January 1959), p. 11.

43. Shippey, *Protestantism,* p. 99.

44. "Darien's *Dolce Vita,*" *Time,* Vol. XXCIV, No. 22 (November 27, 1964), p. 60.

45. David Loth, *Crime in the Suburbs* (New York, 1967), pp. 17, 249.

46. Gans, in Duhl, *Urban Condition,* p. 191.

47. Jane Jacobs, *American Cities,* p. 53.

48. Wyden, *Coddled Kids,* p. 103.

49. "Darien's *Dolce Vita,*" p. 60.

50. Greeley, *Church,* pp. 106–12.

51. Douglas P. Sarff, "Open Letter to the Community of Wayzata," *The Minnetonka Herald* (April 1, 1965), p. 2. Had the newspaper's publisher, Carroll E. Crawford, agreed to give Sarff free space for his opinions, as the teacher proposed, the chances are excellent that his broadside would have caused almost no fuss at all. When he paid for the space out of his own pocket, Sarff enormously enhanced the value of what he had to say in the minds of outsiders. His ideas were not, of course, highly original.

52. Conant, *Slums*, pp. 81–82.

53. Thomas E. Robinson, "Opportunity in Suburbia," *National Education Association Journal*, Vol. XLVI, No. 4 (April 1957), pp. 246–48.

54. Wallace, *First Tuesday*, p. 37.

55. Conant, *Slums*, pp. 144–45, 101.

56. Seeley et al., *Crestwood Heights*, pp. 123, 229.

57. Helen Puner, "Is It True?", p. 96.

58. Douglass, *The Suburban Trend*, p. 201.

59. Wood, *Suburbia*, pp. 186–91.

60. Wallace, *First Tuesday*, p. 176.

61. C. B. Palmer, *Slightly Cooler in the Suburbs* (Garden City, New York, 1950), p. 124.

62. Coffin, "Montgomery County," p. 118.

63. John Cogley, "An Interview with Reinhold Niebuhr," *McCall's*, Vol. XCIII, No. 5 (February 1966), p. 167.

64. Harry Henderson, "The Mass-Produced Suburbs. Part II: Rugged American Collectivism," *Harper's*, Vol. CCVII, No. 1243 (December 1953), p. 82. Henderson estimates the nation's suburbanites as 10 per cent Jewish, 25 per cent Catholic, 55 per cent Protestant, and about 10 per cent unaffiliated.

65. Lionel Trilling, *The Liberal Imagination* (Garden City, New York, 1963), p. 30.

66. Rowland, "Suburbia Buys Religion," pp. 78–80.

67. Will Oursler, "The Ferment in Suburban Congregations," *Suburbia Today* (November 1963), p. 17. Italics mine.

68. Gordon, *Jews*, pp. 88–89.

69. Greeley, *Church*, p. 72.

70. *Ibid.*, p. 67.

71. Herbert J. Gans, "Park Forest: Birth of a Jewish Community," *Commentary*, Vol. XI, No. 4 (April 1951), p. 333.

72. Gibson Winter, *The Suburban Captivity of the Churches* (Garden City, New York, 1961), pp. 35, 59.

73. *Ibid.*, pp. 66, 68.

74. *Ibid.*, pp. 174–75.

75. Douglass, *The Suburban Trend*, pp. 205–10.

76. Quoted in Stein, *Eclipse*, p. 61.

77. Berger, *Working Class Suburb*, p. 52.

78. Quoted in "Suburban Religion," *Time*, Vol. LXX, No. 3 (July 15, 1957), p. 78.

79. Quoted in Greeley, *Church*, p. 169.

80. Gordon, *Jews*, p. 220.

81. Gordon, *Jews*, pp. 167–70.

82. Gans, "Park Forest," p. 337–38.

83. Phyllis McGinley, *The Province of the Heart* (New York, 1959), p. 148.

84. Shippey, *Protestantism*, p. 30.

85. *Ibid.*, p. 39.

86. *Ibid.*, p. 78.

87. *Ibid.*, pp. 200–02.

88. Quoted in Oursler, *Ferment*, p. 19.

89. Shippey, *Protestantism*, pp. 13–15.

90. Mircea Eliade, *The Sacred and the Profane* (New York, 1961), pp. 90–93.

91. *Ibid.*, p. 96.

92. Harry Gersh, "The New Suburbanites of the 50's—Jewish Division," *Commentary*, Vol. XVII, No. 3 (March 1954), p. 215.

93. Eliade, *Sacred*, pp. 202–206.

94. Cox, *Secular City*, p. 154.

CHAPTER IX: THE SUBURBAN FRONTIER

1. Whyte, *Organization Man*, p. 332.

2. Quoted in Berger, *Working Class Suburb*, p. 28.

3. G. Edward Janosik, "The New Suburbia," *Current History*, Vol. XXXI, No. 180 (August 1956), pp. 92–93.

4. Fred I. Greenstein and Raymond E. Wolfinger, "The Suburbs and Shifting Party Loyalties," *Public Opinion Quarterly*, Vol. XXII, No. 4 (Winter 1958–59), p. 482. Working with the same data, Angus Campbell and others failed to arrive at the Republicanization thesis in *The American Voter*.

5. Louis Harris, *Is There a Republican Majority?* (New York, 1954), pp. 121–22. Harris equates the terms "suburban" and "white collar" in his analysis of the 1952 presidential election.

6. Samuel Lubell, *Revolt of the Moderates* (New York, 1956), pp. 114, 276–77.

7. Robert C. Wood, "The Impotent Suburban Vote," *Nation,* Vol. CXC, No. 13 (March 26, 1960), p. 273.

8. Reported in Wood, *Suburbia,* p. 145.

9. Jerome G. Manis and Leo C. Stine, "Suburban Residence and Political Behavior," *Public Opinion Quarterly,* Vol. XXII, No. 4 (Winter 1958–59), pp. 486–89. This article was a companion piece to that of Greenstein and Wolfinger, printed in the same issue of the journal. Editors of the quarterly provided an indication of their bias by remarking of the Manis-Stine monograph that as "a modest case study it will serve to call in question some of the recent easy generalizations and fanciful writing concerning the suburban trend."

10. Berger, *Working Class Suburb,* p. 34.

11. Wallace, *First Tuesday,* p. 4.

12. *Ibid.,* p. 113.

13. *Ibid.,* p. 14.

14. See Millet and Pittman, "The New Suburban Voter: A Case Study in Electoral Behavior," *Southwestern Social Science Quarterly,* Vol. XXXIX, No. 1 (June 1958), pp. 33–42; Bernard Lazerwitz, "Suburban Voting Trends: 1948 to 1956," *Social Forces,* Vol. XXXIX, No. 1 (October 1960), pp. 29–36; Frederick M. Wirt, "The Political Sociology of American Suburbia: A Reinterpretation," *Journal of Politics,* Vol. XXVII, No. 3 (August 1965), pp. 647–66.

15. Alexis de Tocqueville, *Democracy in America,* 2 vols. (New York, 1955), Vol. I, p. 259.

16. Wood, "Impotent," p. 273.

17. Wattel, "Levittown," in Dobriner, *Community,* p. 308.

18. Wood, "Impotent," p. 273.

19. David Riesman, "The Suburban Sadness," in Dobriner, *Community,* pp. 375–408.

20. Berger, *Working Class Suburb,* p. 36.

21. Douglass, *The Suburban Trend,* in Dobriner, *Community,* p. 94.

22. Walter T. Martin, "The Structuring of Social Relationships Engendered by Suburban Residence," *American Sociological Review,* Vol. XXII (August 1956), in Dobriner, *Community,* p. 104.

23. Stanley Eklins and Eric McKitrick, "A Meaning for Turner's Frontier," *Political Science Quarterly,* Vol. LXIX, Nos. 3–4 (September–December 1954).

24. Elkins and McKitrick, *Turner* (December), p. 592.

25. *Ibid.* (September), pp. 329–30.

26. *Ibid.* (September), p. 325.

27. *Ibid.* (September), pp. 326–28.

28. There is a certain irony here, for according to the Elkins-McKitrick theory, the less well planned a new community is, the better the conditions are for exercise of political democracy. Thus in Hilltown, another government housing project, planning was so good that no initial "time of troubles," and consequently, no widespread political participation, developed. The theory calls into question some of our deepest convictions about the nature of democracy, the efficacy of planning, or both. Bernard De Voto, discussing city planners, observes that their "cities in the fields become real estate speculations which collapse and are bought up as fine sites for industrial development. But there is an odd, commonly disregarded fact: the haphazard development of American culture at large has been succeeding where the movers and shakers have failed." De Voto, "Racket," p. 11.

29. Elkins and McKitrick, *Turner* (September), p. 329.

30. Scott Donaldson, *Making*, pp. 46–49. For data on modern Bloomington politics, the best sources are the *Bloomington Sun, Bloomington Suburbanite*, and *Bloomington Sun-Suburbanite*.

31. Wallace, *First Tuesday*, pp. 82, 91, 180–88.

32. See for example Dobriner, *Class*, p. 111; Harris, *Majority*, p. 122; Wood, *Suburbia*, p. 178.

33. Louis Wirth, "Urbanism as a Way of Life," *American Journal of Sociology*, Vol. XLIV (July 1938), in Paul K. Hatt and Albert J. Reiss, Jr., *Cities and Society* (New York, 1951), p. 57.

34. Chauncy D. Harris and Edward L. Ullman, "The Nature of Cities," *The Annals*, Vol. CCXLII (November 1945), in Hatt and Reiss, *Cities*, p. 247.

35. Luther H. Gulick, *The Metropolitan Problem and American Ideas* (New York, 1962), p. 23.

36. William N. Leonard, "Economic Aspects of Suburbanization," in Dobriner, *Community*, p. 186.

37. Charles R. Adrian, *Governing Urban America* (New York, 1955), p. 37.

38. *Ibid.*, pp. 39–40.

39. "Minneapolis, Suburbs Don't Subsidize One Another," *Bloomington Sun-Suburbanite* (December 31, 1964), pp. 1, 2. Banovetz found that Minneapolis subsidized the suburbs in the areas of education, county government, and parks, and that the suburbs subsidized the central city in the areas of welfare and (probably) highways. The cross-subsidies came out almost exactly even.

40. Wood, *Suburbia*, p. 67.

41. Earl S. Johnson, "The Function of the Central Business District in the Metropolitan Community," in Hatt and Reiss, *Cities*, p. 257.

42. Thomas H. Reed, "Hope for 'Suburbanitis,'" *National Municipal Review*, Vol. XXXIX, No. 11 (December 1950), p. 543.

43. Dobriner, *Class*, p. 72. Levittown on Long Island, the subject of Dobriner's study, is part of Nassau County, where strong county government prevails. Perhaps for this reason, he does not call attention to the increasing degree of power being appropriated by county governments in other parts of the country. As the county takes over governmental functions one by one, a sort of "creeping Metro" results. A difficulty with this procedure from the standpoint of efficiency is that the county unit rarely encompasses all of the metropolitan area.

44. "City-Suburb Federation: How Good an Answer Is It?", *Business Week* (January 22, 1955), pp. 66, 68.

45. For this review of recent developments in Toronto Metro, I am indebted to Alastair Lawrie, of the *Globe and Mail's* editorial staff for his letter of March 26, 1968, and for copies of editorials published on January 11, 1966 and January 26, 1967.

46. "What's Ahead for New County Manager?", *Miami Herald* (March 17, 1965), p. 8-A.

47. Lyle C. Fitch, "Fiscal and Political Problems of Increasing Urbanization," *Political Science Quarterly*, Vol. LXXI, No. 1 (March 1956), p. 87. Other exceptions include Baton Rouge and Atlanta.

48. Quoted in Wood, *Suburbia*, p. 25.

49. *Ibid.*, p. 87.

50. Gulick, *Problem*, pp. 166–67.

51. Donald Heinzman, letter to the author, March 29, 1968.

52. Donald G. Emery, "Memo from Scarsdale: A New Role for Suburban Schools," *Look*, Vol. 32, No. 7 (April 2, 1968), p. 18.

53. John Finley Scott and Lois Heyman Scott, "They are not so much Anti-Negro as Pro-Middle Class," *The New York Times Magazine* (March 24, 1968), pp. 119–20.

CHAPTER X: TWO STUDIES IN DEPTH

1. The suburb is no new phenomenon, of course, but its rapid growth and its popular acceptance as a symbol of the American way of life are notions particularly of the mid-twentieth century.

2. Seeley et al., *Crestwood Heights*, p. 19.

3. *Ibid.*, p. 20.

4. Whyte, *Organization Man*, p. 311.

5. *Ibid.*, p. 297.

6. *Ibid.*, p. 300.

7. Seeley et al., *Crestwood Heights*, p. 160.
8. *Ibid.*, p. 295.
9. *Ibid.*, p. 177.
10. Whyte, *Organization Man*, p. 393.
11. A central concept of Whyte's Social Ethic.
12. Whyte, *Organization Man*, p. 393.
13. *Ibid.*, p. 393.
14. Seeley et al., *Crestwood Heights*, p. 177.
15. *Ibid.*, p. 177.
16. Whyte, *Organization Man*, p. 395.
17. Seeley et al., *Crestwood Heights*, p. 206.
18. *Ibid.*, p. 6.
19. Whyte, *Organization Man*, p. 364.
20. Seeley et al., *Crestwood Heights*, p. 4.
21. *Ibid.*, p. 11.
22. Whyte, *Organization Man*, p. 378.
23. *Ibid.*, p. 392.
24. Seeley et al., *Crestwood Heights*, p. 167.
25. *Ibid.*, p. 46.
26. Whyte, *Organization Man*, pp. 346–47.
27. *Ibid.*, pp. 389–90.
28. Seeley et al., *Crestwood Heights*, pp. 219–20.
29. Whyte, *Organization Man*, p. 317.
30. Seeley et al., *Crestwood Heights*, pp. 37–40.
31. Whyte, *Organization Man*, p. 325.
32. Seeley et al., *Crestwood Heights*, p. 134. The high turnover in Park Forest is matter of some alarm to the "old" residents, for there is a strong implication that by staying put they have failed to keep up with the social and economic progress of those who were tapped to move on.
33. Whyte, *Organization Man*, p. 311.
34. Riesman, Introduction to *Crestwood Heights*, pp. xi–xii.
35. Whyte, *Organization Man*, p. 11.
36. Riesman, Introduction, p. vii.
37. Seeley et al., *Crestwood Heights*, pp. 413, 421.
38. Whyte, *Organization Man*, p. 448.

CHAPTER XI: CONFLICT IN THE SUBURBAN NOVEL

1. Whyte, *Organization Man*, p. 5.
2. *Ibid.*, pp. 7–8.
3. *Ibid.*, p. 13.

4. *Ibid.*, p. 278.

5. William Van O'Connor, "The Novel and the 'Truth' About America," in Kwiat and Turpie, *Studies*, p. 81. O'Connor paraphrases Steven Marcus, "Terrors of Yoknapatawpha and Fairfield," *Commentary*, Vol. XIV (December 1952), pp. 575–85.

6. *Ibid.*, p. 83.

7. Bernard Bowron, Leo Marx, and Arnold Rose, "Literature and Covert Culture," in Kwiat and Turpie, *Studies*, pp. 84–94.

8. Richard Yates, *Revolutionary Road* (Boston, 1961), p. 44. Quotes are taken from Bantam edition, 1962.

9. *Ibid.*, p. 237.

10. *Ibid.*, p. 97.

11. Whyte, *Organization Man*, p. 344.

12. The differences between Oakstown and Peaceable Lane, between Ryswick and Revolutionary Road, are substantial.

13. David Karp, *Leave Me Alone* (New York, 1957), p. 225.

14. *Ibid.*, p. 282.

15. *Ibid.*, p. 282.

16. *Ibid.*, p. 298.

17. *Ibid.*, pp. 302–03.

18. Georg Mann, *The Blind Ballots* (New York, 1962), pp. 65–66.

19. *Ibid.*, p. 140.

20. *Ibid.*, p. 151.

21. *Ibid.*, p. 153.

22. *Ibid.*, p. 7.

23. *Ibid.*, p. 276.

24. *Ibid.*, p. 277.

25. Douglass, "Suburbs," *Encyclopedia*, p. 435.

CHAPTER XII: THE FICTIONAL TREATMENT

1. Joe Sarno, *Sin in the Suburbs*. The film was shown at Aster Art Theatre, Minneapolis, November 15, 1965.

2. F. O. Matthiessen, *American Renaissance* (London, Toronto, and New York, 1941), pp. x–xi.

3. Quoted in "Is Nothing Obscene Any More?" *Time*, Vol. XXCIV, No. 2 (July 10, 1964), p. 45.

4. Dean McCoy, *The Love Pool* (New York, 1964), pp. 95–96.

5. Berger, *Working Class Suburb*, p. 99.

6. Jay Presson, *First Wife*, unpublished playscript in possession of Hal Wallis Productions.

7. Valentine Davies and Hal Kanter, *Bachelor in Paradise* (M-G-M, 1961), p. 15.

8. Ira Wallach, *Boys' Night Out* (M-G-M, 1961), p. 59.

9. Isobel Lennart, *Please Don't Eat the Daisies* (M-G-M, 1959), pp. 71–87.

10. Joseph Fields, *The Tunnel of Love* (M-G-M, 1957), pp. 105, 120.

11. The film *No Down Payment* was presented during late night television programming.

12. Joseph Bensman and Bernard Rosenberg, "The Culture of the New Suburbia," *Dissent*, Vol. IX (Summer 1962), p. 268.

13. McGinley, *Province*, pp. 3–4.

14. John P. Marquand, *Point of No Return* (New York, 1947), pp. 131–35, 243.

15. Sloan Wilson, *The Man in the Gray Flannel Suit* (New York, 1955), pp. 113, 140, 252–55.

16. Max Shulman, *Rally Round the Flag, Boys* (Garden City, New York, 1957).

17. Russell W. Nash, "Max Shulman and the Changing Image of Suburbia," *Midcontinent American Studies Journal*, Vol. IV, No. 1 (Spring 1963), pp. 27–38.

18. S. J. Perelman, *Acres and Pains* (New York, 1947), pp. 35–38, 60–61.

19. Eugene Ionesco, *The Bald Soprano,* translation by Donald M. Allen, *Masters of Modern Drama*, eds. Haskell M. Block and Robert G. Shedd (New York, 1962), pp. 1120–21.

20. Bertrand Russell, *Satan in the Suburbs and Other Stories* (London, 1953), pp. 9–10.

21. Josephine Miles, "Housewife," *15 Modern American Poets*, ed. George P. Elliott (New York, 1956), p. 88.

22. Richard Wilbur, "To an American Poet Just Dead," *Ceremony and Other Poems* (New York, 1950), p. 49.

23. Phyllis McGinley, "June in the Suburbs," *Time*, Vol. XXCV, No. 25 (June 18, 1965), p. 758.

24. William Esty, "Out of an Abundant Love of Created Things," *Commonweal*, Vol. LXVI, No. 7 (May 17, 1957), p. 187.

25. Rollene Waterman, untitled article, *Saturday Review*, Vol. XLI, No. 37 (September 13, 1958), p. 33.

26. John Cheever, *The Wapshot Chronicle* (New York, 1957), p. 21.

27. *Ibid.*, pp. 106–08.

28. Henry Adams, *The Education of Henry Adams* (New York, 1931), pp. 8–9.

29. Cheever, *Chronicle*, p. 249.

30. Quoted in *Time*, Vol. XXCIII, No. 13 (March 27, 1964), p. 69.

31. John Cheever, *The Housebreaker of Shady Hill* (New York, 1958), p. 12.

32. John Cheever, "The Swimmer," *The Brigadier and the Golf Widow* (New York, Evanston, and London, 1964), pp. 61–76.

33. Donald Malcolm, "John Cheever's Photograph Album," *New Republic*, Vol. CXXXVI, No. 22 (June 3, 1957), p. 17.

34. Granville Hicks, "Cheever and Others," *Saturday Review*, Vol. XLI, No. 37 (September 13, 1958), p. 33.

35. Cynthia Osick, "America Aglow," *Commentary*, Vol. XXXVIII, No. 1 (July 1964), p. 67.

36. James Scully, "An Oracle of Subocracy," *Nation*, Vol. CC, No. 6 (February 8, 1965), pp. 144–45.

37. Margaret Halsey, *This Demi-Paradise* (New York, 1960), pp. 97–98.

38. Matthiessen, *Renaissance*, p. xv.

39. Conrad Knickerbocker, "No One's in Charge," *Life*, Vol. LIX, No. 26 (December 24, 1965), p. 37.

CHAPTER XIII: THE SUBURB, NOT THE FARM

1. James Kenward, *The Suburban Child* (Cambridge, England, 1955), p. 2.

2. *Ibid.*, p. 3.

3. Adolph S. Tomars, "Rural Survivals in American Urban Life," *Sociological Analysis*, eds. Logan Wilson and William L. Kolb (New York, 1949), p. 372. Tomars regards the fondness for single-family housing and the prevalence of fireplaces in centrally heated homes as other rural survivals.

4. Wallace, *First Tuesday*, pp. 31–34.

5. "Exurbia; The New America," *Newsweek*, Vol. XLIX, No. 22 (June 3, 1957), p. 84.

6. Veblen, *Leisure Class*, p. 134.

7. McGinley, *Province*, pp. 87–88.

8. Erich Fromm, *The Sane Society* (New York, 1955), pp. 38, 48–49.

9. Wallace, *First Tuesday*, pp. 236–37.

10. Quoted in Roger B. Salomon, *Twain and the Image of History* (New Haven, 1961), p. 206.

11. Sanford, *Quest*, p. viii.

12. Wood, *Suburbia*, pp. v, 28.

13. Douglass, *The Suburban Trend*, p. 34.

14. Stein, *Eclipse*, p. 248.

15. Burchard and Bush-Brown, *The Architecture of America*, pp. 306–07.

16. Stein, *Eclipse*, p. 282.

17. Jacobs, *American Cities*, p. 445.

18. Dobriner, *Class*, p. 140.

19. Whyte, *Organization Man*, p. 444.

20. *Selections from Ralph Waldo Emerson*, ed. Stephen E. Wicher (Boston, 1957), p. 159.

21. Carl T. Rowan, address at University of Minnesota, January 28, 1965.

22. Daniel Lerner, "Comfort and Fun: Morality in a Nice Society," *American Scholar*, Vol. XXVII, No. 2 (Spring 1958), p. 161.

23. Sigmund Freud, *Civilization and Its Discontents* (Chicago, n.d.), pp. 60–142.

24. Joe McCarthy, "The Case for Sidewalks," *This Week* (May 24, 1964), p. 12.

25. Freud, *Civilization*, p. 10.

26. Hofstadter, *Age of Reform*, p. 328.

BIBLIOGRAPHY

In order to provide a usable guide to the voluminous writing about the suburbs, this bibliography has been divided by subject matter into seven categories of commentary. These are: architectural, historical, literary, political, psychological, religious, and sociological commentaries. Some pushing and shoving have been necessary to fit each citation into a category. Psychological commentary, for example, includes items dealing with child rearing, education, and juvenile delinquency. The customary distinction between primary and secondary sources did not seem applicable, and has not been employed. As a consequence, the section on literary commentary includes not only novels, potboilers, plays, poems, and stories, but also critical articles of varying merit.

I. ARCHITECTURAL COMMENTARY

BOOKS

Blake, Peter. *Architecture and Space: Frank Lloyd Wright.* Baltimore: 1960.
> Blake presents an interesting portrait of Wright as the last of the true American individualists, in architecture as in life. His book is particularly valuable for its analysis of many buildings designed by Wright.

Burchard, John, and Albert Bush-Brown. *The Architecture of America.* Boston: 1961.
> This book is the best one-volume history of architecture in this country. The authors never forget what they say in the beginning: that architecture is a social art.

Editors of *Fortune. The Exploding Metropolis.* New York: 1958.
> Several of *Fortune's* able editors examine the metropolis, conclude there is hope for the city, and reveal the usual intellectual bias against the suburbs.

Howard, Ebenezer. *Garden Cities of Tomorrow.* Boston: 1965.

Howard's Garden City ideas have had tremendous influence on his native England, with its New Towns, and on America, where men like Clarence Stein and Lewis Mumford have taken their direction from this book (written before the turn of the century).

Jacobs, Jane. *The Death and Life of Great American Cities.* New York: 1961.

Mrs. Jacobs loves the bustle and noise and busyness of cities, and persuasively suggests that propinquity of large numbers of people makes for safety and community in urban life.

Kaufmann, Edgar, and Ben Raeburn (eds.). *Frank Lloyd Wright: Writings and Buildings.* New York: 1960.

The editors have collected some of Wright's most significant remarks in mercifully condensed form, and have included many drawings and photographs of his best work.

Kennedy, Robert Woods. *The House.* New York: 1953.

Kennedy sensibly sees the house in environmental terms, not as space-enclosing sculpture but as housing for people, and distinguishes between several different kinds of housing: dwelling units, homes, and houses.

Mumford, Lewis. *From the Ground Up.* New York: 1956.

A number of Mumford's essays about building in and around New York are brought together in this volume.

Mumford, Lewis (ed.). *Roots of Contemporary American Architecture.* New York: 1952.

Mumford has saved the student of architecture enormous trouble by placing between the covers of one book some of the most significant architectural writings of such men as Horatio Greenough, Montgomery Schuyler, Louis Sullivan, John Root, Frank Lloyd Wright, and Clarence Stein.

Richards, J. M. *Modern Architecture.* Baltimore: 1962.

Using mostly British buildings as examples, Richards discusses the course of architecture in the twentieth century.

Rudofsky, Bernard. *Behind the Picture Window.* New York: 1955.

With wit and understanding, Rudofsky constructs a sample modern house for his readers—and then demolishes it.

Saarinen, Eliel. *The City: Its Growth, Its Decay, Its Future.* New York: 1943.

Saarinen attempts to explain the physical setting of the city much as a biologist would explain the functioning of any living organism. He proposes a system of organic decentralization which resembles Ebenezer Howard's Garden City approach.

Wright, Frank Lloyd. *The Future of Architecture*. New York: 1953.
Wright surveys the future architectural landscape and finds it wanting, although improved by an awareness of the lessons he has taught—elimination of the box through corner windows and the open plan, for example.

ARTICLES

Background Booklets Nos. 1 and 2. Goals for the Region Project, New York Regional Plan Association. New York: 1963.
These booklets present some of the critical problems facing the New York metropolitan area.

Bates, H. E. "Landscape Lost," *Spectator,* Vol. CXCIX (November 22, 1957), pp. 668–70.
Bates issues a lament for the good old rural days, before suburban cottages and villas cluttered up the British landscape.

Blake, Peter. "The Suburbs are a Mess," *Saturday Evening Post,* Vol. CCXXXVI, No. 34 (October 5, 1963), pp. 14–16.
Blake attacks the "foolish idea" that each family should have its own home as a source of metropolitan chaos. The article excerpts comments from Blake's 1963 book, *God's Own Junkyard*.

"The Contemporary Suburban Residence," *Architectural Record,* Vol. XI, No. 3 (January 1902), p. 69–81.
The article is valuable for a comparison of suburban building at the turn of the century and at mid-century. In 1902, the article makes clear, the contemporary suburban residence was a residence for the wealthy man.

von Eckardt, Wolf. "New Towns in America," *New Republic,* Vol. CXLIX, No. 17 (October 26, 1963), pp. 16–18.
von Eckardt discusses early proposals for New Town construction in America, and places the proposals in the historical context of Ebenezer Howard's Garden City movement.

Gans, Herbert J. "Planning and Social Life: Friendship and Neighbor Relations in Suburban Communities," *Journal of the American Institute of Planners,* Vol. XXVII, No. 2 (May 1961), pp. 134–40.
Gans proposed that homogeneity is the most important element in producing suburban neighborliness, and concludes that planners do not need to install homogeneity in most suburbs because they already possess enough to insure friendship.

Griffin, C. W., Jr. "The Ugly America," *Reporter,* Vol. XXX, No. 3 (January 30, 1964), pp. 53–54, 56.
The article reviews Peter Blake's *God's Own Junkyard,* sharing his

animus against the suburbs for gobbling up space and adding the point that the suburbs are shirking their responsibility to the metropolitan area.

Huxtable, Ada Louise. " 'Clusters' Instead of 'Slurbs,' " *New York Times Magazine* (February 9, 1964), pp. 37–44.
After an opening diatribe against "slurburban" homes and culture, Miss Huxtable sees hope for the future in clustering and New Towns.

Klaber, Eugene Henry. "Comment re 'Visual Communities,' " *Journal of the American Institute of Planners*, Vol. XXIV, No. 1 (1958), p. 41.
Klaber cautions his fellow planners that physical planning will not create a community, and that the "touchstone is people, not things."

Mayer, Albert in consultation with Clarence Stein. "New Towns: and Fresh In-City Communities," *Architectural Record*, Vol. CXXXVI, No. 2 (August 1964), pp. 129–38.
The authors maintain that the New Towns need more direct and powerful control by the federal government, if they are to succeed in becoming heterogeneous, balanced communities, both financially and racially.

Mumford, Lewis, "The Future of the City," *Architectural Record*, five-part series, Vol. CXXXII (October, November, December 1962), and Vol. CXXXIII (January, February 1963).
Mumford surveys the disorganizing effects of the escape to the suburbs, and concludes with an endorsement of Ebenezer Howard's Garden Cities of limited size and area.

"Reston," *Architectural Record*, Vol. CXXXVI, No. 1 (July 1964), pp. 119–34.
Ths article examines the progress of Reston, a New Town near Washington, D.C., and praises what it finds.

Time, Vol. XXCIV, No. 19 (November 6, 1964), pp. 60–75.
In its "cover story" on urban renewal, the magazine makes "suburban spwarl" the villain of the piece, "leeching the center city's life-blood."

Webber, Melvin M. "Transportation Planning Models," *Traffic Quarterly*, Vol. XV, No. 3 (July 1961), pp. 373–90.
Webber streses the close relationship between transportation and land use, and warns that planning models are subject to error when applied to humans.

II. HISTORICAL COMMENTARY

BOOKS

Commager, Henry Steele. *The American Mind*. New Haven and London: 1950.

Commager presents his interpretation of the course of American thought from 1880 to the middle of the twentieth century.

Conkin, Paul K. *Tomorrow a New World*. Ithaca, New York: 1959.
In dealing authoritatively with the New Deal community building programs, Conkin has made a much-needed contribution to the scanty body of scholarly literature on community planning in America.

Degler, Carl N. *Out of Our Past*. New York and Evanston: 1959.
Degler's is the best one-volume interpretation of "Americans as a people" and their thinking.

Gabriel, Ralph Henry. *The Course of American Democratic Thought*. New York: 1956.
Gabriel's distinguished work traces the progress through history of what he regards as the three basic tenets of the democratic faith in America: those of the free individual, fundamental law, and manifest destiny. The book is perhaps most interesting where the author has the greatest difficulty in fitting American thinkers into his history of thought, as in the cases of Herman Melville, Henry Adams, and William Graham Sumner.

Gottschalk, Louis. *Understanding History*. New York: 1950.
The author presents a straightforward and readable explanation of the historical process, intended mainly for the nonprofessional reader.

Griswold, A. Whitney. *Farming and Democracy*. New Haven: 1952.
Although better known as a university administrator, Griswold was a fine scholar, as this valuable examination of the persistence of the agrarian myth demonstrates.

Handlin, Oscar, et al. *Harvard Guide to American History*. Cambridge, Massachusetts: 1954.
This book has rapidly and justly become the standard reference volume for American historical bibliography.

Hofstadter, Richard. *The Age of Reform*. New York: 1955.
The historian looks at the development of Populism and Progressivism in the United States as phenomena explicable in terms of social and economic pressures. Hofstadter, unlike many American historians, is not so infected with admiration for reform movements that he is prevented from seeing them whole.

Jefferson, Thomas. *Notes on the State of Virginia*. New York: 1964.
The highly articulate third President reports on the climate, conditions, and mores of his native state in reply to an inquiry from a curious Frenchman.

Kenward, James. *The Suburban Child*. Cambridge, England: 1955.
The author reflects on the great days of suburbia, which, he maintains, are now over.

Kwiat, Joseph J., and Mary C. Turpie (eds.). *Studies in American Culture.* Minneapolis: 1960.

This collection of essays in American Studies, brought together as a *Festschrift* for Professor Tremaine McDowell, includes an examination of the idea of covert culture by Bernard Bowron, Leo Marx, and Arnold Rose, and an essay on the relation of fiction to national character by William Van O'Connor.

Lerner, Max. *America as a Civilization.* New York: 1957.

In this ambitious and useful book, Lerner takes a balanced view of "The Suburban Revolution," finding its way of life standardized, but not conformist.

Marx, Leo. *The Machine in the Garden.* New York: 1964.

Marx explores the consternation that sometimes arose in the American garden of the world when it was invaded by industrial technology.

McMahon, John H. *Success in the Suburbs.* New York and London: 1917.

This early guide book tells the prospective suburbanite, to quote from the subtitle, "how to locate, buy, and build; garden and grow fruit; keep fowls and animals." The explicit message is that the city dweller can return to health-giving farm life, and turn a profit, merely by moving ten to thirty miles out of the city and tending his land. *Success in the Suburbs* constitutes a vital piece of evidence that the agrarian myth persisted at least into the second decade of the twentieth century.

Moore, Arthur K. *The Frontier Mind.* New York: 1963.

The author uses Kentucky as a showcase to demonstrate the persistence of the ideal of "the Garden of the West."

Mumford, Lewis. *The City in History.* New York: 1961.

This huge volume tells the story of urbanization very well and represents first-rate scholarship, especially in its extensive bibliography.

Sanford, Charles L. *The Quest for Paradise.* Urbana, Illinois: 1961.

Sanford traces "the journey pattern" of modern history as it seeks "to overcome obstacles in order to sink back toward origins."

Taylor, William H. *Cavalier and Yankee.* New York: 1963.

Taylor inspects the stereotypes of two American personages, cavalier and yankee, for accuracy and effect.

U.S. Bureau of the Census. Final Report PHC (1)-93. *U.S. Censuses of Population and Housing: 1960.* Washington: 1962.

This report is one of many data compilations relating to Standard Metropolitan Statistical Areas.

――――. *U.S. Census of Population: 1960.* Vol. I, Part 32—New Jersey, and Vol. I, Part 34—New York. Washington: 1963.

The census reports on the states break down their findings into a multitude of subdivisions.

Wecter, Dixon. *The Hero in America*. Ann Arbor: 1963.
Wecter perceives the importance of a rural heritage in the making of American heroes.

Weimer, David R. *City and Country in America*. New York: 1962.
Weimer has brought together an excellent collection of classic commentaries on rural and urban America.

White, Morton, and Lucia White. *The Intellectual Versus the City*. New York: 1964.
The authors weave their chronological account around some of the nation's most quotable attacks on the city, and argue that it is not always agrarianism which lies at the root of such attacks.

Zelomek, A. W. *A Changing America: at Work and Play*. New York: 1959.
In his excellent section on the suburbs, statistician Zelomek points out that the shallow criticism of suburbia "tends to draw attention away from the very real and long-term problems" which confront cities, suburbs, and small towns alike in twentieth century America.

ARTICLES

Coffin, Tristram. "Maryland's Montgomery County: The Changing Suburban Dream," *Holiday*, Vol. XXXVIII, No. 1 (July 1965), pp. 54–55, 104, 117–18.
Coffin maintains that modern suburbanites are making their trip from the city with a less idealistic set of expectations than formerly, and that they no longer expect to find the Garden of Eden in their subdivision.

Harper's Weekly, Vol. XX, No. 1006 (April 8, 1876), p. 294, and Vol. XX, No. 1027 (September 5, 1876), p. 709.
Articles in these two issues of this magazine, the leading periodical of middle class American thought during the year of the Centennial Exposition, clearly reveal the continuing hold of romantic pastoralism on the national thought processes.

Lerner, Daniel. "Comfort and Fun: Morality in a Nice Society," *American Scholar*, Vol. XXVII, No. 2 (Spring 1958), pp. 153–65.
Lerner argues that there are virtues in suburban life, and questions whether the limited dream they represent is really unworthy.

Life, Vol. LIX, No. 26 (December 24, 1965), pp. 37, 139–40.
Articles by Conrad Knickerbocker and Robert C. Wood stress the persistence of agrarian ideals in the highly urbanized present, and the damage that can be and has been wrought in their name.

Tomars, Adolph S. "Rural Survivals in American Urban Life," *Sociological Analysis*. Editors Logan Wilson and William L. Kolb. New York: 1949, pp. 371–78.
Tomars discusses certain rural practices and beliefs which have been somewhat irrationally retained in an urban environment.

III. LITERARY COMMENTARY

BOOKS, FILMS, AND PLAYS

Adams, Henry. *The Education of Henry Adams*. New York: 1931.
Adams contrasts Quincy, country, freedom, and summer with Boston, town, restraint, and winter, taking an attitude toward Quincy (St. Botolphs) which is similar to that of John Cheever.
Cheever, John. *The Brigadier and the Golf Widow*. New York, Evanston, and London: 1964.
This collection of short stories includes the disturbing story, "An Educated American Woman" and the powerful one, "The Swimmer."
———. *The Enormous Radio and Other Stories*. New York: 1953.
Many of these early stories of Cheever's use New York City, rather than its suburbs, as their setting.
———. *The Housebreaker of Shady Hill*. New York: 1958.
The title story pictures the suburbs as an ideal place to live and raise children, but suggests that it is extremely difficult to pay for these benefits.
———. *Some People, Places, and Things That Will Not Appear in My Next Novel*. New York: 1961.
This collection of stories is noteworthy for "The Wrysons," a satiric yet tender look at a dull suburban couple whose private eccentricities manage to make them likeable after all.
———. *The Wapshot Chronicle*. New York: 1957.
Full of an exuberant sense of the joy of life, this episodic novel, which won the National Book Award, is a joy to read.
———. *The Wapshot Scandal*. New York: 1963.
The further adventure of Moses and Coverly Wapshot take them to suburbia, and to marital difficulties.
Conway, John. *Love in Suburbia*. Derby, Connecticut: 1964.
Conway places his novel of sex and sensationalism in a suburban milieu.
Duff, Charles. *Anthropological Report on a London Suburb*. London: 1935.
This slender volume represents a satire both on suburban life styles and on the sober-sided discipline of anthropology.

Fitzgerald, F. Scott. *The Great Gatsby*. New York: 1953.
One of a very few great American novels, *The Great Gatsby* relates the dream of its title character to the larger American dream.

Fuller, Henry B. *The Cliff-Dwellers*. New York: 1893.
Fuller's novel tells the story of a young man on his way up—and his way down—in the boom city of Chicago.

Halsey, Margaret. *This Demi-Paradise*. New York: 1960.
Subtitled "A Westchester Diary," this book recounts the pleasures and difficulties of living in the suburbs, which would be a full paradise were it not for the stubborn, conservative conformity of some of the neighbors.

Howells, William Dean. *A Modern Instance*. Boston: 1957.
Written in 1882, this novel shocked the sensibilities of its readers by dealing forthrightly with the problem of divorce.

——. *Suburban Sketches*. New York: 1871.
Howells records tales and incidents that grew out of his life in the suburbs of Boston.

Ionesco, Eugene. *The Bald Soprano*. *Masters of Modern Drama*. Editors Haskell M. Block and Robert C. Shedd. New York: 1962.
Ionesco's drama of the absurd is set in a dull, dreary suburb of London.

Karp, David. *Leave Me Alone*. New York: 1957.
The hero of Karp's novel concludes that the way to survive in suburbia is to avoid those yahoos who are his neighbors; longish epigraphs by the fictional Professor Miles Minton Cameron depict the "The Indifferent Generation" which makes its home in the suburbs.

Lardner, Ring. *The Ring Lardner Reader*. New York: 1963.
This hefty paperback, edited with an introduction by Maxwell Geismar, contains much of Lardner's best work.

Lewis, R. W. B. *The American Adam*. Chicago: 1955.
Lewis examines the prevalence of the Adamic myth in American literature.

Mann, Georg. *The Blind Ballots*. New York: 1962.
Mann depicts political struggles in the midwestern suburb of "Ryswick," and suggests that the individual can find effective means of self-expression in this environment.

Marquand, John P. *Point of No Return*. New York: 1947.
Marquand tells the bittersweet success story of a middle management bank employee and his middle class life in the suburbs.

Matthiessen, F. O. *American Renaissance*. London, Toronto, and New York: 1941.
In his preface, Matthiessen stresses the interaction between literature and national culture, reminding us that "although literature reflects an age, it also illuminates it."

McCoy, Dean. *The Love Pool.* New York: 1964.
  McCoy's drugstore novel, no worse than the average of its kind, centers its salacious story in a suburban location.
McGinley, Phyllis. *The Province of the Heart.* New York: 1959.
  The author discusses gardening, neighboring, and other matters in her "flowery suburb" of Spruce Manor.
Morris, Wright. *The Territory Ahead.* New York: 1963.
  Morris argues that American literature has always looked backward to an imaginary time of perfection, when men were in absolute harmony with nature.
Palmer, C. B. *Slightly Cooler in the Suburbs.* Garden City, New York: 1950.
  Palmer lightheartedly describes the woes and rewards of the commuter and weekend do-it-yourselfer.
Perelman, S. J. *Acres and Pains.* New York: 1947.
  Perelman's witty pen deals more mightily than the scythe with the myth of rural felicity.
Russell, Bertrand. *Satan in the Suburbs and Other Stories.* London: 1953.
  The title story is about the successful career of a villain who manufactures horrors in order to dispose of suburban boredom.
Salomon, Roger B. *Twain and the Image of History.* New Haven: 1961.
  Salomon shows Twain's preoccupation with the myth of progress, and his eventual disillusionment as it becomes clear to him that the degraded nature of man makes such progress impossible.
Stowe, Harriet Beecher. *Oldtown Fireside Stories.* Boston: 1872.
  Mrs. Stowe recounts the tales of her youth, as it was lived in a semi-rural paradise on the outskirts of Boston.
Thoreau, Henry David. *Walden.* New York: 1964.
  Thoreau's book of life in the woods represents one of the nation's literary masterpieces.
Trilling, Lionel. *The Liberal Imagination.* Garden City, New York: 1963.
  Trilling collects some of his most incisive critical commentary in this volume, including his perceptive study of the nature of "Reality in America."
Wells, H. G. *Anticipations.* New York: 1901.
  Wells's predictions of things to come include an idyllic picture of suburbia in the middle of the twentieth century.
Wheeler, Keith. *Peaceable Lane.* New York: 1960.
  Wheeler's novel explores the troubles that invade the peace of suburban Peaceable Lane after a Negro family decides to move into the neighborhood.

Wilson, Sloan. *The Man in the Gray Flannel Suit*. New York: 1955.

This popular novel portrays the organization man's rejection of the organization, a rejection made possible by the inheritance of a sizeable piece of property in the suburbs.

Yates, Richard. *Revolutionary Road*. Boston: 1962.

The author tells a terrifying story of adultery and suicide as reactions to a materialistic suburban civilization.

Young, Phyllis Brett. *The Gift of Time*. New York: 1961.

Novelist Young perceives that the romantic desire to return to the small rural community does not make much sense in today's world, but fails to see that her rejection of the suburbs is motivated by just that same romantic desire.

ARTICLES, POEMS, AND STORIES

De Vries, Peter. "Humorists Depict the Suburban Wife," *Life*, Vol. XLI, No. 26 (December 24, 1956), pp. 150–51.

The author describes the suburban mother as a slave to her children and as an unglorified chauffeur.

Esty, William. "Out of an Abundant Love of Created Things," *Commonweal*, Vol. LXVI, No. 7 (May 17, 1957), pp. 187–88.

Esty's review of *The Wapshot Chronicle* concludes that the book "must have been wonderful fun to write, it is wonderful fun to read," a remark that conveys his admiration for the book as well as a certain naiveté in regard to the creative process.

Henderson, Robert. "The Leonardo da Vinci Traffic Jam," *The New Yorker*, Vol. XL, No. 26 (August 15, 1964), pp. 24–26.

Henderson's story maintains that conformity, whether in city, country, or suburbs, is not a problem worth worrying about, since nature will create individual differences.

Hicks, Granville. "Cheever and Others," *Saturday Review*, Vol. XLI, No. 37 (September 13, 1958), pp. 33, 47.

Hicks reviews Cheever's *The Housebreaker of Shady Hill*, finding it remarkable that such interesting stories should be set in the suburbs.

Malcolm, Donald. "John Cheever's Photograph Album," *New Republic*, Vol. CXXXVI, No. 22 (June 3, 1957), pp. 17–18.

Malcolm writes a favorable review of *The Wapshot Chronicle*, especially of Coverly's bout with the psychological testers.

McGinley, Phyllis, "June in the Suburbs," *Time*, Vol. XXC, No. 25 (June 18, 1965), p. 75B.

This poem, one of several by McGinley reprinted on this page, cele-

brates the roar "of birth and bloom" nature brings to the suburbs with
the month of June.

Miles, Josephine. "Housewife," *15 Modern American Poets.* Editor
George P. Elliott. New York: 1956, p. 88.
Miss Miles's poem suggests the tragic waste of life suffered by house-
wives caught up in "the submetropolitan stir."

Nash, Russell W. "Max Shulman and the Changing Image of Suburbia,"
Midcontinent American Studies Journal, Vol. IV, No. 1 (Spring 1963),
pp. 27–38.
Nash argues that Shulman's *Rally Round the Flag, Boys* is a spoof on
the Spectorsky type of exposé.

Newman, William J. "Subtopia in America," *Twentieth Century,* Vol.
CLXI, No. 963 (May 1957), pp. 419–34.
Newman, an Englishman, discusses the portrayal of business and of the
suburbs in such novels as *Point of No Return* and *The Man is the Gray
Flannel Suit* and concludes that the unflattering picture is not real, but
only a model.

"Ovid in Ossining," *Time,* Vol. XXC, No. 13 (March 27, 1964), pp.
66–70, 72.
Time's cover story on Cheever proposes that his fables possess "the dignity of the classical theater."

Ozick, Cynthia. "America Aglow," *Commentary,* Vol. XXXVIII, No. 2
(July 1964), pp. 66–67.
The reviewer finds Cheever at fault for failing to spice *The Wapshot
Scandal* with more social criticism.

Scully, James. "An Oracle of Subocracy," *Nation,* Vol. CC, No. 6 (February 8, 1965), pp. 144–45.
Scully asks why Cheever is interested in making "the world safe for
subocracy" and accuses the author of failure to write about what he
(Scully) regards as truly important.

Wilbur, Richard. "To An American Poet Just Dead," *Ceremony and
Other Poems.* New York: 1950, p. 49.
Wilbur bitterly accuses the suburbs of sleeping the sound sleep of ma-
terialistic death.

IV. POLITICAL COMMENTARY

BOOKS

Adrian, Charles R. *Governing Urban America.* New York: 1955.
Adrian deals harshly with the suburbs, and his comments have been
used as examples of the three-part political indictment—conservatism,

lack of meaningful participation, and inefficiency—usually brought against suburbia. His sketch of the career of a "suburban boss" is most interesting.

Dahl, Robert A. *Who Governs?* New Haven: 1961.

Dahl's examination of the power structure of New Haven, Connecticut contradicts the prevailing view, supported by Floyd Hunter, that modern American communities are governed by a powerful economic elite. Dahl's thorough study instead isolates a small stratum of professional politicians, answerable to the voters at election time, standing "not at the peak of a pyramid but rather at the center of intersecting circles" of interest groups.

Gulick, Luther H. *The Metropolitan Problem and American Ideas.* New York: 1962.

Gulick brings his scholarship and practical experience to bear on metropolitan problems, and issues a plea for cooperation between federal, state, and local governments in seeking their solution. Rapid urbanization, he points out, has been responsible for creation of the "major unsolved problems of our society."

Harrington, Michael. *The Other America.* New York: 1962.

Harrington persuasively argues that grinding poverty still afflicts a large percentage of Americans, but that their suffering has become less visible to millions of middle class suburbanites.

Harris, Louis. *Is There a Republican Majority?* New York: 1954.

On the basis of his study of the 1952 election returns Harris predicts that the white-collar voting bloc, which wants to be "modern, enlightened, and moderate," is likely to determine future national elections, On this basis, he is inclined to answer the question posed by his title in the affirmative. His equation of "white-collar" and "Republican" may be open to question.

Hunter, Floyd. *Community Power Structure.* Garden City, New York: 1963.

The setting is Atlanta, Georgia, and Hunter's conclusion is that a group of key business executives dominate positions of civic and political power. His book and Dahl's (above) jointly illustrate the danger of generalizing about power structure in cities, or in suburbs, from an insufficient sample.

Lubell, Samuel. *Revolt of the Moderates.* New York: 1956.

Lubell, as the title indicates, agrees with Harris that the mid-century voter seeks moderation in his political choices. But Lubell does not agree with Harris that this quest will necessarily benefit the Republican cause, and he also disputes Harris's suburbs-make-Republican assumption.

Wallace, David. *First Tuesday*. Garden City, New York: 1964.

A provocative examination of politics in Westport, Connecticut, Wallace's book argues that voting, even in so highly educated a community as the one under study, is almost always determined by a set of culturally inherited or acquired attitudes, which are basically irrational, and not by an intelligent assessment of the parties and candidates. Westport's political ambivalence during the decade of the 1950s challenges the commonly held "Republicanization" hypothesis advanced by William H. Whyte, Jr. and others.

Wood, Robert C. *Suburbia: Its People and Their Politics*. Boston: 1958.

The most thoughtful study yet available on suburban politics, Wood's scholarly work diagnoses the persistence of the Jeffersonian ideal of small, grass-roots government as the cause for the suburbs' reluctance to join their central cities in (what presumably would be) efficient political consolidation.

ARTICLES

"City-Suburb Federation: How Good an Answer is It?" *Business Week* (January 22, 1955), pp. 64–68.

The article comments on the first two years of metropolitan government in the Toronto, Canada area.

Deutsch, Karl W. "Social Mobilization and Political Development," *American Political Science Review*, Vol. LV (September 1961), p. 494.

This paper attempts to establish the pattern of social adjustment that follows a move to suburbia.

Elkins, Stanley, and Eric McKitrick. "A Meaning for Turner's Frontier," *Political Science Quarterly*, Vol. LXIX, Nos. 3–4 (September–December 1954), pp. 321–53 and 565–602.

A landmark in interpretation of American history, the two-part article tests Turner's hypothesis that the American frontier produced political democracy against the actual community experience in the Old Northwest, the Southwest, and New England, and finds that the hypothesis is valid.

Emery, Donald G. "Memo from Scarsdale: A New Role for Suburban Schools," *Look*, Vol. XXXII, No. 7 (April 2, 1968), p. 18.

Emery proposes that mostly white, well-to-do school districts should take the lead in integrating, and equalizing opportunities in, the nation's schools.

Fitch, Lyle C. "Fiscal and Political Problems of Increasing Urbanization," *Political Science Quarterly*, Vol. LXXI, No. 1 (March 1956), pp. 71–90.

Fitch isolates transportation as the most pressing problem of urban areas and advocates solution of this and other metropolitan problems through "changing forms of government or creating new ones."

Gans, Herbert J. "Park Forest: Birth of a Jewish Community," *Commentary*, Vol. XI, No. 4 (April 1951), pp. 330–39.

Gans finds little or no discrimination against the minority of Jews who settled in this much-studied Chicago suburb.

Greenstein, Fred I., and Raymond H. Wolfinger. "The Suburbs and Shifting Party Loyalties," *Public Opinion Quarterly*, Vol. XXII, No. 4 (Winter 1958–1959) pp. 473–82.

Using data from the 1952 presidential election, the article concludes that suburban residence "may produce Republican converts."

Harris, Chauncy D., and Edward L. Ullman. "The Nature of Cities," *Cities and Society*. Editors Paul K. Hatt and Albert J. Reiss, Jr. New York: 1951, pp. 237–47.

The customary notion that political fragmentation leads to a lack of civic responsibility on the part of suburbanites is set forth here.

Heinzman, Donald. Letter to Scott Donaldson (March 29, 1968).

Heinzman, executive editor of Twin Cities Suburban Newspapers, Inc., predicts increasing metropolitanization of governmental services in the Minneapolis area.

Henderson, Harry. "The Mass-Produced Suburbs. Part II: Rugged American Collectivism," *Harper's*, Vol. XXVII, No. 1243 (December 1953), pp. 80–86.

Henderson discusses the importance of organizational life, and especially of churches, in shaping new suburbs.

Janosik, G. Edward. "The New Suburbia," *Current History*, Vol. XXXI, No. 180 (August 1956), pp. 91–95.

This paper emphasizes the future political influence of "the new suburbia" and suggests that the influence may work to the benefit of the Republican party.

Johnson, Earl S. "The Function of the Central Business District in the Metropolitan Community," *Cities and Society*. Editors Paul K. Hatt and Albert J. Reiss, Jr. New York: 1951, pp. 248–59.

Johnson points out that economic movements are "contemptuous" of political borderlines, and calls for a new "set of political implements" to adapt to these movements.

Lader, Lawrence. "Chaos in the Suburbs," *Better Homes and Gardens*, Vol. XXXVI, No. 10 (October 1958), pp. 10, 12, 14, 17, 121, 129, 166. Lader describes the chaos that results from lack of intergovernmental cooperation and argues for metropolitan government.

Lawrie, Alastair. Letter to Scott Donaldson (March 26, 1968).

Lawrie, of the Toronto *Globe and Mail's* editorial department, reviews the history of Metro in that city from 1963 to 1968. See also editorials "Metro Goes Nowhere," Toronto *Globe and Mail* (January 11, 1966), and "Parochialism at Work," Toronto *Globe and Mail* (January 26, 1967).

Lazerwitz, Bernard. "Suburban Voting Trends: 1948 to 1956," *Social Forces*, Vol. XXXIX, No. 1 (October 1960), pp. 29–36.

Lazerwitz finds a drift toward the Democratic party in suburbia, and suggests this trend may lead to creation of a two-party suburban political environment.

Manis, Jerome G., and Leo C. Stine. "Suburban Residence and Political Behavior," *Public Opinion Quarterly*, Vol. XXXI, No. 4 (Winter 1958–1959), pp. 483–89.

This article, which appears immediately following that of Greenstein and Wolfinger (see above), comes to the contrasting conclusion that suburban residence "seems in itself to be politically irrelevant."

Millet, John H., and David Pittman. "The New Suburban Voter: A Case Study in Electoral Behavior," *Southwestern Social Science Quarterly*, Vol. XXXIX, No. 1 (June 1958), pp. 33–42.

The authors' research into voting data from Rochester, New York suburbs disclosed no evidence to support the notion that living in the suburbs creates a shift to Republicanism.

"Minneapolis, Suburbs Don't Subsidize One Another," *Bloomington Sun-Suburbanite* (December 31, 1964), pp. 1–3.

This story reports on the finding of the doctoral dissertation, written by James Banovetz, that Hennepin County suburbs are not subsidized by Minneapolis.

Oberdorfer, Don, and Milton Mackaye. "Will Negroes Crack the Suburbs?" *Saturday Evening Post*, Vol. CCXXXV, No. 46 (December 22, 1962), pp. 71–73.

The authors discuss the probable effect of the Presidential order banning discrimination in federally assisted housing projects on integration in the suburbs.

Rapp, Marvin A. "Challenge to Leadership," *Vital Speeches*, Vol. XXX, No. 21 (August 15, 1964), pp. 654–57.

Rapp isolates the split between the place of residence and place of occupation of "natural leaders," and proposes that they should ignore this split in assuming obligations.

Reed, Thomas H. "Hope for 'Suburbanitis.'" *National Municipal Review*, Vol. XXXIX, No. 11 (December 1950), pp. 542–43.

Reed states that "suburbanitis," or galloping growth unaccompanied by sound planning, is a disease that has infected every metropolitan area in the nation. The solution he advocates is metropolitan government.

Scott, John Finley and Lois Heyman Scott. "They Are Not So Much Anti-Negro as Pro-Middle Class," *The New York Times Magazine* (March 24, 1968), pp. 46–7, 107, 109–10, 117, 119–20.

The Scotts suggest remedies for the imbalance in quality of education between urban and suburban schools.

"Suburbia: Its Taxes Ache," *National Municipal Review*, Vol. XLII, No. 8 (September 1953), pp. 380-81.

This editorial discusses the plight of the "have-not" suburb and recommends such possible remedies as fiscal evaluation and political amalgamation.

"What's Ahead for New County Manager," *Miami Herald* (March 17, 1965), p. 8-A.

The incoming (at the time) Dade County Metro manager faces substantial problems.

Wirt, Frederick M. "The Political Sociology of American Suburbia: A Reinterpretation," *Journal of Politics*, Vol. XXVII, No. 3 (August 1965), pp. 647–66.

Wirt's study of 119 suburbs shows that Republican percentages slid below the 50 per cent mark in the presidential election of 1960 and kept on sliding to a bare one-third of the electorate in 1964 presidential balloting.

Wood, Robert C. "The Impotent Suburban Vote," *Nation*, Vol. CXC, No. 13 (March 26, 1960), pp. 271–74.

Wood argues that most suburbs lack a two-party system, that little political participation is in evidence, and that the Republicans are more to be pitied than envied as a consequence of their sizeable pluralities in under-represented suburban areas.

V. PSYCHOLOGICAL COMMENTARY

BOOKS

Conant, James B. *Slums and Suburbs.* New York: 1961.

The author reports on his exhaustive survey of secondary public education in the United States, finding both "lighthouse" programs and critical weaknesses among suburban high schools.

Duhl, Leonard J. (ed.). *The Urban Condition.* New York and London: 1963.

Duhl's collection of articles examines urbanism and suburbanism from a psychological point of view. The chapters by Robert Gutman and Herbert J. Gans are particularly valuable for an understanding of assimilation and neighboring in the suburbs.

Freud, Sigmund. *Civilization and Its Discontents*. Chicago: n.d.
In this short volume Freud traces the necessary conflict between the individual and his society back to the internal psychological makeup of man himself, specifically, to his tendency to turn his aggressions inward on himself in the form of a superego, or sense of guilt.

Fromm, Erich. *The Sane Society*. New York: 1955.
Fromm analyzes the psychological effects of the decline of individualism in a conformist society.

Geen, Elizabeth, Jeanne R. Lowe, and Kenneth Walker (eds.). *Man and the Modern City*. Pittsburgh: 1963.
This book presents under one cover the lectures presented during Goucher College's recent exploration of the theme spelled out in the title. Dorothy Lee's essay on "Suburbia Reconsidered: Diversity and the Creative Life" (pp. 122–34), argues that the conformity of suburban life operates against creative fulfillment.

Gordon, Richard E., M.D., Katherine K. Gordon, and Max Gunther. *The Split-Level Trap*. New York: 1964.
This is the influential, overstated indictment of the havoc "Disturbia" wreaks upon innocent victims.

Loth, David. *Crime in the Suburbs*. New York: 1967.
Loth finds that reports on increasing crime rates in suburbia have been exaggerated, and singles out those elements that distinguish criminal behavior in the suburbs from that in the city.

Veblen, Thorstein. *The Theory of the Leisure Class*. New York: 1934.
In his famous book on the honorific displays of wealth, Veblen makes a connection between the close-cropped lawn and the cow pasture.

Wyden, Peter. *Suburbia's Coddled Kids*. New York: 1962.
Wyden's popular and clear-headed book perceives that many suburban youngsters are being spoiled, but concludes by suggesting that the existence of pressures simultaneously to conform and to succeed may lead the most pampered among them to maturity.

ARTICLES

Barclay, Dorothy. "Adolescents in Suburbia," *National Education Association Journal*, Vol. XLVIII, No. 1 (January 1959), pp. 10–11, 76–79.
Barclay writes that the protective cocoon surrounding the suburban child bursts at about age twelve, when he is exposed to the temptations of independence.

Blakely, Robert J. "The Lonely Youth of Suburbia," *PTA Magazine*, Vol. LV, No. 8 (April 1961), pp. 14–16.
The author maintains that young people in the suburbs are both lonely and over-protected.

Cogley, John. "An Interview with Reinhold Niebuhr," *McCall's*, Vol. XCIII, No. 5 (February 1966), pp. 90–91, 166–71.
Niebuhr discusses such matters as youth and juvenile delinquency in this interview.

"Darien's *Dolce Vita*," *Time*, Vol. XXCIV, No. 22 (November 27, 1964), p. 60.
The national newsmagazine focuses on a ring of drug addicts in a Connecticut high school.

Friedan, Betty. "Woman: The Fourth Dimension," *Ladies' Home Journal*, Vol. XXCI, No. 5 (June 1964), pp. 48–55.
Friedan proposes that women should develop four dimensions in order to escape from the three-dimensional prisons which she identifies with homes in suburbia

Keats, John. "Compulsive Suburbia," *The Atlantic*, Vol. CCV, No. 4 (April 1960), pp. 47–50.
Keats reiterates his belief that the suburban existence is psychologically unhealthy; written in his customary inflammatory prose.

Kelley, Anne. "Suburbia—Is It a Child's Utopia?" *The New York Times Magazine* (February 2, 1958), pp. 22, 35, 38.
Suburbia is neither utopia nor subtopia for the child, but instead an "imitation small-town" that is "a good deal like other places, only more so."

McCarthy, Joe. "The Case for Sidewalks," *This Week* (May 24, 1964), p. 12.
Much unhappiness about suburban life stems from a set of unrealistic, utopian expectations.

Moskin, J. Robert. "Morality U.S.A.," *Look*, Vol. XXVII, No. 19 (September 24, 1963), pp. 74–78, 81–82, 84, 86–88.
The article asks whether bigness, the bomb, and the buck have destroyed our old morality, and answers that they seem to have done so, using such evidence as wife-swapping in San Francisco suburbs along with Elizabeth Taylor's life and Adam Clayton Powell's taxpayer-financed junkets as examples.

"On the 5:19 to Ulcerville," *Newsweek*, Vol. LIV, No. 7 (August 17, 1959), p. 32.
The charge is set forth that suburban life produces neurotic people.

Rexroth, Kenneth. "Book Week," *New York Sunday Herald Tribune* (March 8, 1964), p. 2.

Rexroth states that juvenile delinquency flourishes far more in the suburbs than within the city.

Robinson, Thomas E. "Opportunity in Suburbia," *National Education Association Journal*, Vol. XLVI, No. 4 (April 1957), pp: 246–48.

Robinson advises young teachers to look to suburbia for better and more challenging jobs.

Rowan, Carl T. Address at University of Minnesota (January 28, 1965).

Rowan comments on the American penchant for self-criticism, and observes that "it can be carried to the point of defeatism."

Sarff, Douglas P. "Open Letter to the Community of Wayzata," *The Minnetonka Herald* (April 1, 1965), p. 2.

Sarff uses his powers of vituperation to issue a scathing farewell to the Wayzata schools where he played "the idealist in a swamp" of middle-class conformity.

"Suburbia: Lost Paradise?" *America*, Vol. CVII, No. 5 (May 5, 1962), p. 199.

This editorial deplores what are described as "faltering moral standards" in suburbia.

VI. RELIGIOUS COMMENTARY

BOOKS

Cox, Harvey. *The Secular City*. New York: 1965.

Cox is fully aware of the secularism of today's society, and sensibly regards such secularism as neither the Messiah nor the anti-Christ, but an opportunity for freedom and maturity.

Eliade, Mircea. *The Sacred and the Profane*. New York: 1961.

Eliade brings his vast knowledge of comparative religion to bear on a contrast between the primitive man, who lived in a sacred world, and modern man, whose life is increasingly desacralized.

Gordon, Albert I. *Jews in Suburbia*. Boston: 1959.

Rabbi Gordon takes a balanced view of the suburbs, at once regretting what he regards as the standardization and conformity of the religious revival and yet acknowledging the preservation of basic values in the conformist suburban communities.

Greeley, Andrew M. *The Church and the Suburbs*. New York: 1959.

Father Greeley surveys the problems of Catholicism in a suburban environment, and concludes that a genuine attempt must be made to restore greater heterogeneity to suburban parishes.

Shippey, Frederick A. *Protestantism in Suburban Life*. New York and Nashville: 1964.

Shippey regards suburban life as a challenge to the ministry, and concludes that negative criticisms "remain unproved and unsupported." There is a first-rate if necessarily incomplete bibliography of articles and novels about suburbia.

Winter, Gibson. *The Suburban Captivity of the Churches*. Garden City, New York: 1961.

Winter attacks the suburban church for failing to meet its responsibility to the larger metropolitan community of which it is a part.

ARTICLES

Gersh, Harry. "The New Suburbanites of the 50s—Jewish Division," *Commentary*, Vol. XVII, No. 3 (March 1954), pp. 209–21.

Gersh reports that an affinity for nature is the first basic change a suburban Jew experiences after moving from the city.

Oursler, Will. "The Ferment in Suburban Congregations," *Suburbia Today* (November 1963), pp. 16–19.

Oursler writes that there are "new spiritual forces awakening in the suburban religious community."

Rowland, Stanley, Jr. "Suburbia Buys Religion," *Nation*, Vol. CXXCIII, No. 4 (July 28, 1956), pp. 78–80.

Rowland bitterly attacks religious practice in suburbia, which is likened to groceries and entertainment as merely another item of consumption.

"The Church in 'Outer Space,'" *America*, Vol. XCVIII, No. 20 (February 22, 1958), p. 585.

The high percentage of church membership in the suburbs is seen as an opportunity; the high percentage of turnover due to families moving as a hindrance.

VII. SOCIOLOGICAL COMMENTARY

BOOKS

Berger, Bennett M. *Working Class Suburb*. Berkeley: 1960.

Berger's valuable study of a suburb inhabited principally by industrial workers finds what he calls "the myth of suburbia" invalid as it is applied to politics, religion, schools, and social and psychological organization in this community.

Dobriner, William M. *Class in Suburbia*. Englewood Cliffs, New Jersey: 1963.

Dobriner's examination of Levittown, Long Island and an older Connecticut suburb leads him to the conclusion that: (1) there are several kinds of suburbs, and (2) they can best be defined by class variables. His book demonstrates that life in Levittown underwent significant changes in the first ten years of that community's existence.

Dobriner, William M. (ed.). *The Suburban Community*. New York: 1958.
The best collection of articles on suburbia now available, the book includes analyses of the suburbs by demographers, economists, social commentators, and a wide spectrum of sociologists. David Riesman's closing essay is a brilliant example of the anti-suburban point of view.

Douglass, Harlan Paul. *The Suburban Trend*. New York: 1925.
Douglass's pioneering work remains extremely valuable historically and as a basis of comparison to current ideas and assumptions about suburbs and suburban life. The author saw the suburbs as the "salvation of the city," the hope of the future.

Gans, Herbert J. *The Levittowners*. New York: 1967.
Gans, in this thorough study of Levittown, N.J., concludes that people's basic life styles are not changed by the move to suburbia, and that the changes that take place are those the emigrants from the central city had anticipated and desired before moving out.

Keats, John. *The Crack in the Picture Window*. Boston: 1956.
This book is interesting as a gross over-statement of the case against the suburbs, during the period in which criticism of suburbia was most fashionable. Keats finds the suburban home, and the people who live in it, uniformily dreary.

Lipset, Seymour Martin. *Culture and Social Character*. Glencoe, Illinois: 1961.
Lipset puts the thesis of David Riesman's *The Lonely Crowd* to the test of historical judgment, and finds that there is nothing significantly new about "other-direction" in his chapter on "A Changing American Character?"

Seeley, John R., R. Alexander Sim, and Elizabeth W. Loosley. *Crestwood Heights*. New York: 1956.
Seeley and his fellow researchers have produced the most conscientious and thorough study of a North American suburb (of Toronto, Canada) yet published.

Spectorsky, A. C. *The Exurbanites*. New York: 1955.
A best seller, Spectorsky's witty, often acid book explores the way of life of the exurbanites.

Stein, Maurice R. *The Eclipse of Community*. New York: 1964.
Largely secondary in approach, Stein's book reviews the literature of

community studies by American sociologists, and suggests techniques which might make future studies more effective and meaningful.

Whyte, William H., Jr. *The Organization Man.* New York: 1956.

Whyte's highly readable book represents a lament for the "good old days" of individualism, now unhappily replaced by the organization and the organization man in his suburban home. The Organization Man is perhaps the most influential and widely read statement of suburban disillusionment.

Willmott, Peter, and Michael Young. *Family and Class in a London Suburb.* London: 1960.

Willmott and Young discover that primary family ties do not dissolve in the suburbs, as has been hypothesized.

ARTICLES

Bensman, Joseph, and Bernard Rosenberg. "The Culture of the New Suburbia," *Dissent,* Vol. IX (Summer 1962), pp. 267–70.

The real test of suburban culture, the authors suggest, must wait until it is known whether suburbanites can *produce* works of art as well as consume them.

Bliven, Bruce, Jr. "Life and Love in the Split-Level Slums," *Reporter,* Vol. XVI, No. 2 (February 7, 1957), p. 46.

Reviewing the book, *The Crack in the Picture Window,* Bliven reaches the conclusion that John Keats was "far too angry to be amusing."

Burton, Hal. "Trouble in the Suburbs," *Saturday Evening Post,* Vol. CCXXVIII, No. 12 (September 17, 1955), pp. 19–21, 113–14, 117–18, Part I; Vol. CCXXVIII, No. 13 (September 24, 1955), pp. 32–33, 140–52, Part II; Vol. CCXXVIII, No. 14 (October 1, 1955), pp. 30, 132–34, Part III.

This three-part series devotes most of its space to a discussion of what is wrong with suburbia, but pauses to reflect in Part III that most people who live there seem to like it.

"The Changing Suburbs," *Architectural Forum,* Vol. CXIV, No. 1 (January 1961), pp. 47–104.

This survey proposes that American suburbs are learning to solve their own problems and that suburban life can be healthy for children.

De Voto, Bernard. "The Easy Chair: Beating the Bali Ha'i Racket," *Harper's Magazine,* Vol. CCXII, No. 1268 (January 1956), pp. 10–12, 14, 16, 18.

With his customary good sense and good nature, De Voto examines the plight of the exurbanite and finds it overstated. The small city in the provinces may supply the environment the exurbanite seeks, he suggests.

Douglass, Harlan Paul. "Suburbs," *Encyclopedia of the Social Sciences.* Editors Edwin R. A. Seligman and Alvin Johnson. New York: 1934, Vol. XIV, pp. 433–35.
Describes the (at the time) current condition of, and speculates (often inaccurately) about the future of, the American suburb.

Erwin, Robert. "Up, Up, and Away with the Arts," *American Scholar,* Vol. XXXI (Autumn 1962), pp. 572–83.
Erwin deplores the development of a mediocre mass culture, as it is reflected in the mass media and in mass housing.

"Exurbia: The New America," *Newsweek,* Vol. XLIX, No. 22 (June 3, 1957), pp. 83–90.
Newsweek pictures exurbia as "a state of mind as well as a place" in the manner of A. C. Spectorsky's book.

Farley, Reynolds. "Suburban Persistence," *American Sociological Review,* Vol. XXIX, No. 1 (February 1964), pp. 38–47.
Farley's research suggests that suburbs are shaped in their earliest formation and that they tend to retain their original character despite successive migrations.

Gans, Herbert J. "Urbanism and Suburbanism as Ways of Life: A Re-Evaluation of Definitions," *Human Behavior and Social Processes.* Editor Arnold M. Rose. Boston: 1962, pp. 625–48.
Gans discloses that his research, like that of Berger, can discover little justification for the prevailing myths about suburban life.

Gleaves, Susanne. "Levittown Revisited," *New York Sunday Herald Tribune Magazine* (August 16, 1964), pp. 9–12.
Miss Gleaves examines Levittown seventeen years after its first homes, and finds that the ugliest duckling has turned into "a very sleek and contented duck indeed," if not exactly a swan.

Gruenberg, Sidonie Matsner. "The Challenge of the New Suburbs," *Marriage and Family Living,* Vol. XVII, No. 2 (May 1955), pp. 133–37.
Gruenberg writes that study and planning is needed to assure that the suburban environment provide "opportunities for the growth and development of children and for the enrichment of family life."

Hanford, Edgar C. "Surprises in the Suburbs," *American Mercury,* Vol. XXCI (September 1955), pp. 67–70.
Hanford warns that starry-eyed couples are in for some unhappy experiences in their suburban homes.

Harris, Chauncy D. "Suburbs," *American Journal of Sociology,* Vol. XLIX, No. 1 (July 1943), pp. 1–13.
Harris's article is important in differentiating among various kinds of suburbs, and in suggesting directions for demographic research.

Henderson, Harry. "The Mass-Produced Suburbs," *Harper's Magazine,* Vol. CCVII, Nos. 1242, 1243 (November, December, 1953), pp. 25–32, 80–86.
The author's two-part series reports on the results of a three-year series of interviews in six suburbs, including Levittown and Park Forest. His outlook on suburbia is middle-of-the-road, tending toward approval.

Ktsanes, Thomas and Leonard Reissman. "Suburbia—New Homes for Old Values," *Social Problems,* Vol. VII, No. 3 (Winter 1959–1960), pp. 187–95.
The writers attack three of the sociological assumptions about suburbia: that it is peculiarly homogeneous, middle class, and conformist.

"A Look at Suburbanites," *Science Digest,* Vol. XL, No. 6 (December 1956), p. 20.
The article suggests that the suburban husband and wife have reversed roles, and that together, they spoil their children.

Marshall, Catherine. "What's Happening to Our Homeowners?" *Suburbia Today* (July 1964), pp. 6–7, 9.
Marshall uncovers some hazards of suburban life, including conformity, immorality, and permissive rearing of children.

McGinley, Phyllis. "Suburbia: Of Thee I Sing," *30th Anniversary Reader's Digest Reader*. Pleasantville, New York: 1952, pp. 227–30.
The usually uncharitable view of suburbia is not supported by the facts, according to McGinley.

Munson, Byron E. "Attitudes Toward Urban and Suburban Residence in Indianapolis," *Social Forces,* Vol. XXXV, No. 1 (October 1956), pp. 76–80.
Munson finds that families move to suburban areas in search of a healthier, pleasanter environment, and proposes that a "neighboring" continuum can be constructed from the relatively isolated urbanite to the relatively friendly ruralite, with the suburbanite falling between these extremes.

Ogburn, Charlton, Jr. "Help! Help!" *Harper's Magazine,* Vol. CCXXIX, No. 1374 (November 1964), pp. 65–69.
Ogburn charts the busyness of a typical suburban day, and stresses the time and energy consumed in upkeep of the garden and grounds.

Puner, Helen. "Is It True What they Say About the Suburbs?" *Parents'*
Magazine, Vol. XXXIII, No. 7 (July 1958), pp. 42–43, 96–97.
Puner proposes that in attacking the suburbs social commentators may
be misdirecting their fire.

"Quit Picking on 'Suburbia.'" *Changing Times,* Vol. XVII, No. 10 (October 1963), pp. 34–36.
This article explores the findings of sociologist Herbert Gans, which
contradict the customary attacks against the suburbs.

Sadler, J. D. J. "Utopia Reconsidered," *House and Garden,* Vol. CXIII,
No. 3 (March 1958), pp. 158, 160.
The financial problems and lack of privacy supposedly inherent in
suburban residence are satirized.

"Some Drawbacks of Suburban Life," *Science Digest,* Vol. XXXVII, No.
1 (January 1955), p. 33.
The drawbacks may include a break-up of the family, inasmuch as the
move from the city may mean "exchanging a full-time father for a
part-time father."

"Spur to Conformity," *Commonweal,* Vol. LXIV, No. 24 (September 21,
1956), p. 602.
The child-centeredness of the suburbs makes for conformity of con-
versation and of ideas, *Commonweal* believes.

Strauss, Anselm. "The Changing Imagery of American City and Suburb,"
Sociological Quarterly, Vol. I, No. 1 (January 1960), pp. 15–24.
Strauss suggests that the standard image of the city swallowing up the
suburb may be shifting to the vision of Nathan Glazer that cities are
being suburbanized, not vice versa.

"Suburbia: The New America," *Newsweek,* Vol. XL, No. 13 (April 1,
1957), pp. 35–42.
Part one of a two-part spread (see "Exurbia" above) which reports on
the way of life, politics, and finances of residents in Lakewood, a
large suburb of Los Angeles.

Tressler, Irving D. "So You Live in a Suburb?" *Best of Modern Humor.*
Editors P. G. Wodehouse and Scott Meredith. New York: 1951,
pp. 208–13.
Tressler casts amusing barbs at excessive neighboring in suburbia, and
suggests alternative ways to lose friends and alienate people.

Winthrop, Anthony, Jr. "The Crab-Grass Roots of Suburbia," *New Re-*
public, Vol. CXXXVI, No. 6 (February 11, 1957), pp. 18–20.
Winthrop reviews Keats's *The Crack in the Picture Window,* stress-
ing the author's lack of charity for his subject.

Wirth, Louis. "Urbanism as a Way of Life," *Cities and Society*. Editors Paul K. Hatt and Albert J. Reiss, Jr. New York: 1951, pp. 46–63.

Wirth's article is the classic sociological statement of the effect of cities on social organization and psychology.

Wrong, Dennis H. "Suburbs and Myths of Suburbia," *Readings in Introductory Sociology*. Editors Dennis H. Wrong and Harry L. Gracey. New York: 1967, pp. 258–64.

Wrong reviews the sociological debunking, during the 1960s, of the attack on suburbia during the 1950s.

INDEX